# CRACKING THE

# CODING

# INTERVIEW

## *4th Edition*

# CRACKING THE
# CODING
# INTERVIEW
## *4th Edition*

*150 Programming Interview*
*Questions and Solutions*

# GAYLE LAAKMANN
### Founder and CEO, CareerCup.com

CareerCup, LLC
Seattle, WA

# CRACKING THE CODING INTERVIEW, FOURTH EDITION

Published by CareerCup, LLC, Seattle, WA. Version 3.21090711301626.

For more information, contact support@careercup.com.

Printed in United States of America

9781451578270 (ISBN 13)

# Table of Contents

# Table of Contents

Dear Readers,

Welcome to the 4th edition of *Cracking the Coding Interview*. This volume updates the 3rd edition with new content and refreshed information. Be sure to check out our website, www. careercup.com, to connect with other candidates and to discover new resources.

For those of you new to technical interviews, the process can seem overwhelming. Interviewers throw questions at you, expect you to whip up brilliant algorithms on the spot, and then ask you to write beautiful code on a whiteboard. Luckily, everyone else is in the same boat, and you're already working hard to prepare. Good job!

As you get ready for your interviews, consider these suggestions:

»   **Write Code on Paper:** Most interviewers won't give you a computer and will instead expect you to write code on a whiteboard or on paper. To simulate this environment, try answering interview problems by writing code on paper first, and then typing them into a computer as-is. Whiteboard / paper coding is a special skill, which can be mastered with constant practice.

»   **Know Your Resume:** While technical skills are extremely important, that's no reason to neglect your own resume. Make sure to prepare yourself to give a quick summary of any project or job you were involved with, and to discuss the hardest and most interesting problems you encountered along the way.

»   **Don't Memorize Solutions:** While this book offers a representative sample of interview questions, there are still thousands of interview questions out there. Memorizing solutions is not a great use of your time. Rather, use this book to explore approaches to problems, to learn new concepts, and to practice your skills.

»   **Talk Out Loud:** Interviewers want to understand how you think and approach problems, so talk out loud while you're solving problems. Let the interviewer see how you're tackling the problem, and they just might guide you as well.

**And remember -- interviews are hard!** In my years of interviewing at Google, I saw some interviewers ask "easy" questions while others ask harder questions. But you know what? Getting the easy questions doesn't make it any easier to get the offer. Receiving an offer is not about solving questions flawlessly (very few candidates do!), but rather, it is about answering questions *better than other candidates*. So don't stress out when you get a tricky question - everyone else probably thought it was hard too!

I'm excited for you and for the skills you are going to develop. Thorough preparation will give you a wide range of technical and communication skills. It will be well-worth it no matter where the effort takes you!

Study hard, practice, and good luck!

Gayle Laakmann

# Introduction

## Something's Wrong

We walked out of the hiring meeting frustrated, again. Of the ten "passable" candidates we reviewed that day, none would receive offers. Were we being too harsh, we wondered?

I, in particular, was disappointed. We had rejected one of *my* candidates. A former student. One who I had referred. He had a 3.73 GPA from the University of Washington, one of the best computer science schools in the world, and had done extensive work on open source projects. He was energetic. He was creative. He worked hard. He was sharp. He was a true geek, in all the best ways.

But, I had to agree with the rest of the committee: the data wasn't there. Even if my emphatic recommendation would sway them to reconsider, he would surely get rejected in the later stages of the hiring process. There were just too many red flags.

Though the interviewers generally believed that he was quite intelligent, he had struggled to develop good algorithms. Most successful candidates could fly through the first question, which was a twist on a well known problem, but he had trouble developing an algorithm. When he came up with one, he failed to consider solutions that optimized for other scenarios. Finally, when he began coding, he flew through the code with an initial solution, but it was riddled with mistakes that he then failed to catch. Though he wasn't the worst candidate we'd seen by any measure, he was far from meeting "the bar." Rejected.

When he asked for feedback over the phone a couple of weeks later, I struggled with what to tell him. Be smarter? No, I knew he was brilliant. Be a better coder? No, his skills were on-par with some of the best I'd seen.

Like many motivated candidates, he had prepared extensively. He had read K&R's classic C book and he'd reviewed CLRS' famous algorithms textbook. He could describe in detail the myriad of ways of balancing a tree, and he could do things in C that no sane programmer should ever want to do.

I had to tell him the unfortunate truth: those books aren't enough. Academic books prepare you for fancy research, but they're not going to help you much in an interview. Why? I'll give you a hint: your interviewers haven't seen Red-Black Trees since *they* were in school either.

To crack the coding interview, you need to prepare with *real* interview questions. You must practice on *real* problems, and learn their patterns.

*Cracking the Coding Interview* is the result of my first-hand experience interviewing at top companies. It is the result of hundreds of conversations with candidates. It is the result of the thousands of candidate- and interviewer- contributed questions. And it's the result of seeing so many interview questions from so many firms. Enclosed in this book are 150 of the best interview questions, selected from thousands of potential problems.

## My Approach

The focus of *Cracking the Coding Interview* is algorithm, coding and design questions. Why? Because while you can and will be asked behavioral questions, the answers will be as varied as your resume. Likewise, while many firms will ask so-called "trivia" questions (e.g., "What is a virtual function?"), the skills developed through practicing these questions are limited to very specific bits of knowledge. The book will briefly touch on some of these questions, to show you what they're like, but I have chosen to allocate space where there's more to learn.

## My Passion

Teaching is my passion. I love helping people understand new concepts, and giving them tools so that they can excel in their passions.

My first experience "officially" teaching was in college at the University of Pennsylvania, when I became a teaching assistant for an undergraduate Computer Science course during my second year. I went on to TA for several other courses, and eventually launched my own CS course at the university focused on "hands-on" skills.

As an engineer at Google, training and mentoring "Nooglers" (yes, that's really what they call new Google employees!) were some of the things I enjoyed most. I went on to use my "20% time" to teach two Computer Science courses at the University of Washington.

*Cracking the Coding Interview* and **CareerCup.com** reflect my passion for teaching. Even now, you can often find me "hanging out" at CareerCup.com, helping users who stop by for assistance.

Join us.


Gayle Laakmann

# Behind the Scenes

For many candidates, interviewing is a bit of a black box. You walk in, you get pounded with questions from a variety of interviewers, and then somehow or other you return with an offer... or not.

Have you ever wondered:

» How do decisions get made?

» Do your interviewers talk to each other?

» What does the company really care about?

Well, wonder no more!

CareerCup sought out interviewing experts from five top companies - Microsoft, Google, Amazon, Yahoo and Apple - to show you what really happens "behind the scenes." These experts will walk us through a typical interview day and describe what's taking place outside of the interviewing room, and what transpires after you leave.

Our interviewing experts also told us what's different about their interview process. From bar raisers (Amazon) to Hiring Committees (Google), each company has its own quirks. Knowing these idiosyncrasies will help you to react better to a super-tough interviewer, or to avoid being intimidated when two interviewers show up at the door (Apple!).

In addition, our specialists offered insight as to what their company stresses in their interviews. While almost all software firms care about coding and algorithms, some companies focus more than others on specific aspects of the interview. Whether this is because of the company's technology or its history, now you'll know what and how to prepare.

So, join us as we take you behind the scenes at Microsoft, Google, Amazon, Yahoo and Apple...

Microsoft wants smart people. Geeks. People who are passionate about technology. You probably won't be tested on the ins and outs of C++ APIs, but you will be expected to write code on the board.

In a typical interview, you'll show up at Microsoft at some time in the morning and fill out initial paper work. You'll have a short interview with a recruiter who will give you a sample question. Your recruiter is usually there to prep you, and not to grill you on technical questions. Be nice to your recruiter. Your recruiter can be your biggest advocate, even pushing to re-interview you if you stumbled on your first interview. They can fight for you to be hired - or not!

During the day, you'll do four or five interviews, often with two different teams. Unlike many companies, where you meet your interviewers in a conference room, you'll meet with your Microsoft interviewers in their office. This is a great time to look around and get a feel for the team culture.

Depending on the team, interviewers may or may not share their feedback on you with the rest of the interview loop.

When you complete your interviews with a team, you might speak with a hiring manager. If so, that's a great sign! It likely means that you passed the interviews with a particular team. It's now down to the hiring manager's decision.

You might get a decision that day, or it might be a week. After one week of no word from HR, send them a friendly email asking for a status update.

### Definitely Prepare:

"Why do you want to work for Microsoft?"

In this question, Microsoft wants to see that you're passionate about technology. A great answer might be, "I've been using Microsoft software as long as I can remember, and I'm really impressed at how Microsoft manages to create a product that is universally excellent. For example, I've been using Visual Studio recently to learn game programming, and it's APIs are excellent." Note how this shows a passion for technology!

### What's Unique:

You'll only reach the hiring manager if you've done well, but if you do, that's a great sign!

Amazon's recruiting process typically begins with one or two phone screens in which you interview with a specific team. The engineer who interviews you will usually ask you to write simple code and read it aloud on the phone. They will ask a broad set of questions to explore what areas of technology you're familiar with.

Next, you fly to Seattle for four or five interviews with one or two teams which have selected you based on your resume and phone interviews. You will have to code on a whiteboard, and some interviewers will stress other skills. Interviewers are each assigned a specific area to probe and may seem very different from each other. They can not see other feedback until they have submitted their own and they are discouraged from discussing it until the hiring meeting.

Amazon's "bar raiser" interviewer is charged with keeping the interview bar high. They attend special training and will interview candidates outside their group in order to balance out the group itself. If one interview seems significantly harder and different, that's most likely the bar raiser. This person has both significant experience with interviews and veto power in the hiring decision. You will meet with your recruiter at the end of the day.

Once your interviewers have entered their feedback, they will meet to discuss it. They will be the people making the hiring decision.

While Amazon's recruiters are excellent at following up with candidates, occasionally there are delays. If you haven't heard from Amazon within a week, we recommend a friendly email.

### Definitely Prepare:

Amazon is a web-based company, and that means they care about scale. Make sure you prepare for questions in "Large Scale." You don't need a background in distributed systems to answer these questions. See our recommendations in the System Design and Memory Limits Chapter.

Additionally, Amazon tends to ask a lot of questions about object oriented design. Check out the Object Oriented Design chapter for sample questions and suggestions.

### What's Unique:

The Bar Raiser, who is brought in from a different team to keep the bar high.

There are many scary stories floating around about Google interviews, but they're mostly just that: stories. The interview is not terribly different from Microsoft's or Amazon's. However, because Google HR can be a little disorganized, we recommend being proactive in communication.

A Google engineer performs the first phone screen, so expect tough technical questions. On your on-site interview, you'll interview with four to six people, one of whom will be a lunch interviewer. Interviewer feedback is kept confidential from the other interviewers, so you can be assured that you enter each interview with blank slate. Your lunch interviewer doesn't submit feedback, so this is a great opportunity to ask honest questions.

Written feedback is submitted to a hiring committee of engineers to make a hire/no-hire recommendation. Feedback is typically broken down into four categories (Analytical Ability, Coding, Experience and Communication) and you are given a score from 1.0 to 4.0 overall.

The hiring committee understands that you can't be expected to excel in every interview, but if multiple people raise the same red flag (arrogance, poor coding skills, etc), that can disqualify you. A hiring committee typically wants to see one interviewer who is an "enthusiastic endorser." In other words, a packet with scores of 3.6, 3.1, 3.1 and 2.6 is better than all 3.1s. Your phone screen is usually not a strong factor in the final decision.

The Google hiring process can be slow. If you don't hear back within one week, politely ask your recruiter for an update. A lack of response says nothing about your performance.

### Definitely Prepare:

As a web-based company, Google cares about how to design a scalable system. So, make sure you prepare for questions from "System Design and Memory Limits" Additionally, many Google interviewers will ask questions involving Bit Manipulation, so please brush up on these topics.

### What's Different:

Your interviewers do not make the hiring decision. Rather, they enter feedback which is passed to a hiring committee. The hiring committee recommends a decision which can be—though rarely is—rejected by Google executives.

Much like the company itself, Apple's interview process has minimal bureaucracy. The interviewers will be looking for excellent technical skills, but a passion for the position and the company is also very important. While it's not a prerequisite to be a Mac user, you should at least be familiar with the system.

The interview process usually begins with a recruiter phone screen to get a basic sense of your skills, followed up by a series of technical phone screens with team members.

Once you're invited on campus, you'll typically be greeted by the recruiter who provides an overview of the process. You will then have 6-8 interviews with members of the team for which you're interviewing, as well as key people with whom your team works.

You can expect a mix of 1-on-1 and 2-on-1 interviews. Be ready to code on a whiteboard and make sure all of your thoughts are clearly communicated. Lunch is with your potential future manager and appears more casual, but is still an interview. Each interviewer is usually focused on a different area and is discouraged from sharing feedback unless there's something they want subsequent interviewers to drill into.

Towards the end of the day, your interviewers will compare notes and if everyone still feels you're a viable candidate, you'll interview with the director and the VP of the organization you're applying to. While this decision is rather informal, it's very good sign if you make it. This decision also happens behind the scenes and if you don't pass, you'll simply be escorted out of the building without ever having been the wiser (until now).

If you made it to the director and VP interviews, all of your interviewers will gather in a conference room to give an official thumbs up or thumbs down. The VP typically won't be present, but can still veto the hire if they weren't impressed. Your recruiter will usually follow up a few days later, but feel free to ping him or her for updates.

### Definitely Prepare:

If you know what team you're interviewing with, make sure you read up on that product. What do you like about it? What would you improve? Offering specific recommendations can show your passion for the job.

### What's Unique:

Apple does 2-on-1 interviews often, but don't get stressed out about them - it's the same as a 1-on-1 interview!

Also, Apple employees are huge Apple fans. You should show this same passion in your interview.

**Resume Selection & Screening:** While Yahoo tends to only recruit at the top 10 – 20 schools, other candidates can still get interviewed through Yahoo's job board (or – better yet – if they can get an internal referral). If you're one of the lucky ones selected, your interview process will start off with a phone screen. Your phone screen will be with a senior employee (tech lead, manager, etc).

**On-Site Interview:** You will typically interview with 6 – 7 people on the same team for 45 minutes each. Each interviewer will have an area of focus. For example, one interviewer might focus on databases, while another interviewer might focus on your understanding of computer architecture. Interviews will often be composed as follows:

*5 minutes:* General conversation. Tell me about yourself, your projects, etc.

*20 minutes:* Coding question. For example, implement merge sort.

*20 minutes:* System design. For example, design a large distributed cache. These questions will often focus on an area from your past experience or on something your interviewer is currently working on.

**Decision:** At the end of the day, you will likely meet with a Program Manager or someone else for a general conversation (product demos, concerns about the company, your competing offers, etc). Meanwhile, your interviewers will discuss your performance and attempt to come to a decision. The hiring manager has the ultimate say and will weigh the positive feedback against the negative.

If you have done well, you will often get a decision that day, but this is not always the case. There can be many reasons that you might not be told for several days – for example, the team may feel it needs to interview several other people.

### Definitely Prepare:

Yahoo, almost as a rule, asks questions about system design, so make sure you prepare for that. They want to know that you can not only write code, but that you can design software. Don't worry if you don't have a background in this - you can still reason your way through it!

### What's Unique:

Your phone interview will likely be performed by someone with more influence, such as a hiring manager.

Yahoo is also unusual in that it often gives a decision (if you're hired) on the same day. Your interviewers will discuss your performance while you meet with a final interviewer.

## The View from the Other Side of the Front, by Peter Bailey

For the eager candidate getting ready for a big job interview, *Cracking the Coding Interview* is an invaluable reference, containing excellent coaching and practice material that gives you an inside edge on the interview process. However, as you go over your old data structures textbook and drill yourself with homemade discrete math flash cards, don't make the mistake of thinking of the interview as a kind of high-pressure game show – that if you just give all the right answers to the tech questions, you too can win a shiny new career (this week, on *Who Wants to be a Software Engineer?*)

While the technical questions on computer science obviously *are* very important, the *most* important interview question is not covered in this guidebook. In fact, it's often the single most important question in your interviewers' minds as they grill you in that little room. Despite the questions on polymorphism and heaps and virtual machines, the question they really want an answer to is ...

*Would I have a beer with this guy?*

Don't look at me like that, I'm serious! Well, I may be embellishing a little, but hear me out. The point I'm trying to make is that interviewers, especially those that you might work with, are probably just as anxious as you are. *Nonsense*, you say, as a nervous young professional, checking your pants for lint while you bite your fingernails, waiting for the interview team to show up in the front lobby. After all, this is the big leagues, and these guys are just waiting for you to slip up so they can rip you apart, laugh at your shriveled corpse, and grind your career dreams to dust beneath the heels of their boots.

Right? Just like pledge week, back in freshman year? Right? Hmmm?

Nothing could be further from the truth. The team of developers and managers interviewing you have their own tasks and projects waiting for them, back at their own desks. Believe me, they're hoping that every interview is going to be the last one. They'd rather be doing *anything* else. There might be a batch of upcoming projects looming on their calendar, and they need more manpower if they're going to even have a *prayer* of making their deadline. But the last guy the agency sent over was a complete flake who railed about Microsoft's evil for half an hour. And the one before that couldn't code his way out of a wet paper bag without using copy-and-paste. Sheesh, they think, where is HR *getting* these guys? How hard can it be to hire one lousy person?

While they may not literally be asking themselves "Would I have a beer with this guy (or gal)", they *are* looking to see how well you would fit in with the team, and how you would affect team chemistry. If they hire you, you're all going to be spending a lot of time together for the next few months or years, and they want to know that they can rely on you – and maybe even come to consider you a friend and colleague. They want to know that they can *depend* on you. And as tempting as it might be to them to just settle and hire the next person who comes along, they know better.

In many companies, particularly large U.S. companies, it's harder to fire somebody than it is to hire somebody. (Welcome to the US: Land of Lawsuits!) If they hire a dud, they're stuck with them. That person might be unproductive or, even worse, a drain on the team's productivity. So they keep interviewing, until they find the right person. They know that it's better to reject a good candidate than hire a bad one.

Some of those interviews are real doozies. Once you've interviewed long enough, you build up a repertoire of horror stories. War stories, of candidates who looked promising on paper until the interviews went terribly, terribly wrong. These war stories are not only humorous – they're also instructive.

*Names have been changed to protect the innocent – or downright ridiculous.*

## Pop Divas Need Not Apply

Leonard was a very promising C++ coder, three years out of college, with a solid work history and an impressive skill set. He proved on the phone screen that he was above-average technically, and so he was invited in for an interview. We needed a savvy C++ person to work on a piece of middleware that interfaced with our database, and Leonard seemed like a sure fit.

However, once we started talking to him, things went south in a hurry. He spent most of the interview criticizing every tool and platform that we questioned him on. We used SQL Server as our database? Puhleease. We were planning to switch to Oracle soon, right? What's that? Our team used Tool A to do all our coding in? Unacceptable. He used Tool B, and only Tool B, and after he was hired, we'd all have to switch to Tool B. And we'd have to switch to Java, because he really wanted to work with Java, despite the fact that 75 percent of the codebase would have to be rewritten. We'd thank him later. And oh, by the way, he wouldn't be making any meetings before ten o'clock.

Needless to say, we encouraged Leonard to seek opportunities elsewhere. It wasn't that his ideas were bad – in fact, he was "technically" right about many things, and his (strong) opinions were all backed with solid fact and sound reason (except for the ten o'clock thing – we think he may have just been making a "power play".) But it was obvious that, if hired, Leonard wasn't going to play well with others – he would have been toxic kryptonite for team chemistry. He actually managed to offend two of the team members during the forty-five minutes of his interview. Leonard also made the mistake of assuming that Code Purity and Algorithm Beauty were always more important than a business deadline.

In the real world, there are always compromises to be made, and knowing how to work with the business analysts is just as important as knowing how to refactor a blob of code. If Leonard would not have gotten along with other IT people, he definitely wouldn't have gotten along with the business folks. Maybe you can get away with hiring a Leonard if he's one of the best ten coders in the world (he wasn't). But he was the classic failure example for the "Would you have a beer with this guy?" test.

## What We Have Here is Failure to Communicate

Trisha was a mid-level Java developer with a solid history of middleware and JSP work on her resume. Since she was local, we invited her in for an interview without a phone screen. When we started asking her questions, it quickly became obvious that Trisha was a woman of few words. Her answers were short and often composed of "yes/no" responses, even to questions that were meant to start a dialog. Once she did start opening up, I still wasn't sure she was *actually* talking. I saw her lips moving, and heard mumbling sounds coming out, but it wasn't anything that sounded like English.

I'm not sure if Trisha was nervous or just shy, but either way, I had to ask her numerous times to repeat herself. Now I was the one getting nervous! I didn't want to be the guy who "ruined" the interview, so I pulled back on my questions. The other folks in the room and I exchanged uneasy glances. We felt like we were on a *Seinfeld* episode. It was almost impossible to understand Trisha, and when she did speak up, her halting, uncertain, confused speech patterns made us feel more like code breakers than interviewers. I am not exaggerating to say that I did not understand a single answer she gave during the interview.

Knowing, alone, isn't good enough. You're going to be talking with other technical people, and you're going to be talking to customers, and sales reps, and Betty from Marketing. You will write something eventually, whether it's documentation, or a project plan, or a requirements document. The word processor might correct your spelling, but it won't correct your lousy writing. The ability to communicate thoughts and ideas, in a clear, concise manner, is an absolutely invaluable skill that employers seek.

The same goes for verbal communication. I used to work with a co-worker who doubled the length of every meeting he was in, because he could not answer a question in less than ten minutes. "Hey, Dennis, what time is it?" "Well, that's kind of interesting, because I just happened to be reading an article on cesium clocks and leap seconds and the history of the Gregorian Calendar and ..."

I'll spare you the rest.

## You Can Count on Me, Just Not Until Early Afternoon

Ahhh, 1999. The crest of the dot-com bubble, and the tightest labor market in history. Our company was racing to expand its development team, and we would have hired a German Shepherd if it knew HTML. Instead, we wound up hiring Ian. We should've hired the dog.

Ian was a cheerful, friendly guy who had a gift of natural charisma. He got along fantastically with all of the interviewers, and seemed very intelligent. Skill-wise, he was adequate. He hadn't written a single line of computer code outside of his college courses, and didn't even have his own e-mail address. When we gave Ian the chance to ask us questions at the end of the interview, he asked about flexible work hours, and how soon he could take vacation time. Instead of showing an interest in the career opportunities, or in company's growth prospects, he asked whether he could take the all-you-could-drink break room soda home with him. The questions grew more bizarre from there.

Ian was very interested in our Legal Assistance benefit. He wanted to know if it covered the cost of filing lawsuits, if it covered him if he got sued himself, if it applied to any lawsuits he currently was involved in, and if he could "theoretically" use it to *sue the company itself.* He also asked us if he could use it to help him "fix" some unpaid speeding tickets.

In any other year, that should have been it for Ian right there. But, in 1999, we were hiring anybody who was even remotely competent. Ian collected paychecks from us for eighteen months, and he was about as productive as a traffic cone. He usually sauntered into the office around ten-thirty with some sort of lame excuse (by my count, he had to wait for the cable guy sixteen times in a six-month period). He usually killed the morning by answering e-mail and playing ping-pong, before breaking for a two-hour lunch. After lunch, it was more ping-pong, and maybe an hour of writing bad code, before bolting the office sometime around three. He was the dictionary definition of unreliable.

Remember, your potential future team members need to know that they can rely on you. And they need to know that you won't need constant supervision and hand-holding. They need to know that you're able to figure things out on your own. One of the most important messages that you, as a candidate, can convey in your interview is *hiring me will make your lives easier.* In fact, this is a large part of the reason for the famously difficult interview questions at places like Amazon and Google; if you can handle that kind of unpredictable pressure in an interview, then you stand a good chance of being useful to them on real projects.

To cite a more subtle example, once I was on a four person team that was desperately trying to recruit new members to help work on an old pile of software. It was a real mess; we'd inherited a nasty ball of spaghetti, and we needed people who could jump in, figure things out, and be part of the solution.

There was one very smart fellow, Terry, who would have been a great asset for our team – but we didn't hire him, despite his excellent technical and personal skills. It was because he insisted on meticulous written instructions for every step of the coding process. He wasn't going to make a suggestion or take any initiative – or blow his nose, for that matter – without a mile-long audit trail and a dozen signatures. While he insisted that he worked that way for reasons of quality (a defensible point), we got the impression that it had more to do with butt-covering, and we simply didn't have the time for that kind of bureaucracy. Terry would have been an excellent fit in a government or aerospace IT department, something that required ISO 9000 procedures. But he would have never fit into our team; he would have been a burden, not an asset.

## My Spider Senses are Tingling

I can think of lots of interviews that just fell into the general category of *weird and uncomfortable:*

» The Java coder who apparently considered hygiene optional, and had the interview room smelling like week-old blue cheese within ten minutes (my eyes were watering).

» The young fresh-out-of-college graduate with a tongue piercing that kept tick-tick-ticking against his teeth as he talked (after half an hour, it was like Chinese water torture).

» The girl who wore an iPod through her interview, with the volume turned loud enough that she actually had to ask the interviewers to repeat themselves a few times.

» The poor, hyper-nervous fellow who was sweating like a marathon runner for half an hour.

» The girl who wore a T-shirt with an obscene political slogan to her interview.

» The guy who asked (seriously) at the end of his interview, "So, are there any hot chicks in our department?"

Those are the interviews where we politely thank the people for their time, shake their hand (except for the sweaty guy), then turn to each other after the door closes and ask – *did that really just happen?*

Nobody is saying that you have to be a bland, boring robot in a Brooks Brothers suit and tie. Remember, the interview team wants you to be "the one", but they're also very worried about the possibility that you're going to be more of a distraction than an asset. Don't talk or behave in a way that will set off their early warning radar. Whether or not somebody bothers to behave professionally during an interview is often a very good indicator of what kind of teammate they're going to be.

Rudimentary social skills are part of the answer to "Would I have a beer with this guy?", or at least, "Will I mind working next to this guy for six months?" From the interviewer's point of view, they're picking a neighbor that they're going to live and work with 200 hours per month for foreseeable future. Would you really want a neighbor that smelled like a hog rendering plant?

# Before the Interview

## What Resume Screeners Look For

Resume screeners look for the same things that interviewers do:

» Are you smart?

» Can you code?

That means you should present your resume to highlight those two things. Your love of tennis, traveling, or magic cards won't do much to show that, so it's likely just wasting space.

Keep in mind that recruiters only spend a fixed amount of time (about 20 seconds) looking at your resume. If you limit the content to the best, most impressive, most relevant items, they'll jump out at the recruiter. Weak items only dilute your resume and distract the recruiter from what you'd like them to see.

## Employment History

**Relevant Jobs:** Your resume does not - and should not - include a full history of every role you've ever had. Your job serving ice cream, for example, will not show that you're smart or that you can code. Include only the relevant things.

**Writing Strong Bullets:** For each role, try to discuss your accomplishments with the following approach: "Accomplished X by implementing Y which led to Z." Here's an example:

» "Reduced object rendering time by 75% by applying Floyd's algorithm, leading to a 10% reduction in system boot time."

Here's another example with an alternate wording:

» "Increased average match accuracy from 1.2 to 1.5 by implementing a new comparison algorithm based on windiff."

Not everything you did will fit into this approach, but the principle is the

### Got some extra time to prepare?

If you have at least a couple of months before an interview (or if you're in school and not graduating yet), you may be able to improve your resume.

Go out and get some project experience! Take courses that have major projects. Get involved in open source. Ask a professor if there is any research you can aid with, or ask if he/she can sponsor you on an independent study.

This will put you in a better position to have your resume selected down the road. It will also give you lots of things to talk about in an interview.

same: show what you did, how you did it, and what the results were. Ideally, you should try to make the results "measurable" somehow.

## Projects

Almost every candidate has some projects, even if they're just academic projects. List them on your resume! I recommend putting a section called "Projects" on your resume and list your 2 - 4 most significant projects. State what the project was, which languages or technologies it employed, and whether it was an individual or a team project. If your project was not for a course, that's even better! It shows passion, initiative, and work ethic. You can specify the type of project by listing course projects as "Course Project" and your independent projects as "Independent Projects" (or some other wording).

## Programming Languages and Software

**Software:** Generally speaking, I do not recommend listing that you're familiar with Microsoft Office. Everyone is, and it just dilutes the "real" information. On the other hand, familiarity with developer-specific or highly technical software (e.g., Visual Studio, Eclipse, Linux) can be useful, but it often doesn't make much of a difference.

**Languages:** Knowing which languages to include on your resume is always a tricky thing. Do you list everything you've ever worked with? Or only the ones that you're more comfortable using (even though that might only be one or two languages)? I recommend the following compromise: list most of the languages you've used, but add your experience level. This approach is shown below:

» "Languages: Java (expert), C++ (proficient), JavaScript (prior experience), C (prior experience)"

## Advice for Non-Native English Speakers and Internationals

**Proofreading:** Some companies will throw out your resume just because of a typo. Please get at least one native English speaker to proofread your resume.

**Personal Information:** For US positions, do *not* include age, marital status, or nationality. This sort of personal information is not appreciated by companies, as it creates a legal liability for them. However, you may want to include your current work authorization / visa status, particularly when applying to smaller companies who may be unable to sponsor candidates.

## Why Are Behavioral Questions Asked?

Behavioral questions are asked for a variety of reasons. They can be asked either to get to know your personality, to understand your resume more deeply, or just to ease you into an interview. Either way, these questions are important and can be prepared for.

## How To Prepare

Behavioral questions are usually of the form "tell me about a time when you ...", and may require an example from a specific project or position. I recommend filling in the following "preparation grid" as shown below:

| | Project 1 | Project 2 | Project 3 | Project 4 |
|---|---|---|---|---|
| Most Challenging | | | | |
| What You Learned | | | | |
| Most Interesting | | | | |
| Hardest Bug | | | | |
| Enjoyed Most | | | | |
| Conflicts with Teammates | | | | |

Along the top, as columns, you should list all the major aspects of your resume – e.g., your projects, jobs, or activities. Along the side, as rows, you should list the common questions – e.g., what you enjoyed most, what you enjoyed least, what you considered most challenging, what you learned, what the hardest bug was, etc. In each cell, put the corresponding story.

We recommend reducing each story to just a couple of keywords that you can write in each cell. This will make the grid easier to study and remember.

In your interview, when you're asked about a project, you'll be able to come up with an appropriate story effortlessly. Study this grid before your interview.

NOTE: If you're doing a phone interview, you may want to have this grid out in front of you.

Some additional advice:

1.  When asked about your weaknesses, give a real weakness! Answers like "My greatest weakness is that I work too hard" tell your interviewer that you're arrogant and/or won't admit to your faults. No one wants to work with someone like that. A better answer conveys a real, legitimate weakness but emphasizes how you work to overcome it. For example: "Sometimes, I don't have a very good attention to detail. While that's good because it lets me execute quickly, it also means that I sometimes make careless mistakes. Because of that, I make sure to always have someone else double check my work."

2.  When asked what the most challenging part was, don't say "I had to learn a lot of new languages and technologies." This is the "cop out" answer (e.g., you don't know what else to say). It tells the interviewer that nothing was really that hard.

3.  Remember: you're not just answering their questions, you're telling them about yourself! Many people try to just answer the questions. Think more deeply about what each story communicates about you.

4.  If you think you'll be asked behavioral questions (e.g., "tell me about a challenging interaction with a team member"), you should create a Behavioral Preparation Grid. This is the same as the one above, but the left side contains things like "challenging interaction", "failure", "success", and "influencing people."

## What questions should you ask the interviewer?

Most interviewers will give you a chance to ask them questions. The quality of your questions will be a factor, whether subconsciously or consciously, in their decisions.

Some questions may come to you during the interview, but you can - and should - prepare questions in advance. Doing research on the company or team may help you with preparing questions.

Questions can be divided into three different categories:

**Genuine Questions:** These are the questions you actually want to know the answers to. Here are a few ideas of questions that are valuable to many candidates:

1.  "How much of your day do you spend coding?"

2.  "How many meetings do you have every week?"

3.  "What is the ratio of testers to developers to product managers? What is the interaction like? How does project planning happen on the team?"

**Insightful Questions:** These questions are designed to demonstrate your deep knowledge of programming or technologies.

1.  "I noticed that you use technology X. How do you handle problem Y?"

2.  "Why did the product choose to use the X protocol over the Y protocol? I know it has benefits like A, B, C, but many companies choose not to use it because of issue D."

**Passion Questions:** These questions are designed to demonstrate your passion for technology.

1.  "I'm very interested in scalability. Did you come in with a background in this, or what opportunities are there to learn about it?"

2.  "I'm not familiar with technology X, but it sounds like a very interesting solution. Could you tell me a bit more about how it works?"

## How to Prepare for Technical Questions

You've purchased this book, so you've already gone a long way towards good preparation. Nice work!

That said, there are better and worse ways to prepare. Many candidates just read through problems and solutions. Don't do that! Memorizing or trying to learn specific questions won't help you! Rather, do this:

1. Try to solve the problem on your own. I mean, *really* try to solve it. Many questions are designed to be tough - that's ok! When you're solving a problem, make sure to think about the space and time efficiency. Ask yourself if you could improve the time efficiency by reducing the space efficiency, or vice versa.

2. Write the code for the algorithm on paper. You've been coding all your life on a computer, and you've gotten used to the many nice things about it. But, in your interview, you won't have the luxury of syntax highlighting, code completion, or compiling. Mimic this situation by coding on paper.

3. Type your paper code as-is into a computer. You will probably make a bunch of mistakes. Start a list of all the errors you make, so that you can keep these in mind in the real interview.

4. Do a mock interview. CareerCup offers a mock interview service, or you can grab a friend to ask you questions. Though your friend may not be an expert interviewer, he or she may still be able to walk you through a coding or algorithm problem.

## What You Need To Know

Most interviewers won't ask about specific algorithms for binary tree balancing or other complex algorithms. Frankly, they probably don't remember these algorithms either.

You're usually only expected to know the basics. Here's a list of the absolute must-have knowledge:

| Data Structures | Algorithms | Concepts |
|---|---|---|
| Linked Lists | Breadth First Search | Bit Manipulation |
| Binary Trees | Depth First Search | Singleton Design Pattern |
| Tries | Binary Search | Factory Design Pattern |
| Stacks | Merge Sort | Memory (Stack vs Heap) |
| Queues | Quick Sort | Recursion |
| Vectors / ArrayLists | Tree Insert / Find / etc | Big-O Time |
| Hash Tables | | |

This is not, of course, an all-inclusive list. Questions may be asked on areas outside of these topics. This is merely a "must know" list.

For each of the topics, make sure you understand how to implement / use them, and (where applicable) the space and time complexity.

Practice implementing the data structures and algorithms. You might be asked to implement them directly, or you might be asked to implement a modification of them. Either way, the more comfortable you are with implementations the better.

## Do you need to know details of C++, Java, etc?

While I personally never liked asking these sorts of questions (e.g., "what is a vtable?"), many interviewers regretfully do ask them. For big companies like Microsoft, Google, Amazon, etc, I wouldn't stress too much about these questions. Look up the most common questions and make sure you have answers to them, but I would focus more on data structures and algorithms preparation.

At smaller companies, or non-software companies, these questions can be more important. Look up your company on CareerCup.com to decide for yourself. If your company isn't listed, find a similar company as a reference.

# The Interview and Beyond

## Why Behavioral Questions

As stated earlier, interviews usually start and end with "chit chat" or "soft skills." This is a time to answer questions about your resume or general questions, and also an opportunity for you to ask questions. This part of the interview is targeted at getting to know you, as well as relaxing you.

## Be Specific, Not Arrogant

Arrogance is a red flag, but you still want to make yourself sound impressive. So how do you make yourself sound good without being arrogant? By being specific!

Specificity means giving just the facts and letting the interviewer derive an interpretation. Consider an example:

» Candidate #1: "I basically did all the hard work for the team."

» Candidate #2: "I implemented the file system, which was considered one of the most challenging components because ..."

Candidate #2 not only sounds more impressive, but she also appears less arrogant.

## Limit Details

When a candidate blabbers on about a problem, it's hard for an interviewer who isn't well versed in the subject or project to understand it. CareerCup recommends that you stay light on details and just state the key points. That is, consider something like this: "By examining the most common user behavior and applying the Rabin-Karp algorithm, I designed a new algorithm to reduce search from $O(n)$ to $O(\log n)$ in 90% of cases. I can go into more details if you'd like." This demonstrates the key points while letting your interviewer ask for more details if he wants to.

## Ask Good Questions

Remember those questions you came up with while preparing? Now is a great time to use them!

## Structure Answers Using S.A.R.

Structure your responses using S.A.R.: Situation, Action, Result. That is, you should start off outlining the situation, then explaining the actions you took, and lastly, describing the result.

*Example: "Tell me about a challenging interaction with a teammate."*

» **Situation:** On my operating systems project, I was assigned to work with three other people. While two were great, the third team member didn't contribute much. He stayed quiet during meetings, rarely chipped in during email discussions, and struggled to complete his components.

» **Action:** One day after class, I pulled him aside to speak about the course and then moved the discussion into talking about the project. I asked him open-ended questions on how he felt it was going, and which components he was excited about tackling. He suggested all the easiest components, and yet offered to do the write-up. I realized then that he wasn't lazy – he was actually just really confused about the project and lacked confidence. I worked with him after that to break down the components into smaller pieces, and I made sure to complement him a lot on his work to boost his confidence.

» **Result:** He was still the weakest member of the team, but he got a lot better. He was able to finish all his work on time, and he contributed more in discussions. We were happy to work with him on a future project.

The situation and the result should be very succinct. Your interviewer generally does not need many details to understand what happened.

By using the SAR model with clear, crisp situations, actions and results, the interviewer will be able to easily identify how you made an impact and why it mattered.

## General Advice for Technical Questions

Interviews are supposed to be difficult. If you don't get every – or any – answer immediately, that's ok! In fact, in my experience, maybe only 10 people out of the 120+ that I've interviewed have gotten the question right instantly.

So when you get a hard question, don't panic. Just start talking aloud about how you would solve it.

And, one more thing: you're not done until the interviewer says that you're done! What I mean here is that when you come up with an algorithm, start thinking about the problems accompanying it. When you write code, start trying to find bugs. If you're anything like the other 110 candidates that I've interviewed, you probably made some mistakes.

## Five Steps to a Technical Question

A technical interview question can be solved utilizing a five step approach:

1.  Ask your interviewer questions to resolve ambiguity.

2.  Design an Algorithm

3.  Write pseudo-code first, but make sure to tell your interviewer that you're writing pseudo-code! Otherwise, he/she may think that you're never planning to write "real" code, and many interviewers will hold that against you.

4.  Write your code, not too slow and not too fast.

5.  Test your code and *carefully* fix any mistakes.

## Step 1: Ask Questions

Technical problems are more ambiguous than they might appear, so make sure to ask questions to resolve anything that might be unclear or ambiguous. You may eventually wind up with a very different – or much easier – problem than you had initially thought. In fact, many interviewers (especially at Microsoft) will specifically test to see if you ask good questions.

Good questions might be things like: What are the data types? How much data is there? What assumptions do you need to solve the problem? Who is the user?

**Example: "Design an algorithm to sort a list."**

»   *Question: What sort of list? An array? A linked list?*

»   Answer: An array.

»   *Question: What does the array hold? Numbers? Characters? Strings?*

»   Answer: Numbers.

» *Question: And are the numbers integers?*

» Answer: Yes.

» *Question: Where did the numbers come from? Are they IDs? Values of something?*

» Answer: They are the ages of customers.

» *Question: And how many customers are there?*

» Answer: About a million.

We now have a pretty different problem: sort an array containing a million integers between 0 and 130. How do we solve this? Just create an array with 130 elements and count the number of ages at each value.

## Step 2: Design an Algorithm

Designing an algorithm can be tough, but our five approaches to algorithms can help you out (see pg 34). While you're designing your algorithm, don't forget to think about:

» What are the space and time complexities?

» What happens if there is a lot of data?

» Does your design cause other issues? (i.e., if you're creating a modified version of a binary search tree, did your design impact the time for insert / find / delete?)

» If there are other issues, did you make the right trade-offs?

» If they gave you specific data (e.g., mentioned that the data is ages, or in sorted order), have you leveraged that information? There's probably a reason that you're given it.

## Step 3: Pseudo-Code

Writing pseudo-code first can help you outline your thoughts clearly and reduce the number of mistakes you commit. But, make sure to tell your interviewer that you're writing pseudo-code first and that you'll follow it up with "real" code. Many candidates will write pseudo-code in order to 'escape' writing real code, and you certainly don't want to be confused with those candidates.

## Step 4: Code

You don't need to rush through your code; in fact, this will most likely hurt you. Just go at a nice, slow methodical pace. Also, remember this advice:

» Use Data Structures Generously: Where relevant, use a good data structure or define your own. For example, if you're asked a problem involving finding the minimum age for a group of people, consider defining a data structure to represent a Person. This shows your interviewer that you care about good object oriented design.

» Don't Crowd Your Coding: This is a minor thing, but it can really help. When you're writing code on a whiteboard, start in the upper left hand corner – not in the middle. This will give you plenty of space to write your answer.

## Step 5: Test

Yes, you need to test your code! Consider testing for:

» Extreme cases: 0, negative, null, maximums, etc

» User error: What happens if the user passes in null or a negative value?

» General cases: Test the normal case.

If the algorithm is complicated or highly numerical (bit shifting, arithmetic, etc), consider testing while you're writing the code rather than just at the end.

Also, when you find mistakes (which you will), carefully think through *why* the bug is occuring. One of the worst things I saw while interviewing was candidates who recognized a mistake and tried making "random" changes to fix the error.

For example, imagine a candidate writes a function that returns a number. When he tests his code with the number '5' he notices that it returns 0 when it should be returning 1. So, he changes the last line from "return ans" to "return ans+1," without thinking through why this would resolve the issue. Not only does this look bad, but it also sends the candidate on an endless string of bugs and bug fixes.

When you notice problems in your code, really think deeply about why your code failed before fixing the mistake.

## Five Algorithm Approaches

There's no sure fire approach to solving a tricky algorithm problem, but the approaches below can be useful. Keep in mind that the more problems you practice, the easier it will to identify which approach to use.

Also, remember that the five approaches can be "mixed and matched." That is, once you've applied "Simplify & Generalize", you may want to implement Pattern Matching next.

### APPROACH I: EXAMPLIFY

Description: Write out specific examples of the problem, and see if you can figure out a general rule.

Example: Given a time, calculate the angle between the hour and minute hands.

Approach: Start with an example like 3:27. We can draw a picture of a clock by selecting where the 3 hour hand is and where the 27 minute hand is.

By playing around with these examples, we can develop a rule:

»   Minute angle (from 12 o'clock): 360 * minutes / 60

»   Hour angle (from 12 o'clock): 360 * (hour % 12) / 12 + 360 * (minutes / 60) * (1 / 12)

»   Angle between hour and minute: (hour angle - minute angle) % 360

By simple arithmetic, this reduces to 30 * hours - 5.5 * minutes.

### APPROACH II: PATTERN MATCHING

Description: Consider what problems the algorithm is similar to, and figure out if you can modify the solution to develop an algorithm for this problem.

Example: A sorted array has been rotated so that the elements might appear in the order 3 4 5 6 7 1 2. How would you find the minimum element?

Similar Problems:

»   Find the minimum element in an array.

»   Find a particular element in an array (eg, binary search).

Algorithm:

Finding the minimum element in an array isn't a particularly interesting algorithm (you could just iterate through all the elements), nor does it use the information provided (that the array is sorted). It's unlikely to be useful here.

However, binary search is very applicable. You know that the array is sorted, but rotated. So, it must proceed in an increasing order, then reset and increase again. The minimum element is the "reset" point.

If you compare the first and middle element (3 and 6), you know that the range is still increasing. This means that the reset point must be after the 6 (or, 3 is the minimum element and the array was never rotated). We can continue to apply the lessons from binary search to pinpoint this reset point, by looking for ranges where LEFT > RIGHT. That is, for a particular point, if LEFT < RIGHT, then the range does not contain the reset. If LEFT > RIGHT, then it does.

## APPROACH III: SIMPLIFY & GENERALIZE

Description: Change a constraint (data type, size, etc) to simplify the problem. Then try to solve it. Once you have an algorithm for the "simplified" problem, generalize the problem again.

Example: A ransom note can be formed by cutting words out of a magazine to form a new sentence. How would you figure out if a ransom note (string) can be formed from a given magazine (string)?

Simplification: Instead of solving the problem with words, solve it with characters. That is, imagine we are cutting characters out of a magazine to form a ransom note.

Algorithm:

We can solve the simplified ransom note problem with characters by simply creating an array and counting the characters. Each spot in the array corresponds to one letter. First, we count the number of times each character in the ransom note appears, and then we go through the magazine to see if we have all of those characters.

When we generalize the algorithm, we do a very similar thing. This time, rather than creating an array with character counts, we create a hash table. Each word maps to the number of times the word appears.

## APPROACH IV: BASE CASE AND BUILD

Description: Solve the algorithm first for a base case (e.g., just one element). Then, try to solve it for elements one and two, assuming that you have the answer for element one. Then, try to solve it for elements one, two and three, assuming that you have the answer to elements one and two.

Example: Design an algorithm to print all permutations of a string. For simplicity, assume all characters are unique.

Test String: abcdefg
```
Case "a"   --> {a}
Case "ab"  --> {ab, ba}
Case "abc" --> ?
```
This is the first "interesting" case. If we had the answer to P("ab"), how could we generate P("abc"). Well, the additional letter is "c", so we can just stick c in at every possible point. That

is:

```
merge(c, ab) --> cab, acb, abc
merge(c, ba) --> cba, bca, bac
```

Algorithm: Use a recursive algorithm. Generate all permutations of a string by "chopping off" the last character and generating all permutations of s[1... n-1]. Then, insert s[n] into every location of the string.

NOTE: Base Case and Build Algorithms often lead to natural recursive algorithms.

**APPROACH V: DATA STRUCTURE BRAINSTORM**

Description: This is hacky, but it often works. Simply run through a list of data structures and try to apply each one.

Example: Numbers are randomly generated and stored into an (expanding) array. How would you keep track of the median?

Data Structure Brainstorm:

»   Linked list? Probably not – linked lists tend not to do very well with accessing and sorting numbers.

»   Array? Maybe, but you already have an array. Could you somehow keep the elements sorted? That's probably expensive. Let's hold off on this and return to it if it's needed.

»   Binary tree? This is possible, since binary trees do fairly well with ordering. In fact, if the binary search tree is perfectly balanced, the top might be the median. But, be careful – if there's an even number of elements, the median is actually the average of the middle two elements. The middle two elements can't both be at the top. This is probably a workable algorithm, but let's come back to it.

»   Heap? A heap is really good at basic ordering and keeping track of max and mins. This is actually interesting – if you had two heaps, you could keep track of the biggest half and the smallest half of the elements. The biggest half is kept in a min heap, such that the smallest element in the biggest half is at the root. The smallest half is kept in a max heap, such that the biggest element of the smallest half is at the root. Now, with these data structures, you have the potential median elements at the roots. If the heaps are no longer the same size, you can quickly "rebalance" the heaps by popping an element off the one heap and pushing it onto the other.

Note that the more problems you do, the more developed your instinct on which data structure to apply will be.

## Congrats! You got the offer!

If you're lucky enough to get an offer (and I'm sure you will be!), congratulations! You may now be stressing over which offer to accept and all that fun stuff, so just remember that, most likely, all of your options are great and you'll be happy at any of them.

As far as which offer to take, well, we could tell you that money isn't that important and blah blah blah… but we'll skip over that and let you make your own decision regarding the importance of money. We have some other advice for you.

## Negotiating

It's Always Negotiable! Ok, maybe not always, but usually an offer is negotiable even if a recruiter tells you otherwise. It helps if you have a competing offer. But, don't lie – Microsoft knows what Google offers, so it just won't be realistic if you make up numbers. Also, technology is a small world, and people talk. Be honest.

## What's the money like, really?

Think about the full offer package. Many companies will have impressive salaries, but small annual bonuses. Other companies will have huge annual bonuses, but lower salaries. It's very confusing, and it's often not clear which company is offering more. Make sure you look at the full package (salary, signing bonus, health care benefits, raises, annual bonus, relocation, stock, promotions, etc).

## What about your career options?

Even if money is all that matters, think about the long term career. If you're fortunate enough to have several offers to pick from, consider how each one will impact your career in the long run. The company with the lowest salary but where you'll learn the most may just be the best move, even financially.

I can't give you some magical formula to decide the best offer, but here's what I'd recommend thinking about (in no particular order):

»   Career Path: Make a plan for your career. What do you want to do 5, 10 and 15 years from now? What skills do you need to develop? Which company or position will help you get there?

»   Promotion Opportunity: Do you ultimately desire to move into management, or would you rather become an increasingly senior developer?

»   Money and Benefits: Of course, the money still matters (but if you're early in your career, it probably doesn't matter much). As mentioned above, make sure you look at the full package.

» Happiness: Do you like the people? The products? The location? It's hard to tell, of course, before you work there. What are the options to change teams if you're unhappy?

» Brand Name: The company's brand name can mean a lot for your future career. Some company names will open doors, while others will not as much.

What about company stability? Personally, I think it matters much less than most people think. There are so many software companies out there. If you get laid off and need to find a new job, will it be difficult to find a new one? Only you can answer that.

## On the job, and beyond...

Before starting at a company, devise a career plan. What would you like your career to look like? What will it take to get there? Make sure you check in on your career plan regularly to make sure you are on track.

It's very easy, particularly at the big companies, to get sucked into staying for a while. They're great companies with lots of perks, and most people are truly quite happy there. If what you want is to stay an engineer for life, then there is absolutely nothing wrong with that.

However, if you want to run a company one day, or move up into management, you should stop and check your career plan. Is another year at your job going to help you get there? Or is it time to move? You, and only you, can decide.

# #1 | Practicing on a Computer

If you were training for a serious bike race in the mountains, would you practice only by biking on the streets? I hope not. The air is different. The terrain is different. I bet you'd practice in the mountains, right?

Using a compiler to practice interview questions is like preparing for a mountain race by street biking - and you've been street biking your whole life. Put away the compiler and get out the old pen and paper. Use a compiler only to verify your solutions.

# #2 | Not Rehearsing Behavioral Questions

Many candidates spend all their time prepping for technical questions and overlook the behavioral questions. Guess what? Your interviewer is judging those too! And, not only that - your performance on behavioral questions might bias your interviewer's perception of your technical performance. Behavioral prep is relatively easy and well-worth your time. Look over your projects and positions and think of the key stories. Rehearse the stories.

# #3 | Not Doing a Mock Interview

Imagine you're preparing for a big speech. Your whole school, company, or whatever will be there. Your future depends on this. And all you do to prepare is read the speech to yourself. Silently. In your head. Crazy, right?

Not doing a mock interview to prepare for your real one is just like this. If you're an engineer, you must know other engineers. Grab a buddy and ask him/her to do a mock interview with you. You can even return the favor!

# #4 | Trying to Memorize Solutions

Quality beats quantity. Try to struggle through and solve questions yourself; don't flip directly to the solutions when you get stuck. Memorizing how to solve specific problems isn't going to help you much in an interview either. Real preparation is about learning how to approach new problems.

# #5 | Talking Too Much

I can't tell you how many times I've asked candidates a simple question like "what was the hardest bug on Project Pod?", only to have them ramble on and on about things I don't understand. Five minutes later, when they finally come up for air, I've learned nothing - except that they're poor communicators. When asked a question, break your answer into three parts (Situation / Action / Response, Issue 1 / Issue 2 / Issue 3, etc) and speak for just a couple sentences about each. If I want more details, I'll ask!

## #6 | Talking Too Little

Psst - let me tell you a secret: I don't know what's going on in your head. So if you aren't talking, I don't know what you're thinking. If you don't talk for a long time, I'll assume that you aren't making any progress. Speak up often, and try to talk your way through a solution. This shows your interviewer that you're tackling the problem and aren't stuck. And it lets them guide you when you get off-track, helping you get to the answer faster. Best of all, it demonstrates your awesome communication skills. What's not to love?

## #7 | Rushing

Coding is not a race, and neither is interviewing. Take your time when working on a coding problem - don't rush! Rushing leads to mistakes, and suggests that you are careless. Go slowly and methodically, testing often and thinking through the problem thoroughly. In the end, you'll finish the problem in less time and with fewer mistakes.

## #8 | Not Debugging

Would you ever write code and not run or test it? I hope not! So why do that in an interview? When you finish writing code in an interview, "run" (or walk through) the code to test it. Or, on more complicated problems, test the code while writing it.

## #9 | Sloppy Coding

Did you know that you can write bug-free code but still perform horribly on a coding question? It's true! Duplicated code, messy data structures (i.e., lack of object oriented design), etc. Bad, bad, bad! When you write code, imagine you're writing for real-world maintainability. Break code into sub-routines, and design data structures to link appropriate data.

## #10 | Giving Up

Have you ever taken a computer adaptive test? These are tests that give you harder questions the better you do. Take it from me - they're not fun. Regardless of how well you're actually doing, you suddenly find yourself stumbling through problems. Yikes!

Interviewing is sort of like this. If you whiz through the easy problems, you're going to get more difficult problems. Or, the questions might have just started out hard to begin with! Either way, struggling on a question does *not* mean you are doing badly. So don't give up or get discouraged. You're doing great!

## Do I have to get every question right?

No. A good interviewer will stretch your mind. They'll want to see you struggle with a difficult problem. If a candidate is good, they'll ask harder and tougher questions until he/she is stumped! Thus, if you have trouble on a question, all it means is that the interviewer is doing their job!

## Should I tell my interviewer if I know a question?

Yes! You should definitely tell your interviewer if you've previously heard the question. This seems silly to some people - if you already know the question (and answer), you could ace the question, right? Not quite.

Here's why we strongly recommend that you tell your interviewer that you've heard the problem before:

1.  Big honesty points. This shows a lot of integrity - that's huge! Remember that the interviewer is evaluating you as a potential teammate. I don't know about you, but I personally prefer to work with honest people!

2.  The question might have changed ever-so-slightly. You don't want to risk repeating the wrong answer.

3.  If you easily belt out the right answer, it's obvious to the interviewer. They know how difficult a problem is supposed to be. It's very hard to "pretend" to struggle through a question, because you just can't approach it the same way other candidates do.

## How are interview questions selected?

This depends on the company, but any number of ways:

1.  Pre-Assigned List of Questions: This is unusual at bigger companies.

2.  Assigned Topics: Each interviewer is assigned a specific area to probe, but decides on his/her own questions.

3.  Interviewer's Choice: Each interviewer asks whatever he / she wants. Typically, under this system, the interviewers have a way of tracking which questions were already asked to a candidate to ensure a good diversity of questions.

Approach #3 is the most common. This usually means that interviewers will each have a "stock" set of five or so questions that they ask candidates.

## How should I dress?

Generally, candidates should dress one small step above the average employee in their position, or as nicely as the nicest dressed employees in their position. In most software firms, this means that jeans (nice jeans with no holes) or slacks with a nice shirt or sweater is fine. In a bank or another more formal institution, however, avoid jeans and wear slacks instead.

## What language should I use?

Many people will tell you "whatever language you're most comfortable with," but ideally you want to use a language that your interviewer is comfortable with. I'd usually recommend coding in either C, C++ or Java, as the vast majority of interviewers will be comfortable in one of these languages. My personal preference for interviews is Java (unless it's a question requiring C / C++), because it's quick to write and almost everyone can read and understand Java, even if they code mostly in C++. (Almost all the solutions in this book are written in Java for this reason.)

## I didn't hear back immediately after my interview. Am I rejected?

Absolutely not. Responses can be held up for a variety of reasons that have nothing to do with a good or bad performance. For example, an interviewer could have gone on vacation right after your interview. A company will always tell you if you're rejected (or at least I've never heard of a company which didn't).

## Can I re-apply to a company after getting rejected?

Almost always, but you typically have to wait a bit (6 months – 1 year). Your first bad interview usually won't affect you too much when you re-interview. Lots of people get rejected from Google or Microsoft and later get offers.

## What about experienced candidates?

This depends a lot on the company. On average though, experienced candidates will slightly get more questions about their background, and they might face higher standards when discussing system architecture (if this is relevant to their experience). For the most part though, experienced candidates face much the same process.

Yes, for better or worse, they should expect to go through the same coding and algorithm questions. With respect to their performance, they could face either higher standards (because they have more experience) or lower standards (because it's likely been many years since they worked with certain data structures).

## How This Book is Organized

We have grouped the interview questions into categories, with a page preceding each category offering advice and other useful information. Note that many questions may fall into multiple categories.

Within each category, the questions are sorted by approximate level of difficulty. Solutions for all questions are at the back.

## Special Advice for Software Design Engineers in Test (SDETs)

Not only must SDETs master testing, but they also have to be great coders. Thus, we recommend the following preparation process:

»   **Prepare the Core Testing Problems:** For example, how would you test a light bulb? A pen? A cash register? Microsoft Word? The Testing Chapter will give you more background on these problems.

»   **Practice the Coding Questions:** The #1 thing that SDETs get rejected for is coding skills. Make sure that you practice solving all the same coding and algorithm questions that a regular developer would get.

»   **Practice Testing the Coding Questions:** A very popular format for SDET questions is "Write code to do X," followed up by "OK, now test it." So, even when the question doesn't specifically require this, you should ask yourself, "how would I test this?" Remember: any problem can be an SDET problem!

## Full, Compilable Solutions

For your convenience, you can download the full solutions to the problems at http://www.careercup.com/careercup_book_solutions. This file provides executable code for all the Java solutions. The solutions can be opened and run with Eclipse.

## Suggestions and Corrections

While we do our best to ensure that all the solutions are correct, mistakes will be made. Moreover, sometimes there is no "right" answer. If you'd like to offer a suggestion or correction, please submit it at http://xrl.us/ccbook.

# Interview Questions

*Part 1*
# Data Structures

## Hash Tables

While not all problems can be solved with hash tables, a shocking number of interview problems can be. Before your interview, make sure to practice both using and implementing hash tables.

```
1   public HashMap<Integer, Student> buildMap(Student[] students) {
2       HashMap<Integer, Student> map = new HashMap<Integer, Student>();
3       for (Student s : students) map.put(s.getId(), s);
4       return map;
5   }
```

## ArrayList (Dynamically Resizing Array):

An ArrayList, or a dynamically resizing array, is an array that resizes itself as needed while still providing O(1) access. A typical implementation is that when a vector is full, the array doubles in size. Each doubling takes O(n) time, but happens so rarely that its amortized time is still O(1).

```
1   public ArrayList<String> merge(String[] words, String[] more) {
2       ArrayList<String> sentence = new ArrayList<String>();
3       for (String w : words) sentence.add(w);
4       for (String w : more) sentence.add(w);
5       return sentence;
6   }
```

## StringBuffer / StringBuilder

**Question:** What is the running time of this code?
```
1   public String makeSentence(String[] words) {
2       String sentence = "";
3       for (String w : words) sentence = sentence + w;
4       return sentence;
5   }
```

**Answer: O(n^2),** where n is the number of letters in sentence. Here's why: each time you append a string to sentence, you create a copy of sentence and run through all the letters in sentence to copy them over. If you have to iterate through up to n characters each time in the loop, and you're looping at least n times, that gives you an O(n^2) run time. Ouch!

StringBuffer (or StringBuilder) can help you avoid this problem.
```
1   public String makeSentence(String[] words) {
2       StringBuffer sentence = new StringBuffer();
3       for (String w : words) sentence.append(w);
4       return sentence.toString();
5   }
```

**1.1** Implement an algorithm to determine if a string has all unique characters. What if you can not use additional data structures?

pg 95

**1.2** Write code to reverse a C-Style String. (C-String means that "abcd" is represented as five characters, including the null character.)

pg 96

**1.3** Design an algorithm and write code to remove the duplicate characters in a string without using any additional buffer. NOTE: One or two additional variables are fine. An extra copy of the array is not.

FOLLOW UP

Write the test cases for this method.

pg 97

**1.4** Write a method to decide if two strings are anagrams or not.

pg 99

**1.5** Write a method to replace all spaces in a string with '%20'.

pg 100

**1.6** Given an image represented by an NxN matrix, where each pixel in the image is 4 bytes, write a method to rotate the image by 90 degrees. Can you do this in place?

pg 101

**1.7** Write an algorithm such that if an element in an MxN matrix is 0, its entire row and column is set to 0.

pg 102

**1.8** Assume you have a method isSubstring which checks if one word is a substring of another. Given two strings, s1 and s2, write code to check if s2 is a rotation of s1 using only one call to isSubstring (i.e., "waterbottle" is a rotation of "erbottlewat").

pg 103

# Chapter 2 | Linked Lists

## How to Approach:

Linked list questions are extremely common. These can range from simple (delete a node in a linked list) to much more challenging. Either way, we advise you to be extremely comfortable with the easiest questions. Being able to easily manipulate a linked list in the simplest ways will make the tougher linked list questions much less tricky. With that said, we present some "must know" code about linked list manipulation. You should be able to easily write this code yourself prior to your interview.

## Creating a Linked List:

NOTE: When you're discussing a linked list in an interview, make sure to understand whether it is a single linked list or a doubly linked list.

```
1   class Node {
2       Node next = null;
3       int data;
4       public Node(int d) { data = d; }
5       void appendToTail(int d) {
6           Node end = new Node(d);
7           Node n = this;
8           while (n.next != null) { n = n.next; }
9           n.next = end;
10      }
11  }
```

## Deleting a Node from a Singly Linked List

```
1   Node deleteNode(Node head, int d) {
2       Node n = head;
3       if (n.data == d) {
4           return head.next; /* moved head */
5       }
6       while (n.next != null) {
7           if (n.next.data == d) {
8               n.next = n.next.next;
9               return head; /* head didn't change */
10          }
11          n = n.next;
12      }
13  }
```

**2.1** Write code to remove duplicates from an unsorted linked list.

FOLLOW UP

How would you solve this problem if a temporary buffer is not allowed?

pg 105

**2.2** Implement an algorithm to find the nth to last element of a singly linked list.

pg 106

**2.3** Implement an algorithm to delete a node in the middle of a single linked list, given only access to that node.

EXAMPLE

Input: the node 'c' from the linked list a->b->c->d->e

Result: nothing is returned, but the new linked list looks like a->b->d->e

pg 107

**2.4** You have two numbers represented by a linked list, where each node contains a single digit. The digits are stored in reverse order, such that the 1's digit is at the head of the list. Write a function that adds the two numbers and returns the sum as a linked list.

EXAMPLE

Input: (3 -> 1 -> 5) + (5 -> 9 -> 2)

Output: 8 -> 0 -> 8

pg 108

**2.5** Given a circular linked list, implement an algorithm which returns node at the beginning of the loop.

DEFINITION

Circular linked list: A (corrupt) linked list in which a node's next pointer points to an earlier node, so as to make a loop in the linked list.

EXAMPLE

input: A -> B -> C -> D -> E -> C [the same C as earlier]

output: C

pg 109

## How to Approach:

Whether you are asked to implement a simple stack / queue, or you are asked to implement a modified version of one, you will have a big leg up on other candidates if you can flawlessly work with stacks and queues. Practice makes perfect! Here is some skeleton code for a Stack and Queue class.

## Implementing a Stack

```
1   class Stack {
2       Node top;
3       Node pop() {
4           if (top != null) {
5               Object item = top.data;
6               top = top.next;
7               return item;
8           }
9           return null;
10      }
11      void push(Object item) {
12          Node t = new Node(item);
13          t.next = top;
14          top = t;
15      }
16  }
```

## Implementing a Queue

```
1   class Queue {
2       Node first, last;
3       void enqueue(Object item) {
4           if (!first) {
5               last = new Node(item);
6               first = last;
7           } else {
8               last.next = new Node(item);
9               last = last.next;
10          }
11      }
12      Node dequeue(Node n) {
13          if (first != null) {
14              Object item = first.data;
15              first = first.next;
16              return item;
17          }
18          return null;
19      }
20  }
```

**3.1** Describe how you could use a single array to implement three stacks.

pg 111

**3.2** How would you design a stack which, in addition to push and pop, also has a function min which returns the minimum element? Push, pop and min should all operate in O(1) time.

pg 113

**3.3** Imagine a (literal) stack of plates. If the stack gets too high, it might topple. Therefore, in real life, we would likely start a new stack when the previous stack exceeds some threshold. Implement a data structure SetOfStacks that mimics this. SetOf-Stacks should be composed of several stacks, and should create a new stack once the previous one exceeds capacity. SetOfStacks.push() and SetOfStacks.pop() should behave identically to a single stack (that is, pop() should return the same values as it would if there were just a single stack).

FOLLOW UP

Implement a function popAt(int index) which performs a pop operation on a specific sub-stack.

pg 115

**3.4** In the classic problem of the Towers of Hanoi, you have 3 rods and N disks of different sizes which can slide onto any tower. The puzzle starts with disks sorted in ascending order of size from top to bottom (e.g., each disk sits on top of an even larger one). You have the following constraints:

(A) Only one disk can be moved at a time.

(B) A disk is slid off the top of one rod onto the next rod.

(C) A disk can only be placed on top of a larger disk.

Write a program to move the disks from the first rod to the last using Stacks.

pg 118

**3.5** Implement a MyQueue class which implements a queue using two stacks.

pg 120

**3.6** Write a program to sort a stack in ascending order. You should not make any assumptions about how the stack is implemented. The following are the only functions that should be used to write this program: push | pop | peek | isEmpty.

pg 121

## How to Approach:

Trees and graphs questions typically come in one of two forms:

1.   Implement a tree / find a node / delete a node / other well known algorithm.

2.   Implement a modification of a known algorithm.

Either way, it is *strongly* recommended to understand the important tree algorithms prior to your interview. If you're fluent in these, it'll make the tougher questions that much easier! We'll list some of the most important.

## WARNING: Not all binary trees are binary search trees

When given a binary tree question, many candidates assume that the interviewer means "binary *search* tree", when the interviewer might only mean "binary tree." So, listen carefully for that word "search." If you don't hear it, the interviewer may just mean a binary tree with no particular ordering on the nodes. If you aren't sure, ask.

## Binary Trees—"Must Know" Algorithms

You should be able to easily implement the following algorithms prior to your interview:

»   **In-Order:** Traverse left node, current node, then right [usually used for binary search trees]

»   **Pre-Order:** Traverse current node, then left node, then right node.

»   **Post-Order:** Traverse left node, then right node, then current node.

»   **Insert Node:** On a binary search tree, we insert a value v, by comparing it to the root. If v > root, we go right, and else we go left. We do this until we hit an empty spot in the tree.

.................................................................................

   **Note:** balancing and deletion of binary search trees are rarely asked, but you might want to have some idea how they work. It can set you apart from other candidates.

.................................................................................

## Graph Traversal—"Must Know" Algorithms

You should be able to easily implement the following algorithms prior to your interview:

»   **Depth First Search:** DFS involves searching a node and all its children before proceeding to its siblings.

»   **Breadth First Search:** BFS involves searching a node and its siblings before going on to any children.

**4.1** Implement a function to check if a tree is balanced. For the purposes of this question, a balanced tree is defined to be a tree such that no two leaf nodes differ in distance from the root by more than one.

pg 123

**4.2** Given a directed graph, design an algorithm to find out whether there is a route between two nodes.

pg 124

**4.3** Given a sorted (increasing order) array, write an algorithm to create a binary tree with minimal height.

pg 125

**4.4** Given a binary search tree, design an algorithm which creates a linked list of all the nodes at each depth (i.e., if you have a tree with depth D, you'll have D linked lists).

pg 126

**4.5** Write an algorithm to find the 'next' node (i.e., in-order successor) of a given node in a binary search tree where each node has a link to its parent.

pg 127

**4.6** Design an algorithm and write code to find the first common ancestor of two nodes in a binary tree. Avoid storing additional nodes in a data structure. NOTE: This is not necessarily a binary search tree.

pg 128

**4.7** You have two very large binary trees: T1, with millions of nodes, and T2, with hundreds of nodes. Create an algorithm to decide if T2 is a subtree of T1.

pg 130

**4.8** You are given a binary tree in which each node contains a value. Design an algorithm to print all paths which sum up to that value. Note that it can be any path in the tree - it does not have to start at the root.

pg 131

*Part 2*
# Concepts and Algorithms

## How to Approach:

Bit manipulation can be a scary thing to many candidates, but it doesn't need to be! If you're shaky on bit manipulation, we recommend doing a couple of arithmetic-like problems to boost your skills. Compute the following by hand:

| 1010 - 0001 | 1010 + 0110 | 1100^1010 |
|---|---|---|
| 1010 << 1 | 1001^1001 | 1001 & 1100 |
| 1010 >> 1 | 0xFF - 1 | 0xAB + 0x11 |

If you're still uncomfortable, examine very carefully what happens when you do subtraction, addition, etc in base 10. Can you repeat that work in base 2?

> NOTE: The Windows Calculator knows how to do lots of operations in binary, including ADD, SUBTRACT, AND and OR. Go to View > Programmer to get into binary mode while you practice.

## Things to Watch Out For:

»   It's really easy to make mistakes on these problems, so be careful! When you're writing code, stop and think about what you're writing every couple of lines - or, better yet, test your code mid-way through! When you're done, check through your entire code.

»   If you're bit shifting, what happens when the digits get shifted off the end? Make sure to think about this case to ensure that you're handling it correctly.

| And (&): | 0 & 0 = 0 | 1 & 0 = 0 | 0 & 1 = 0 | 1 & 1 = 1 |
|---|---|---|---|---|
| Or (\|): | 0 \| 0 = 0 | 1 \| 0 = 1 | 0 \| 1 = 1 | 1 \| 1 = 1 |
| Xor (^): | 0 ^ 0 = 0 | 1 ^ 0 = 1 | 0 ^ 1 = 1 | 1 ^ 1 = 0 |

## Left Shift:

**x << y** means x shifted y bits to the left. If you start shifting and you run out of space, the bits just "drop off". For example:

```
00011001 << 2 = 01100100
00011001 << 4 = 10010000
```

## Right Shift:

**x >> y** means x shifted y bits to the right. If you start shifting and you run out of space, the bits just "drop off" the end. Example:

```
00011001 >> 2 = 00000110
00011001 >> 4 = 00000001
```

**5.1** You are given two 32-bit numbers, N and M, and two bit positions, i and j. Write a method to set all bits between i and j in N equal to M (e.g., M becomes a substring of N located at i and starting at j).

EXAMPLE:

Input: N = 10000000000, M = 10101, i = 2, j = 6

Output: N = 10001010100

pg 133

**5.2** Given a (decimal - e.g. 3.72) number that is passed in as a string, print the binary representation. If the number can not be represented accurately in binary, print "ERROR"

pg 134

**5.3** Given an integer, print the next smallest and next largest number that have the same number of 1 bits in their binary representation.

pg 135

**5.4** Explain what the following code does: ((n & (n-1)) == 0).

pg 138

**5.5** Write a function to determine the number of bits required to convert integer A to integer B.

Input: 31, 14

Output: 2

pg 139

**5.6** Write a program to swap odd and even bits in an integer with as few instructions as possible (e.g., bit 0 and bit 1 are swapped, bit 2 and bit 3 are swapped, etc).

pg 140

**5.7** An array A[1...n] contains all the integers from 0 to n except for one number which is missing. In this problem, we cannot access an entire integer in A with a single operation. The elements of A are represented in binary, and the only operation we can use to access them is "fetch the jth bit of A[i]", which takes constant time. Write code to find the missing integer. Can you do it in O(n) time?

pg 141

## Do companies really ask brain teasers?

While many companies, including Google and Microsoft, have policies banning brain teasers, interviewers still sometimes ask these tricky questions. This is especially true since people have different definitions of brain teasers.

## Advice on Approaching Brain Teasers

Don't panic when you get a brain teaser. Interviewers want to see how you tackle a problem; they don't expect you to immediately know the answer. Start talking, and show the interviewer how you approach a problem.

In many cases, you will also find that the brain teasers have some connection back to fundamental laws or theories of computer science.

If you're stuck, we recommend simplifying the problem. Solve it for a small number of items or a special case, and then see if you can generalize it.

## Example

You are trying to cook an egg for exactly fifteen minutes, but instead of a timer, you are given two ropes which burn for exactly 1 hour each. The ropes, however, are of uneven densities - i.e., half the rope length-wise might take only two minutes to burn.

## The Approach

1.  What is important? Numbers usually have a meaning behind them. The fifteen minutes and two ropes were picked for a reason.

2.  Simplify! You can easily time one hour (burn just one rope).

3.  Now, can you time 30 minutes? That's half the time it takes to burn one rope. Can you burn the rope twice as fast? Yes! (Light the rope at both ends.)

4.  You've now learned: (1) You can time 30 minutes. (2) You can burn a rope that takes X minutes in just X/2 minutes by lighting both ends.

5.  Work backwards: if you had a rope of burn-length 30 minutes, that would let you time 15 minutes. Can you remove 30 minutes of burn-time from a rope?

6.  You can remove 30 minutes of burn-time from Rope #2 by lighting Rope #1 at both ends and Rope #2 at one end.

7.  Now that you have Rope #2 at burn-length 30 minutes, start cooking the egg and light Rope #2 at the other end. When Rope #2 burns up, your egg is done!

**6.1** Add arithmetic operators (plus, minus, times, divide) to make the following expression true: 3 1 3 6 = 8. You can use any parentheses you'd like.

pg 143

**6.2** There is an 8x8 chess board in which two diagonally opposite corners have been cut off. You are given 31 dominos, and a single domino can cover exactly two squares. Can you use the 31 dominos to cover the entire board? Prove your answer (by providing an example, or showing why it's impossible).

pg 144

**6.3** You have a five quart jug and a three quart jug, and an unlimited supply of water (but no measuring cups). How would you come up with exactly four quarts of water?

NOTE: The jugs are oddly shaped, such that filling up exactly 'half' of the jug would be impossible.

pg 145

**6.4** A bunch of men are on an island. A genie comes down and gathers everyone together and places a magical hat on some people's heads (i.e., at least one person has a hat). The hat is magical: it can be seen by other people, but not by the wearer of the hat himself. To remove the hat, those (and only those who have a hat) must dunk themselves underwater at exactly midnight. If there are n people and c hats, how long does it take the men to remove the hats? The men cannot tell each other (in any way) that they have a hat.

FOLLOW UP

Prove that your solution is correct.

pg 146

**6.5** There is a building of 100 floors. If an egg drops from the Nth floor or above it will break. If it's dropped from any floor below, it will not break. You're given 2 eggs. Find N, while minimizing the number of drops for the worst case.

pg 148

**6.6** There are one hundred closed lockers in a hallway. A man begins by opening all one hundred lockers. Next, he closes every second locker. Then he goes to every third locker and closes it if it is open or opens it if it is closed (e.g., he toggles every third locker). After his one hundredth pass in the hallway, in which he toggles only locker number one hundred, how many lockers are open?

pg 149

## How to Approach

Object oriented design questions are very important, as they demonstrate the quality of a candidate's code. A poor performance on this type of question raises serious red flags.

## Handling Ambiguity in an Interview

OOD questions are often intentionally vague to test if you'll make assumptions, or if you'll ask clarifying questions. How do you design a class if the constraints are vague? Ask questions to eliminate ambiguity, then design the classes to handle any remaining ambiguity.

## Object Oriented Design for Software

Imagine we're designing the objects for a deck of cards. Consider the following approach:

1.  What are you trying to do with the deck of cards? Ask your interviewer. Let's assume we want a general purpose deck of cards to implement many different types of card games.

2.  What are the core objects—and what "sub types" are there? For example, the core items might be: Card, Deck, Number, Suit, PointValue

3.  Have you missed anything? Think about how you'll use that deck of cards to implement different types of games, changing the class design as necessary.

4.  Now, get a little deeper: how will the methods work? If you have a method like Card Deck:.getCard(Suit s, Number n), think about how it will retrieve the card.

## Object Oriented Design for Real World Object

Real world objects are handled very similarly to software object oriented design. Suppose you are designing an object oriented design for a parking lot:

1.  What are your goals? For example: figure out if a parking spot is taken, figure out how many cars of each type are in the parking lot, look up handicapped spots, etc.

2.  Now, think about the core objects (Car, ParkingSpot, ParkingLot, ParkingMeter, etc—Car has different subclasses, and ParkingSpot is also subclassed for handicapped spot).

3.  Have we missed anything? How will we represent parking restrictions based on time or payment? Perhaps, we'll add a class called Permission which handles different payment systems. Permission will be sub-classed into classes PaidPermission (fee to park) and FreeParking (open parking). ParkingLot will have a method called GetPermission which will return the current Permission object based on the time.

4.  How will we know whether or not a car is in a spot? Think about how to represent the data so that the methods are most efficient.

**7.1** Design the data structures for a generic deck of cards. Explain how you would sub-class it to implement particular card games.

pg 151

**7.2** Imagine you have a call center with three levels of employees: fresher, technical lead (TL), product manager (PM). There can be multiple employees, but only one TL or PM. An incoming telephone call must be allocated to a fresher who is free. If a fresher can't handle the call, he or she must escalate the call to technical lead. If the TL is not free or not able to handle it, then the call should be escalated to PM. Design the classes and data structures for this problem. Implement a method getCallHandler().

pg 152

**7.3** Design a musical juke box using object oriented principles.

pg 154

**7.4** Design a chess game using object oriented principles.

pg 156

**7.5** Design the data structures for an online book reader system.

pg 157

**7.6** Implement a jigsaw puzzle. Design the data structures and explain an algorithm to solve the puzzle.

pg 159

**7.7** Explain how you would design a chat server. In particular, provide details about the various backend components, classes, and methods. What would be the hardest problems to solve?

pg 161

**7.8** Othello is played as follows: Each Othello piece is white on one side and black on the other. When a piece is surrounded by its opponents on both the left and right sides, or both the top and bottom, it is said to be captured and its color is flipped. On your turn, you must capture at least one of your opponent's pieces. The game ends when either user has no more valid moves, and the win is assigned to the person with the most pieces. Implement the object oriented design for Othello.

pg 163

**7.9** Explain the data structures and algorithms that you would use to design an in-memory file system. Illustrate with an example in code where possible.

pg 166

**7.10** Describe the data structures and algorithms that you would use to implement a garbage collector in C++.

pg 167

# Chapter 8 | Recursion

## How to Recognize

While there is a wide variety of recursive problems, many recursive problems follow similar patterns. A good hint that problem is recursive is that it appears to be built off sub-problems.

When you hear a problem beginning with the following, it's often (though not always) a good candidate for recursion: "Design an algorithm to compute the nth …"; "Write code to list the first n…"; "Implement a method to compute all…"; etc.

Again, practice makes perfect! The more problems you do, the easier it will be to recognize recursive problems.

## How to Approach

Recursive solutions, by definition, are built off solutions to sub-problems. Many times, this will mean simply to compute f(n) by adding something, removing something, or otherwise changing the solution for f(n-1). In other cases, you might have to do something more complicated. Regardless, we recommend the following approach:

1. Think about what the sub-problem is. How many sub-problems does f(n) depend on? That is, in a recursive binary tree problem, each part will likely depend on two problems. In a linked list problem, it'll probably be just one.

2. Solve for a "base case." That is, if you need to compute f(n), first compute it for f(0) or f(1). This is usually just a hard-coded value.

3. Solve for f(2).

4. Understand how to solve for f(3) using f(2) (or previous solutions). That is, understand the exact process of translating the solutions for sub-problems into the real solution.

5. Generalize for f(n).

This "bottom-up recursion" is often the most straight-forward. Sometimes, though, it can be useful to approach problems "top down", where you essentially jump directly into breaking f(n) into its sub-problems.

## Things to Watch Out For

1. All problems that can be solved recursively can also be solved iteratively (though the code may be much more complicated). Before diving into a recursive code, ask yourself how hard it would be to implement this algorithm iteratively. Discuss the trade-offs with your interviewer.

2. Recursive algorithms can be very space inefficient. Each recursive call adds a new layer to the stack, which means that if your algorithm has O(n) recursive calls then it uses O(n) memory. Ouch! This is one reason why an iterative algorithm may be better.

**8.1** Write a method to generate the nth Fibonacci number.

pg 169

**8.2** Imagine a robot sitting on the upper left hand corner of an NxN grid. The robot can only move in two directions: right and down. How many possible paths are there for the robot?

FOLLOW UP

Imagine certain squares are "off limits", such that the robot can not step on them. Design an algorithm to get all possible paths for the robot.

pg 170

**8.3** Write a method that returns all subsets of a set.

pg 171

**8.4** Write a method to compute all permutations of a string.

pg 173

**8.5** Implement an algorithm to print all valid (e.g., properly opened and closed) combinations of n-pairs of parentheses.

EXAMPLE:

input: 3 (e.g., 3 pairs of parentheses)

output: ()(), ()(()), (())(), ((()))

pg 174

**8.6** Implement the "paint fill" function that one might see on many image editing programs. That is, given a screen (represented by a 2 dimensional array of Colors), a point, and a new color, fill in the surrounding area until you hit a border of that color.

pg 175

**8.7** Given an infinite number of quarters (25 cents), dimes (10 cents), nickels (5 cents) and pennies (1 cent), write code to calculate the number of ways of representing n cents.

pg 176

**8.8** Write an algorithm to print all ways of arranging eight queens on a chess board so that none of them share the same row, column or diagonal.

pg 177

## How to Approach:

Understanding the common sorting algorithms is incredibly valuable, as many sorting or searching solutions require tweaks of known sorting algorithms. A good approach when you are given a question like this is to run through the different sorting algorithms and see if one applies particularly well.

*Example:* You have a very large array of 'Person' objects. Sort the people in increasing order of age.

We're given two interesting bits of knowledge here: (1) It's a large array, so efficiency is very important. (2) We are sorting based on ages, so we know the values are in a small range. By scanning through the various sorting algorithms, we might notice that bucket sort would be a perfect candidate for this algorithm. In fact, we can make the buckets small (just 1 year each) and get O(n) running time.

## Bubble Sort:

Start at the beginning of an array and swap the first two elements if the first is bigger than the second. Go to the next pair, etc, continuously making sweeps of the array until sorted. O(n^2).

## Selection Sort:

Find the smallest element using a linear scan and move it to the front. Then, find the second smallest and move it, again doing a linear scan. Continue doing this until all the elements are in place. O(n^2).

## Merge Sort:

Sort each pair of elements. Then, sort every four elements by merging every two pairs. Then, sort every 8 elements, etc. O(n log n) expected and worst case.

## Quick Sort:

Pick a random element and partition the array, such that all numbers that are less than it come before all elements that are greater than it. Then do that for each half, then each quarter, etc. O(n log n) expected, O(n^2) worst case.

## Bucket Sort:

Partition the array into a finite number of buckets, and then sort each bucket individually. This gives a time of O(n + m), where n is the number of items and m is the number of distinct items.

**9.1** You are given two sorted arrays, A and B, and A has a large enough buffer at the end to hold B. Write a method to merge B into A in sorted order.

pg 179

**9.2** Write a method to sort an array of strings so that all the anagrams are next to each other.

pg 180

**9.3** Given a sorted array of n integers that has been rotated an unknown number of times, give an O(log n) algorithm that finds an element in the array. You may assume that the array was originally sorted in increasing order.

EXAMPLE:

Input: find 5 in array (15 16 19 20 25 1 3 4 5 7 10 14)

Output: 8 (the index of 5 in the array)

pg 181

**9.4** If you have a 2 GB file with one string per line, which sorting algorithm would you use to sort the file and why?

pg 182

**9.5** Given a sorted array of strings which is interspersed with empty strings, write a method to find the location of a given string.

Example: find "ball" in ["at", "", "", "", "ball", "", "", "car", "", "", "dad", "", ""] will return 4
Example: find "ballcar" in ["at", "", "", "", "", "ball", "car", "", "", "dad", "", ""] will return -1

pg 183

**9.6** Given a matrix in which each row and each column is sorted, write a method to find an element in it.

pg 184

**9.7** A circus is designing a tower routine consisting of people standing atop one another's shoulders. For practical and aesthetic reasons, each person must be both shorter and lighter than the person below him or her. Given the heights and weights of each person in the circus, write a method to compute the largest possible number of people in such a tower.

EXAMPLE:

Input (ht, wt): (65, 100) (70, 150) (56, 90) (75, 190) (60, 95) (68, 110)

Output: The longest tower is length 6 and includes from top to bottom: (56, 90) (60,95) (65,100) (68,110) (70,150) (75,190)

pg 185

## How to Approach:

Many of these problems read as brain teasers at first, but can be worked through in a logical way. Just remember to rely on the rules of mathematics to develop an approach, and then to carefully translate that idea into code.

*Example:* Given two numbers m and n, write a method to return the first number r that is divisible by both (e.g., the least common multiple).

*The Approach:* What does it mean for r to be divisible by m and n? It means that all the primes in m must go into r, and all primes in n must be in r. What if m and n have primes in common? For example, if m is divisible by 3^5 and n is divisible by 3^7, what does this mean about r? It means r must be divisible by 3^7.

> *The Rule:* For each prime p such that p^a \ m (e.g., m is divisible by p^a) and p^b \ n, r must be divisible by p^max(a, b).

*The Algorithm:*

```
Define q to be 1.
for each prime number p less than m and n:
    find the largest a and b such that p^a \ m and p^b \ n
    let q = q * p^max(a, b)
return q
```

NOTE: An alternate solution involves recognizing that gcd(a, b) * lcm(a, b) = ab. One could then compute the gcd(a, b) using the Euclidean algorithm. Of course, unless you already know this fact, it's unlikely that this rule would occur to you during an interview.

## Things to Watch Out For:

1. Be careful with the difference in precision between floats vs. doubles.

2. Don't assume that a value (such as the slope of a line) is an int unless you've been told so.

## Bayes' Rule and Probability

1. If A and B are independent, then P(A and B) = P(A) * P(B).

2. Else (in general), P(A and B) = P(A given B) * P(B)

3. If A and B are mutually exclusive (e.g., if one happens, the other one can't), P(A or B) = P(A) + P(B).

4. Else (in general), P(A or B) = P(A) + P(B) - P(A and B).

**10.1**  You have a basketball hoop and someone says that you can play 1 of 2 games.

Game #1: You get one shot to make the hoop.

Game #2: You get three shots and you have to make 2 of 3 shots.

If p is the probability of making a particular shot, for which values of p should you pick one game or the other?

pg 187

**10.2**  There are three ants on different vertices of a triangle. What is the probability of collision (between any two or all of them) if they start walking on the sides of the triangle? Similarly find the probability of collision with 'n' ants on an 'n' vertex polygon.

pg 188

**10.3**  Given two lines on a Cartesian plane, determine whether the two lines would intersect.

pg 189

**10.4**  Write a method to implement *, - , / operations. You should use only the + operator.

pg 190

**10.5**  Given two squares on a two dimensional plane, find a line that would cut these two squares in half.

pg 192

**10.6**  Given a two dimensional graph with points on it, find a line which passes the most number of points.

pg 193

**10.7**  Design an algorithm to find the kth number such that the only prime factors are 3, 5, and 7.

pg 195

## Testing Problems: Not Just for Testers!

Although testers are obviously asked more testing problems, developers will often be asked testing problems as well. Why? Because a good developer knows how to test their code!

## Types of Testing Problems:

Testing problems generally fall into one of three categories:

1. Explain how you would test this real world object (pen, paperclip, etc).

2. Explain how you would test this computer software (e.g., a web browser).

3. Write test cases / test code to test this specific method.

We'll discuss type #1, since it's usually the most daunting. Remember that all three types require you to not make assumptions that the input or the user will play nice. Expect abuse and plan for it.

## How to Test A Real World Object

Let's imagine that you were asked to test a paperclip. The first thing to understand is: what is it expected to be used for and who are the expected users. Ask your interviewer—the answer may not be what you think! The answer could be "by teachers, to hold papers together" or it could be "by artists, to bend into new shapes." These two use-cases will have very different answers. Once you understand the intended use, think about:

» What are the specific use cases for the intended purpose? For example, holding 2 sheets of paper together, and up to 30 sheets. If it fails, does it fail gracefully? (see below)

» What does it mean for it to fail? Answer: "*Failing gracefully*" means for the paperclip to not hold paper together. If it snaps easily, that's (probably) not failing gracefully.

» Ask your interviewer—what are the expectations of it being used outside of the intended use case? Should we ensure that it has a minimum of usefulness for the other cases?

» What "stress" conditions might your paperclip be used in? *Answer:* hot weather, cold weather, frequent re-use, etc.

**11.1** Find the mistake(s) in the following code:

```
1    unsigned int i;
2    for (i = 100; i <= 0; --i)
3        printf("%d\n", i);
```

pg 197

**11.2** You are given the source to an application which crashes when it is run. After running it ten times in a debugger, you find it never crashes in the same place. The application is single threaded, and uses only the C standard library. What programming errors could be causing this crash? How would you test each one?

pg 198

**11.3** We have the following method used in a chess game: boolean canMoveTo(int x, int y) x and y are the coordinates of the chess board and it returns whether or not the piece can move to that position. Explain how you would test this method.

pg 199

**11.4** How would you load test a webpage without using any test tools?

pg 200

**11.5** How would you test a pen?

pg 201

**11.6** How would you test an ATM in a distributed banking system?

pg 202

## How to Approach:

Don't be scared by these types of questions. Unless you claim to know how to design large systems, your interviewer probably won't expect you to know this stuff automatically. They just want to see how you tackle these problems.

## General Approach

The general approach is as follows: Imagine we're designing a hypothetical system X for millions of items (users, files, megabytes, etc):

1.  How would you solve it for a small number of items? Develop an algorithm for this case, which is often pretty straight-forward.

2.  What happens when you try to implement that algorithm with millions of items? It's likely that you have run out of space on the computer. So, divide up the files across many computers.

    »   How do you divide up data across many machines? That is, do the first 100 items appear on the same computer? Or all items with the same hash value mod 100?

    »   About how many computers will you need? To estimate this, ask how big each item is and take a guess at how much space a typical computer has.

3.  Now, fix the problems that occur when you are using many computers. Make sure to answer the following questions:

    »   How does one machine know which machine it should access to look up data?

    »   Can data get out of sync across computers? How do you handle that?

    »   How can you minimize expensive reads across computers?

## Example: Design a Web Crawler

1.  Forget about the fact that you're dealing with billions of pages. How would you design this system if it were just a small number of pages? You should have an understanding of how you would solve the simple, small case in order to understand how you would solve the bigger case.

2.  Now, think about the issues that occur with billions of pages. Most likely you can't fit the data on one machine. How will you divide it up? How will you figure out which computer has a particular piece of data?

3.  You now have different pieces of data on different machines. What problems might that create? Can you try to solve them?

*And remember, don't get scared! This is just an ordinary problem solving question.*

# Chapter 12 | System Design and Memory Limits

**12.1** If you were integrating a feed of end of day stock price information (open, high, low, and closing price) for 5,000 companies, how would you do it? You are responsible for the development, rollout and ongoing monitoring and maintenance of the feed. Describe the different methods you considered and why you would recommend your approach. The feed is delivered once per trading day in a comma-separated format via an FTP site. The feed will be used by 1000 daily users in a web application.

pg 203

**12.2** How would you design the data structures for a very large social network (Facebook, LinkedIn, etc)? Describe how you would design an algorithm to show the connection, or path, between two people (e.g., Me -> Bob -> Susan -> Jason -> You).

pg 205

**12.3** Given an input file with four billion integers, provide an algorithm to generate an integer which is not contained in the file. Assume you have 1 GB of memory.

FOLLOW UP
What if you have only 10 MB of memory?

pg 208

**12.4** You have an array with all the numbers from 1 to N, where N is at most 32,000. The array may have duplicate entries and you do not know what N is. With only 4KB of memory available, how would you print all duplicate elements in the array?

pg 211

**12.5** If you were designing a web crawler, how would you avoid getting into infinite loops?

pg 212

**12.6** You have a billion urls, where each is a huge page. How do you detect the duplicate documents?

pg 213

**12.7** You have to design a database that can store terabytes of data. It should support efficient range queries. How would you do it?

pg 214

*Part 3*
# Knowledge Based

## How To Approach:

A good interviewer won't demand that you code in a language you don't profess to know. Hopefully, if you're asked to code in C++, it's listed on your resume. If you don't remember all the APIs, don't worry—your interviewer probably doesn't care that much. We do recommend, however, studying up on basic C++ syntax.

## Pointer Syntax

```
1   int *p; // Defines pointer.
2   p = &q; // Sets p to address of q.
3   v = *p; // Set v to value of q.
4   Foo *f = new Foo(); // Initializes f.
5   int k = f->x; // Sets k equal to the value of f's member variable.
```

## C++ Class Syntax

```
1    class MyClass {
2        private:
3            double var;
4        public:
5            MyClass(double v) {var = v; }
6            ~MyClass() {};
7            double Update(double v);
8    };
9    double Complex::Update(double v) {
10           var = v; return v;
11   }
```

## C++ vs Java

A very common question in an interview is "describe the differences between C++ and Java." If you aren't comfortable with any of these concepts, we recommend reading up on them.

1.  Java runs in a virtual machine.

2.  C++ natively supports unsigned arithmetic.

3.  In Java, parameters are always passed by value (or, with objects, their references are passed by value). In C++, parameters can be passed by value, pointer, or by reference.

4.  Java has built-in garbage collection.

5.  C++ allows operator overloading.

6.  C++ allows multiple inheritance of classes.

Question: Which of these might be considered strengths or weaknesses of C++ or Java? Why? In what cases might you choose one language over the other?

---

**13.1** Write a method to print the last K lines of an input file using C++.

pg 215

**13.2** Compare and contrast a hash table vs. an STL map. How is a hash table implemented? If the number of inputs is small, what data structure options can be used instead of a hash table?

pg 216

**13.3** How do virtual functions work in C++?

pg 217

**13.4** What is the difference between deep copy and shallow copy? Explain how you would use each.

pg 218

**13.5** What is the significance of the keyword "volatile" in C?

pg 219

**13.6** What is name hiding in C++?

pg 220

**13.7** Why does a destructor in base class need to be declared virtual?

pg 221

**13.8** Write a method that takes a pointer to a Node structure as a parameter and returns a complete copy of the passed-in data structure. The Node structure contains two pointers to other Node structures.

pg 223

**13.9** Write a smart pointer (smart_ptr) class.

pg 224

## How to Approach:

While Java related questions are found throughout this book, this chapter deals with questions about the language and syntax. You generally will not find too many questions like this at the larger software companies (though they are sometimes asked), but these questions are very common at other companies.

## What do you do when you don't know the answer?

If you don't know the answer to a question about the Java language, try to figure it out by doing the following: (1) Think about what other languages do. (2) Create an example of the scenario. (3) Ask yourself how you would handle the scenario if you were designing the language.

Your interviewer may be equally—or more—impressed if you can derive the answer than if you automatically knew it. Don't try to bluff though. Tell the interviewer, "I'm not sure I can recall the answer, but let me see if I can figure it out. Suppose we have this code…"

## Classes & Interfaces (Example)

```
1    public static void main(String args[]) { … }
2    interface Foo {
3        void abc();
4    }
5    class Foo extends Bar implements Foo { … }
```

## final:

»   Class: Can not be sub-classed

»   Method: Can not be overridden.

»   Variable: Can not be changed.

## static:

»   Method: Class method. Called with Foo.DoIt() instead of f.DoIt()

»   Variable: Class variable. Has only one copy and is accessed through the class name.

## abstract:

»   Class: Contains abstract methods. Can not be instantiated.

»   Interface: All interfaces are implicitly abstract. This modifier is optional.

»   Method: Method without a body. Class must also be abstract.

**14.1**   In terms of inheritance, what is the effect of keeping a constructor private?

pg 225

**14.2**   In Java, does the finally block gets executed if we insert a return statement inside the try block of a try-catch-finally?

pg 226

**14.3**   What is the difference between final, finally, and finalize?

pg 227

**14.4**   Explain the difference between templates in C++ and generics in Java.

pg 228

**14.5**   Explain what object reflection is in Java and why it is useful.

pg 229

**14.6**   Suppose you are using a map in your program, how would you count the number of times the program calls the put() and get() functions?

pg 230

## How to Approach:

You could be asked about databases in a variety of ways: write a SQL query, design a database to hold certain data, or design a large database. We'll go through the latter two types here.

## Small Database Design

Imagine you are asked to design a system to represent a large, multi-location, apartment rental company.

*What are the key objects?*

Property. Building. Apartment. Tenant. Manager.

*How do they relate to each other?*

Many-to-Many:

»   A property could have multiple managers, and a manager could manage multiple properties.

One-to-Many:

»   A building can only be part of one property.

»   An apartment can only be part of one building.

> What is the relationship between Tenant and Apartment? An apartment can obviously have multiple tenants. Can a tenant rent multiple apartments? It would be very unusual to, but this could actually happen (particularly if it's a national company). Talk to your interviewer about this. There is a trade-off between simplifying your database and designing it to be flexible. If you do assume that a Tenant can only rent one Apartment, what do you have to do if this situation occurs?

## Large Database Design

When designing a large, scalable database, joins (which are required in the above examples), are generally very slow. Thus, you must *denormalize* your data. Think carefully about how data will be used—you'll probably need to duplicate it in multiple tables.

**15.1** Write a method to find the number of employees in each department.

pg 231

**15.2** What are the different types of joins? Please explain how they differ and why certain types are better in certain situations.

pg 232

**15.3** What is denormalization? Explain the pros and cons.

pg 234

**15.4** Draw an entity-relationship diagram for a database with companies, people, and professionals (people who work for companies).

pg 235

**15.5** Imagine a simple database storing information for students' grades. Design what this database might look like, and provide a SQL query to return a list of the honor roll students (top 10%), sorted by their grade point average.

pg 236

## How to Approach:

Many candidates find low level problems to be some of the most challenging. Low level questions require a large amount of knowledge about the underlying architecture of a system. But just how much do you need to know? The answer to that depends, of course, on the company. At a typical large software company where you'd be working on desktop or web applications, you usually only need a minimum amount of knowledge. However, you should understand the concepts below very well, as many interview questions are based off this information.

## Big vs Little Endian:

In big endian, the most significant byte is stored at the memory address location with the lowest address. This is akin to left-to-right reading order. Little endian is the reverse: the most significant byte is stored at the address with the highest address.

## Stack (Memory)

When a function calls another function which calls another function, this memory goes onto the stack. An int (not a pointer to an int) that is created in a function is stored on the stack.

## Heap (Memory)

When you allocate data with new() or malloc(), this data gets stored on the heap.

## Malloc

Memory allocated using malloc is persistent—i.e., it will exist until either the programmer frees the memory or the program is terminated.

`void *malloc(size_t sz)`

Malloc takes as input sz bytes of memory and, if it is successful, returns a void pointer which indicates that it is a pointer to an unknown data type.

`void free(void * p)`

Free releases a block of memory previously allocated with malloc, calloc, or realloc.

**16.1**   Explain the following terms: virtual memory, page fault, thrashing.

pg 237

**16.2**   What is a Branch Target buffer? Explain how it can be used in reducing bubble cycles in cases of branch misprediction.

pg 238

**16.3**   Describe direct memory access (DMA). Can a user level buffer / pointer be used by kernel or drivers?

pg 239

**16.4**   Write a step by step execution of things that happen after a user presses a key on the keyboard. Use as much detail as possible.

pg 240

**16.5**   Write a program to find whether a machine is big endian or little endian.

pg 241

**16.6**   Discuss how would you make sure that a process doesn't access an unauthorized part of the stack.

pg 242

**16.7**   What are the best practices to prevent reverse engineering of DLLs?

pg 244

**16.8**   A device boots with an empty FIFO queue. In the first 400 ns period after startup, and in each subsequent 400 ns period, a maximum of 80 words will be written to the queue. Each write takes 4 ns. A worker thread requires 3 ns to read a word, and 2 ns to process it before reading the next word. What is the shortest depth of the FIFO such that no data is lost?

pg 245

**16.9**   Write an aligned malloc & free function that takes number of bytes and aligned byte (which is always power of 2)

EXAMPLE

align_malloc (1000,128) will return a memory address that is a multiple of 128 and that points to memory of size 1000 bytes.

aligned_free() will free memory allocated by align_malloc.

pg 247

**16.10**   Write a function called my2DAlloc which allocates a two dimensional array. Minimize the number of calls to malloc and make sure that the memory is accessible by the notation arr[i][j].

pg 248

## How to Approach

While the big software houses probably won't ask you many detailed networking questions in general, some interviewers will attempt to assess your understanding of networking as far as it relates to software and system design. Thus, you should have an understanding of http post and get requests, tcp, etc.

For a more networking based company (Qualcomm, CISCO, etc), we recommend a more thorough understanding. A good way to study is to read the material below, and delve further into it on Wikipedia. When Wikipedia discusses a concept that you are unfamiliar with, click on the concept to read more.

## OSI 7 Layer Model

Networking architecture can be divided into seven layers. Each layer provides services to the layer above it and receives services from the layer below it. The seven layers, from top to bottom, are:

| OSI 7 Layer Model | |
|---|---|
| Level 7 | Application Layer |
| Level 6 | Presentation Layer |
| Level 5 | Session Layer |
| Level 4 | Transport Layer |
| Level 3 | Network Layer |
| Level 2 | Data Link Layer |
| Level 1 | Physical Layer |

For a networking focused interview, we suggest reviewing and understanding these concepts and their implications in detail.

**17.1** Explain what happens, step by step, after you type a URL into a browser. Use as much detail as possible.

pg 249

**17.2** Explain any common routing protocol in detail. For example: BGP, OSPF, RIP.

pg 250

**17.3** Compare and contrast the IPv4 and IPv6 protocols.

pg 252

**17.4** What is a network / subnet mask? Explain how host A sends a message / packet to host B when: (a) both are on same network and (b) both are on different networks. Explain which layer makes the routing decision and how.

pg 254

**17.5** What are the differences between TCP and UDP? Explain how TCP handles reliable delivery (explain ACK mechanism), flow control (explain TCP sender's / receiver's window) and congestion control.

pg 255

## How to Approach:

In a Microsoft, Google or Amazon interview, it's not terribly common to be asked to implement an algorithm with threads (unless you're working in a team for which this is a particularly important skill). It is, however, relatively common for interviewers at any company to assess your general understanding of threads, particularly your understanding of deadlocks

## Deadlock Conditions

In order for a deadlock to occur, you must have the following four conditions met:

1.  Mutual Exclusion: Only one process can use a resource at a given time.

2.  Hold and Wait: Processes already holding a resource can request new ones.

3.  No Preemption: One process cannot forcibly remove another process' resource.

4.  Circular Wait: Two or more processes form a circular chain where each process is waiting on another resource in the chain.

## Deadlock Prevention

Deadlock prevention essentially entails removing one of the above conditions, but many of these conditions are difficult to satisfy. For instance, removing #1 is difficult because many resources can only be used by one process at a time (printers, etc). Most deadlock prevention algorithms focus on avoiding condition #4: circular wait.

If you aren't familiar with these concepts, please read http://en.wikipedia.org/wiki/Deadlock.

## A Simple Java Thread

```
1   class Foo implements Runnable {
2       public void run() {
3           while (true) beep();
4       }
5   }
6   Foo foo = new Foo ();
7   Thread myThread = new Thread(foo);
8   myThread.start();
```

**18.1** What's the difference between a thread and a process?

pg 257

**18.2** How can you measure the time spent in a context switch?

pg 258

**18.3** Implement a singleton design pattern as a template such that, for any given class Foo, you can call Singleton::instance() and get a pointer to an instance of a singleton of type Foo. Assume the existence of a class Lock which has acquire() and release() methods. How could you make your implementation thread safe and exception safe?

pg 259

**18.4** Design a class which provides a lock only if there are no possible deadlocks.

pg 261

**18.5** Suppose we have the following code:

```
class Foo {
public:
    A(.....); /* If A is called, a new thread will be created and
               * the corresponding function will be executed. */
    B(.....); /* same as above */
    C(.....); /* same as above */
}
Foo f;
f.A(.....);
f.B(.....);
f.C(.....);
```

i) Can you design a mechanism to make sure that B is executed after A, and C is executed after B?

iii) Suppose we have the following code to use class Foo. We do not know how the threads will be scheduled in the OS.

```
Foo f;
f.A(.....); f.B(.....); f.C(.....);
f.A(.....); f.B(.....); f.C(.....);
```

Can you design a mechanism to make sure that all the methods will be executed in sequence?

pg 262

**18.6** You are given a class with synchronized method A, and a normal method C. If you have two threads in one instance of a program, can they call A at the same time? Can they call A and C at the same time?

pg 264

*Part 4*
# Additional Review Problems

**19.1** Write a function to swap a number in place without temporary variables.

**19.2** Design an algorithm to figure out if someone has won in a game of tic-tac-toe.

**19.3** Write an algorithm which computes the number of trailing zeros in n factorial.

**19.4** Write a method which finds the maximum of two numbers. You should not use if-else or any other comparison operator.

EXAMPLE

Input: 5, 10

Output: 10

**19.5** The Game of Master Mind is played as follows:

The computer has four slots containing balls that are red (R), yellow (Y), green (G) or blue (B). For example, the computer might have RGGB (e.g., Slot #1 is red, Slots #2 and #3 are green, Slot #4 is blue).

You, the user, are trying to guess the solution. You might, for example, guess YRGB.

When you guess the correct color for the correct slot, you get a "hit". If you guess a color that exists but is in the wrong slot, you get a "pseudo-hit". For example, the guess YRGB has 2 hits and one pseudo hit.

For each guess, you are told the number of hits and pseudo-hits.

Write a method that, given a guess and a solution, returns the number of hits and pseudo hits.

**19.6** Given an integer between 0 and 999,999, print an English phrase that describes the integer (eg, "One Thousand, Two Hundred and Thirty Four").

**19.7** You are given an array of integers (both positive and negative). Find the continuous sequence with the largest sum. Return the sum.

EXAMPLE

Input: {2, -8, 3, -2, 4, -10}

Output: 5 (i.e., {3, -2, 4} )

**19.8** Design a method to find the frequency of occurrences of any given word in a book.

pg 273

**19.9** Since XML is very verbose, you are given a way of encoding it where each tag gets mapped to a pre-defined integer value. The language/grammar is as follows:

```
Element --> Element Attr* END Element END [aka, encode the element
    tag, then its attributes, then tack on an END character, then
    encode its children, then another end tag]
Attr --> Tag Value [assume all values are strings]
END --> 01
Tag --> some predefined mapping to int
Value --> string value END
```

Write code to print the encoded version of an xml element (passed in as string).

FOLLOW UP

Is there anything else you could do to (in many cases) compress this even further?

pg 275

**19.10** Write a method to generate a random number between 1 and 7, given a method that generates a random number between 1 and 5 (i.e., implement rand7() using rand5()).

pg 277

**19.11** Design an algorithm to find all pairs of integers within an array which sum to a specified value.

pg 278

**20.1** Write a function that adds two numbers. You should not use + or any arithmetic operators.

pg 279

**20.2** Write a method to shuffle a deck of cards. It must be a perfect shuffle - in other words, each 52! permutations of the deck has to be equally likely. Assume that you are given a random number generator which is perfect.

pg 281

**20.3** Write a method to randomly generate a set of m integers from an array of size n. Each element must have equal probability of being chosen.

pg 282

**20.4** Write a method to count the number of 2s between 0 and n.

pg 283

**20.5** You have a large text file containing words. Given any two words, find the shortest distance (in terms of number of words) between them in the file. Can you make the searching operation in O(1) time? What about the space complexity for your solution?

pg 285

**20.6** Describe an algorithm to find the largest 1 million numbers in 1 billion numbers. Assume that the computer memory can hold all one billion numbers.

pg 286

**20.7** Write a program to find the longest word made of other words in a list of words.

EXAMPLE

Input: test, tester, testertest, testing, testingtester

Output: testingtester

pg 287

**20.8** Given a string s and an array of smaller strings T, design a method to search s for each small string in T.

pg 288

**20.9** Numbers are randomly generated and passed to a method. Write a program to find and maintain the median value as new values are generated.

pg 290

**20.10** Given two words of equal length that are in a dictionary, write a method to transform one word into another word by changing only one letter at a time. The new word you get in each step must be in the dictionary.

EXAMPLE

Input: DAMP, LIKE

Output: DAMP -> LAMP -> LIMP -> LIME -> LIKE

pg 291

**20.11** Imagine you have a square matrix, where each cell is filled with either black or white. Design an algorithm to find the maximum subsquare such that all four borders are filled with black pixels.

pg 293

**20.12** Given an NxN matrix of positive and negative integers, write code to find the sub-matrix with the largest possible sum.

pg 295

**20.13** Given a dictionary of millions of words, give an algorithm to find the largest possible rectangle of letters such that every row forms a word (reading left to right) and every column forms a word (reading top to bottom).

pg 298

Each problem may have many 'optimal' solutions that differ in
runtime, space, clarity, extensibility, etc. We have provided one
(or more) optimal solutions. If you have additional solutions you
would like to contribute, please contact us at
http://www.xrl.us/ccbook or support@careercup.com.


We welcome all feedback and suggestions. Contact us at
http://www.xrl.us/ccbook or support@careercup.com.

# Solutions

**1.1** Implement an algorithm to determine if a string has all unique characters. What if you can not use additional data structures?

pg 48

## SOLUTION

For simplicity, assume char set is ASCII (if not, we need to increase the storage size. The rest of the logic would be the same). *NOTE:* This is a *great* thing to point out to your interviewer!

```
1    public static boolean isUniqueChars2(String str) {
2        boolean[] char_set = new boolean[256];
3        for (int i = 0; i < str.length(); i++) {
4            int val = str.charAt(i);
5            if (char_set[val]) return false;
6            char_set[val] = true;
7        }
8        return true;
9    }
```

Time complexity is O(n), where n is the length of the string, and space complexity is O(n).

We can reduce our space usage a little bit by using a bit vector. We will assume, in the below code, that the string is only lower case 'a' through 'z'. This will allow us to use just a single int

```
1    public static boolean isUniqueChars(String str) {
2        int checker = 0;
3        for (int i = 0; i < str.length(); ++i) {
4            int val = str.charAt(i) - 'a';
5            if ((checker & (1 << val)) > 0) return false;
6            checker |= (1 << val);
7        }
8        return true;
9    }
```

Alternatively, we could do the following:

1.  Check every char of the string with every other char of the string for duplicate occurrences. This will take O(n^2) time and no space.

2.  If we are allowed to destroy the input string, we could sort the string in O(n log n) time and then linearly check the string for neighboring characters that are identical. Careful, though - many sorting algorithms take up extra space.

**1.2**    Write code to reverse a C-Style String. (C-String means that "abcd" is represented as five characters, including the null character.)

pg 48

## SOLUTION

This is a classic interview question. The only "gotcha" is to try to do it in place, and to be careful for the null character.

```
1   void reverse(char *str) {
2       char * end = str;
3       char tmp;
4       if (str) {
5           while (*end) {
6               ++end;
7           }
8           --end;
9           while (str < end) {
10              tmp = *str;
11              *str++ = *end;
12              *end-- = tmp;
13          }
14      }
15  }
```

**1.3**    Design an algorithm and write code to remove the duplicate characters in a string without using any additional buffer. NOTE: One or two additional variables are fine. An extra copy of the array is not.

FOLLOW UP

Write the test cases for this method.

pg 48

## SOLUTION

First, ask yourself, what does the interviewer mean by an additional buffer? Can we use an additional array of constant size?

*Algorithm—No (Large) Additional Memory:*

1.    For each character, check if it is a duplicate of already found characters.

2.    Skip duplicate characters and update the non duplicate characters.

Time complexity is $O(N^2)$.

```
1   public static void removeDuplicates(char[] str) {
2       if (str == null) return;
3       int len = str.length;
4       if (len < 2) return;
5
6       int tail = 1;
7
8       for (int i = 1; i < len; ++i) {
9           int j;
10          for (j = 0; j < tail; ++j) {
11              if (str[i] == str[j]) break;
12          }
13          if (j == tail) {
14              str[tail] = str[i];
15              ++tail;
16          }
17      }
18      str[tail] = 0;
19  }
```

Test Cases:

1.    String does not contain any duplicates, e.g.: abcd

2.    String contains all duplicates, e.g.: aaaa

3.    Null string

4.    String with all continuous duplicates, e.g.: aaabbb

5.  String with non-contiguous duplicate, e.g.: abababa

*Algorithm—With Additional Memory of Constant Size*

```
1    public static void removeDuplicatesEff(char[] str) {
2        if (str == null) return;
3        int len = str.length;
4        if (len < 2) return;
5        boolean[] hit = new boolean[256];
6        for (int i = 0; i < 256; ++i) {
7            hit[i] = false;
8        }
9        hit[str[0]] = true;
10           int tail = 1;
11       for (int i = 1; i < len; ++i) {
12           if (!hit[str[i]]) {
13               str[tail] = str[i];
14               ++tail;
15               hit[str[i]] = true;
16           }
17       }
18       str[tail] = 0;
19   }
```

**Test Cases:**

1.  String does not contain any duplicates, e.g.: abcd

2.  String contains all duplicates, e.g.: aaaa

3.  Null string

4.  Empty string

5.  String with all continuous duplicates, e.g.: aaabbb

6.  String with non-contiguous duplicates, e.g.: abababa

**1.4**   Write a method to decide if two strings are anagrams or not.

pg 48

## SOLUTION

There are two easy ways to solve this problem:

*Solution #1: Sort the strings*

```
1   boolean anagram(String s, String t) {
2       return sort(s) == sort(t);
3   }
```

*Solution #2: Check if the two strings have identical counts for each unique char.*

```
1    public static boolean anagram(String s, String t) {
2        if (s.length() != t.length()) return false;
3        int[] letters = new int[256];
4        int num_unique_chars = 0;
5        int num_completed_t = 0;
6        char[] s_array = s.toCharArray();
7        for (char c : s_array) { // count number of each char in s.
8            if (letters[c] == 0) ++num_unique_chars;
9            ++letters[c];
10       }
11       for (int i = 0; i < t.length(); ++i) {
12           int c = (int) t.charAt(i);
13           if (letters[c] == 0) { // Found more of char c in t than in s.
14               return false;
15           }
16           --letters[c];
17           if (letters[c] == 0) {
18               ++num_completed_t;
19               if (num_completed_t == num_unique_chars) {
20                   // it's a match if t has been processed completely
21                   return i == t.length() - 1;
22               }
23           }
24       }
25       return false;
26   }
```

**1.5**    Write a method to replace all spaces in a string with '%20'.

pg 48

## SOLUTION

The algorithm is as follows:

1.  Count the number of spaces during the first scan of the string.

2.  Parse the string again from the end and for each character:

    »   If a space is encountered, store "%20".

    »   Else, store the character as it is in the newly shifted location.

```
1   public static void ReplaceFun(char[] str, int length) {
2       int spaceCount = 0, newLength, i = 0;
3       for (i = 0; i < length; i++) {
4           if (str[i] == ' ') {
5               spaceCount++;
6           }
7       }
8       newLength = length + spaceCount * 2;
9       str[newLength] = '\0';
10      for (i = length - 1; i >= 0; i--) {
11          if (str[i] == ' ') {
12              str[newLength - 1] = '0';
13              str[newLength - 2] = '2';
14              str[newLength - 3] = '%';
15              newLength = newLength - 3;
16          } else {
17              str[newLength - 1] = str[i];
18              newLength = newLength - 1;
19          }
20      }
21  }
```

**1.6** Given an image represented by an NxN matrix, where each pixel in the image is 4 bytes, write a method to rotate the image by 90 degrees. Can you do this in place?

pg 48

## SOLUTION

The rotation can be performed in layers, where you perform a cyclic swap on the edges on each layer. In the first for loop, we rotate the first layer (outermost edges). We rotate the edges by doing a four-way swap first on the corners, then on the element clockwise from the edges, then on the element three steps away.

Once the exterior elements are rotated, we then rotate the interior region's edges.

```
1    public static void rotate(int[][] matrix, int n) {
2        for (int layer = 0; layer < n / 2; ++layer) {
3            int first = layer;
4            int last = n - 1 - layer;
5            for(int i = first; i < last; ++i) {
6                int offset = i - first;
7                int top = matrix[first][i]; // save top
8                // left -> top
9                matrix[first][i] = matrix[last-offset][first];
10
11               // bottom -> left
12               matrix[last-offset][first] = matrix[last][last - offset];
13
14               // right -> bottom
15               matrix[last][last - offset] = matrix[i][last];
16
17               // top -> right
18               matrix[i][last] = top; // right <- saved top
19           }
20       }
21   }
```

**1.7**  Write an algorithm such that if an element in an MxN matrix is 0, its entire row and column is set to 0.

pg 48

## SOLUTION

At first glance, this problem seems easy: just iterate through the matrix and every time we see a 0, set that row and column to 0. There's one problem with that solution though: we will "recognize" those 0s later on in our iteration and then set their row and column to zero. Pretty soon, our entire matrix will be set to 0s!

One way around this is to keep a second matrix which flags the 0 locations. We would then do a second pass through the matrix to set the zeros. This would take O(MN) space.

Do we really need O(MN) space? No. Since we're going to set the entire row and column to zero, do we really need to track *which* cell in a row is zero? No. We only need to know that row 2, for example, has a zero.

The code below implement this algorithm. We keep track in two arrays all the rows with zeros and all the columns with zeros. We then make a second pass of the matrix and set a cell to zero if its row or column is zero.

```
1   public static void setZeros(int[][] matrix) {
2       int[] row = new int[matrix.length];
3       int[] column = new int[matrix[0].length];
4       // Store the row and column index with value 0
5       for (int i = 0; i < matrix.length; i++) {
6           for (int j = 0; j < matrix[0].length;j++) {
7               if (matrix[i][j] == 0) {
8                   row[i] = 1;
9                   column[j] = 1;
10              }
11          }
12      }
13
14      // Set arr[i][j] to 0 if either row i or column j has a 0
15      for (int i = 0; i < matrix.length; i++) {
16          for (int j = 0; j < matrix[0].length; j++) {
17              if ((row[i] == 1 || column[j] == 1)) {
18                  matrix[i][j] = 0;
19              }
20          }
21      }
22  }
```

**1.8**    Assume you have a method isSubstring which checks if one word is a substring of another. Given two strings, s1 and s2, write code to check if s2 is a rotation of s1 using only one call to isSubstring (i.e., "waterbottle" is a rotation of "erbottlewat").

pg 48

## SOLUTION

Just do the following checks

1.  Check if length(s1) == length(s2). If not, return false.

2.  Else, concatenate s1 with itself and see whether s2 is substring of the result.

    input: s1 = apple, s2 = pleap  ==> apple is a substring of pleappleap

    input: s1 = apple, s2 = ppale ==> apple is not a substring of ppaleppale

```
1   public static boolean isRotation(String s1, String s2) {
2       int len = s1.length();
3       /* check that s1 and s2 are equal length and not empty */
4       if (len == s2.length() && len > 0) {
5           /* concatenate s1 and s1 within new buffer */
6           String s1s1 = s1 + s1;
7           return isSubstring(s1s1, s2);
8       }
9       return false;
10  }
```

**2.1**    Write code to remove duplicates from an unsorted linked list.

FOLLOW UP

How would you solve this problem if a temporary buffer is not allowed?

pg 50

## SOLUTION

If we can use a buffer, we can keep track of elements in a hashtable and remove any dups:

```
1    public static void deleteDups(LinkedListNode n) {
2        Hashtable table = new Hashtable();
3        LinkedListNode previous = null;
4        while (n != null) {
5            if (table.containsKey(n.data)) previous.next = n.next;
6            else {
7                table.put(n.data, true);
8                previous = n;
9            }
10           n = n.next;
11       }
12   }
```

Without a buffer, we can iterate with two pointers: "current" does a normal iteration, while "runner" iterates through all prior nodes to check for dups. Runner will only see one dup per node, because if there were multiple duplicates they would have been removed already.

```
1    public static void deleteDups2(LinkedListNode head) {
2        if (head == null) return;
3        LinkedListNode previous = head;
4        LinkedListNode current = previous.next;
5        while (current != null) {
6            LinkedListNode runner = head;
7            while (runner != current) { // Check for earlier dups
8                if (runner.data == current.data) {
9                    LinkedListNode tmp = current.next; // remove current
10                   previous.next = tmp;
11                   current = tmp; // update current to next node
12                   break; // all other dups have already been removed
13               }
14               runner = runner.next;
15           }
16           if (runner == current) { // current not updated - update now
17               previous = current;
18               current = current.next;
19           }
20       }
21   }
```

**2.2**    Implement an algorithm to find the nth to last element of a singly linked list.

pg 50

## SOLUTION

Note: This problem screams recursion, but we'll do it a different way because it's trickier. In a question like this, expect follow up questions about the advantages of recursion vs iteration.

Assumption: The minimum number of nodes in list is *n*.

Algorithm:

1. Create two pointers, p1 and p2, that point to the beginning of the node.

2. Increment p2 by n-1 positions, to make it point to the nth node from the beginning (to make the distance of n between p1 and p2).

3. Check for p2->next == null if yes return value of *p1*, otherwise increment *p1* and *p2*. If next of *p2* is null it means *p1* points to the nth node from the last as the distance between the two is *n*.

4. Repeat Step 3.

```
1   LinkedListNode nthToLast(LinkedListNode head, int n) {
2       if (head == null || n < 1) {
3           return null;
4       }
5       LinkedListNode p1 = head;
6       LinkedListNode p2 = head;
7       for (int j = 0; j < n - 1; ++j) { // skip n-1 steps ahead
8           if (p2 == null) {
9               return null; // not found since list size < n
10          }
11          p2 = p2.next;
12      }
13      if (p2 == null) {
14          return null;
15      }
16      while (p2.next != null) {
17          p1 = p1.next;
18          p2 = p2.next;
19      }
20      return p1;
21  }
```

**2.3** Implement an algorithm to delete a node in the middle of a single linked list, given only access to that node.

EXAMPLE

Input: the node 'c' from the linked list a->b->c->d->e

Result: nothing is returned, but the new linked list looks like a->b->d->e

pg 50

## SOLUTION

The solution to this is to simply copy the data from the next node into this node and then delete the next node.

> NOTE: This problem can not be solved if the node to be deleted is the last node in the linked list. That's ok—your interviewer wants to see you point that out. You could consider marking it as dummy in that case. This is an issue you should discuss with your interviewer.

```
1   public static boolean deleteNode(LinkedListNode n) {
2       if (n == null || n.next == null) {
3           return false; // Failure
4       }
5       LinkedListNode next = n.next;
6       n.data = next.data;
7       n.next = next.next;
8       return true;
9   }
```

**2.4** You have two numbers represented by a linked list, where each node contains a single digit. The digits are stored in reverse order, such that the 1's digit is at the head of the list. Write a function that adds the two numbers and returns the sum as a linked list.

EXAMPLE

Input: (3 -> 1 -> 5), (5 -> 9 -> 2)

Output: 8 -> 0 -> 8

pg 50

## SOLUTION

We can implement this recursively by adding node by node, just as we would digit by digit.

1. result.data = (node1 + node2 + any earlier carry) % 10

2. if node1 + node2 > 10, then carry a 1 to the next addition.

3. add the tails of the two nodes, passing along the carry.

```
1   LinkedListNode addLists(LinkedListNode l1, LinkedListNode l2,
2                           int carry) {
3       LinkedListNode result = new LinkedListNode(carry, null, null);
4       int value = carry;
5       if (l1 != null) {
6           value += l1.data;
7       }
8       if (l2 != null) {
9           value += l2.data;
10      }
11      result.data = value % 10;
12      if (l1 != null || l2 != null || value >= 10) {
13          LinkedListNode more = addLists(l1 == null ? null : l1.next,
14                                         l2 == null ? null : l2.next,
15                                         value >= 10 ? 1 : 0);
16          result.setNext(more);
17      }
18      return result;
19  }
```

**2.5**   Given a circular linked list, implement an algorithm which returns node at the beginning of the loop.

DEFINITION

Circular linked list: A (corrupt) linked list in which a node's next pointer points to an earlier node, so as to make a loop in the linked list.

EXAMPLE

Input: A -> B -> C -> D -> E -> C [the same C as earlier]

Output: C

*pg 50*

## SOLUTION

If we move two pointers, one with speed 1 and another with speed 2, they will end up meeting if the linked list has a loop. Why? Think about two cars driving on a track—the faster car will always pass the slower one!

The tricky part here is finding the start of the loop. Imagine, as an analogy, two people racing around a track, one running twice as fast as the other. If they start off at the same place, when will they next meet? They will next meet at the start of the next lap.

Now, let's suppose Fast Runner had a head start of k meters on an n step lap. When will they next meet? They will meet k meters before the start of the next lap. (Why? Fast Runner would have made $k + 2(n - k)$ steps, including its head start, and Slow Runner would have made $n - k$ steps. Both will be k steps before the start of the loop.)

Now, going back to the problem, when Fast Runner (n2) and Slow Runner (n1) are moving around our circular linked list, n2 will have a head start on the loop when n1 enters. Specifically, it will have a head start of k, where k is the number of nodes before the loop. Since n2 has a head start of k nodes, n1 and n2 will meet k nodes before the start of the loop.

So, we now know the following:

1.   Head is k nodes from LoopStart (by definition).

2.   MeetingPoint for n1 and n2 is k nodes from LoopStart (as shown above).

Thus, if we move n1 back to Head and keep n2 at MeetingPoint, and move them both at the same pace, they will meet at LoopStart.

---

```
1   LinkedListNode FindBeginning(LinkedListNode head) {
2       LinkedListNode n1 = head;
3       LinkedListNode n2 = head;
4
5       // Find meeting point
6       while (n2.next != null) {
7           n1 = n1.next;
8           n2 = n2.next.next;
9           if (n1 == n2) {
10              break;
11          }
12      }
13
14      // Error check - there is no meeting point, and therefore no loop
15      if (n2.next == null) {
16          return null;
17      }
18
19      /* Move n1 to Head. Keep n2 at Meeting Point.  Each are k steps
20      /* from the Loop Start. If they move at the same pace, they must
21       * meet at Loop Start. */
22      n1 = head;
23      while (n1 != n2) {
24          n1 = n1.next;
25          n2 = n2.next;
26      }
27      // Now n2 points to the start of the loop.
28      return n2;
29  }
```

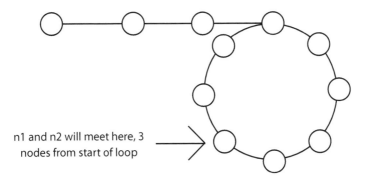

n1 and n2 will meet here, 3
nodes from start of loop

**3.1**    Describe how you could use a single array to implement three stacks.

pg 52

## SOLUTION

*Approach 1:*

Divide the array in three equal parts and allow the individual stack to grow in that limited space (note: "[" means inclusive, while "(" means exclusive of the end point).

» for stack 1, we will use [0, n/3)

» for stack 2, we will use [n/3, 2n/3)

» for stack 3, we will use [2n/3, n)

This solution is based on the assumption that we do not have any extra information about the usage of space by individual stacks and that we can't either modify or use any extra space. With these constraints, we are left with no other choice but to divide equally.

```
1   int stackSize = 300;
2   int[] buffer = new int [stackSize * 3];
3   int[] stackPointer = {0, 0, 0}; // stack pointers to track top elem
4
5   void push(int stackNum, int value) {
6       /* Find the index of the top element in the array + 1, and
7        * increment the stack pointer */
8       int index = stackNum * stackSize + stackPointer[stackNum] + 1;
9       stackPointer[stackNum]++;
10      buffer[index] = value;
11  }
12
13  int pop(int stackNum) {
14      int index = stackNum * stackSize + stackPointer[stackNum];
15      stackPointer[stackNum]--;
16      int value = buffer[index];
17      buffer[index]=0;
18      return value;
19  }
20
21  int peek(int stackNum) {
22      int index = stackNum * stackSize + stackPointer[stackNum];
23      return buffer[index];
24  }
25
26  boolean isEmpty(int stackNum) {
27      return stackPointer[stackNum] == stackNum*stackSize;
28  }
```

*Approach 2:*

In this approach, any stack can grow as long as there is any free space in the array.

We sequentially allocate space to the stacks and we link new blocks to the previous block. This means any new element in a stack keeps a pointer to the previous top element of that particular stack.

In this implementation, we face a problem of unused space. For example, if a stack deletes some of its elements, the deleted elements may not necessarily appear at the end of the array. So, in that case, we would not be able to use those newly freed spaces.

To overcome this deficiency, we can maintain a free list and the whole array space would be given initially to the free list. For every insertion, we would delete an entry from the free list. In case of deletion, we would simply add the index of the free cell to the free list.

In this implementation we would be able to have flexibility in terms of variable space utilization but we would need to increase the space complexity.

```
1   int stackSize = 300;
2   int indexUsed = 0;
3   int[] stackPointer = {-1,-1,-1};
4   StackNode[] buffer = new StackNode[stackSize * 3];
5   void push(int stackNum, int value) {
6       int lastIndex = stackPointer[stackNum];
7       stackPointer[stackNum] = indexUsed;
8       indexUsed++;
9       buffer[stackPointer[stackNum]]=new StackNode(lastIndex,value);
10  }
11  int pop(int stackNum) {
12      int value = buffer[stackPointer[stackNum]].value;
13      int lastIndex = stackPointer[stackNum];
14      stackPointer[stackNum] = buffer[stackPointer[stackNum]].previous;
15      buffer[lastIndex] = null;
16      indexUsed--;
17      return value;
18  }
19  int peek(int stack) { return buffer[stackPointer[stack]].value; }
20  boolean isEmpty(int stackNum) { return stackPointer[stackNum] == -1; }
21
22  class StackNode {
23      public int previous;
24      public int value;
25      public StackNode(int p, int v){
26          value = v;
27          previous = p;
28      }
29  }
```

**3.2**    How would you design a stack which, in addition to push and pop, also has a function min which returns the minimum element? Push, pop and min should all operate in O(1) time.

pg 52

## SOLUTION

You can implement this by having each node in the stack keep track of the minimum beneath itself. Then, to find the min, you just look at what the top element thinks is the min.

When you push an element onto the stack, the element is given the current minimum. It sets its "local min" to be the min.

```
1    public class StackWithMin extends Stack<NodeWithMin> {
2        public void push(int value) {
3            int newMin = Math.min(value, min());
4            super.push(new NodeWithMin(value, newMin));
5        }
6
7        public int min() {
8            if (this.isEmpty()) {
9                return Integer.MAX_VALUE;
10           } else {
11               return peek().min;
12           }
13       }
14   }
15
16   class NodeWithMin {
17       public int value;
18       public int min;
19       public NodeWithMin(int v, int min){
20           value = v;
21           this.min = min;
22       }
23   }
```

There's just one issue with this: if we have a large stack, we waste a lot of space by keeping track of the min for every single element. Can we do better?

We can (maybe) do a bit better than this by using an additional stack which keeps track of the mins.

```
1    public class StackWithMin2 extends Stack<Integer> {
2        Stack<Integer> s2;
3        public StackWithMin2() {
4            s2 = new Stack<Integer>();
```

```
5         }
6         public void push(int value){
7             if (value <= min()) {
8                 s2.push(value);
9             }
10            super.push(value);
11        }
12        public Integer pop() {
13            int value = super.pop();
14            if (value == min()) {
15                s2.pop();
16            }
17            return value;
18        }
19        public int min() {
20            if (s2.isEmpty()) {
21                return Integer.MAX_VALUE;
22            } else {
23                return s2.peek();
24            }
25        }
26    }
```

Why might this be more space efficient?  If many elements have the same local min, then we're keeping a lot of duplicate data.  By having the mins kept in a separate stack, we don't have this duplicate data (although we do use up a lot of extra space because we have a stack node instead of a single int).

**3.3**   Imagine a (literal) stack of plates. If the stack gets too high, it might topple. There-fore, in real life, we would likely start a new stack when the previous stack exceeds some threshold. Implement a data structure SetOfStacks that mimics this. SetOf-Stacks should be composed of several stacks, and should create a new stack once the previous one exceeds capacity. SetOfStacks.push() and SetOfStacks.pop() should behave identically to a single stack (that is, pop() should return the same values as it would if there were just a single stack).

FOLLOW UP

Implement a function popAt(int index) which performs a pop operation on a specific sub-stack.

*pg 52*

## SOLUTION

In this problem, we've been told what our data structure should look like:

```
1   class SetOfStacks {
2       ArrayList<Stack> stacks = new ArrayList<Stack>();
3       public void push(int v) { ... }
4       public int pop() { ... }
5   }
```

We know that push() should behave identically to a single stack, which means that we need push() to call push on the last stack. We have to be a bit careful here though: if the last stack is at capacity, we need to create a new stack. Our code should look something like this:

```
1   public void push(int v) {
2       Stack last = getLastStack();
3       if (last != null && !last.isAtCapacity()) { // add to last stack
4           last.push(v);
5       } else { // must create new stack
6           Stack stack = new Stack(capacity);
7           stack.push(v);
8           stacks.add(stack);
9       }
10  }
```

What should pop() do? It should behave similarly to push(), in that it should operate on the last stack. If the last stack is empty (after popping), then we should remove it from the list of stacks.

```
1   public int pop() {
2       Stack last = getLastStack();
3       int v = last.pop();
4       if (last.size == 0) stacks.remove(stacks.size() - 1);
5       return v;
6   }
```

What about the follow up question? This is a bit trickier to implement, but essentially we should imagine a "rollover" system. If we pop an element from stack 1, we need to remove the *bottom* of stack 2 and push it onto stack 1. We then need to rollover from stack 3 to stack 2, stack 4 to stack 3, etc.

> NOTE: You could make an argument that, rather than "rolling over," we should be OK with some stacks not being at full capacity. This would improve the time complexity (by a fair amount, with a large number of elements), but it might get us into tricky situations later on if someone assumes that all stacks (other than the last) operate at full capacity. There's no "right answer" here; discuss this trade-off with your interviewer!

```
1   public class SetOfStacks {
2       ArrayList<Stack> stacks = new ArrayList<Stack>();
3       public int capacity;
4       public SetOfStacks(int capacity) { this.capacity = capacity; }
5
6       public Stack getLastStack() {
7           if (stacks.size() == 0) return null;
8           return stacks.get(stacks.size() - 1);
9       }
10
11      public void push(int v) { /* see earlier code */ }
12      public int pop() {
13          Stack last = getLastStack();
14          System.out.println(stacks.size());
15          int v = last.pop();
16          if (last.size == 0) stacks.remove(stacks.size() - 1);
17          return v;
18      }
19
20      public int popAt(int index) {
21          return leftShift(index, true);
22      }
23
24      public int leftShift(int index, boolean removeTop) {
25          Stack stack = stacks.get(index);
26          int removed_item;
27          if (removeTop) removed_item = stack.pop();
28          else removed_item = stack.removeBottom();
29          if (stack.isEmpty()) {
30              stacks.remove(index);
31          } else if (stacks.size() > index + 1) {
32              int v = leftShift(index + 1, false);
```

```
33                    stack.push(v);
34              }
35            return removed_item;
36      }
37  }
38
39  public class Stack {
40      private int capacity;
41      public Node top, bottom;
42      public int size = 0;
43
44      public Stack(int capacity) { this.capacity = capacity; }
45      public boolean isAtCapacity() { return capacity == size; }
46
47      public void join(Node above, Node below) {
48          if (below != null) below.above = above;
49          if (above != null) above.below = below;
50      }
51
52      public boolean push(int v) {
53          if (size >= capacity) return false;
54          size++;
55          Node n = new Node(v);
56          if (size == 1) bottom = n;
57          join(n, top);
58          top = n;
59          return true;
60      }
61
62      public int pop() {
63          Node t = top;
64          top = top.below;
65          size--;
66          return t.value;
67      }
68
69      public boolean isEmpty() { return size == 0; }
70      public int removeBottom() {
71          Node b = bottom;
72          bottom = bottom.above;
73          if (bottom != null) bottom.below = null;
74          size--;
75          return b.value;
76      }
77  }
```

**3.4** In the classic problem of the Towers of Hanoi, you have 3 rods and N disks of different sizes which can slide onto any tower. The puzzle starts with disks sorted in ascending order of size from top to bottom (e.g., each disk sits on top of an even larger one). You have the following constraints:

(A) Only one disk can be moved at a time.

(B) A disk is slid off the top of one rod onto the next rod.

(C) A disk can only be placed on top of a larger disk.

Write a program to move the disks from the first rod to the last using Stacks.

pg 52

## SOLUTION

We need to move N disks from Rod 1 to Rod 3, but let's start from the beginning. Moving the top disk is easy - we just move it to Disk 3.

Can we move the top two disks? Yes:

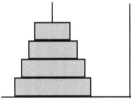

1. Move Disk 1 from Rod 1 to Rod 2

2. Move Disk 2 from Rod 1 to Rod 3

3. Move Disk 1 from Rod 2 to Rod 3

Can we move the top three disks?

1. We know we can move the top two disks around from one Rod to another (as shown earlier), so let's assume we have moved Disk 1 and 2 to Rod 2.

2. Move Disk 3 to Rod 3

3. Again we know we can move the top two disks around, so let's move them from Rod 2 to Rod 3.

This approach leads to a natural recursive algorithm:

```
1   public static void main(String[] args)
2       int n = 5;
3       Tower[] towers = new Tower[n];
4       for (int i = 0; i < 3; i++) towers[i] = new Tower(i);
5       for (int i = n - 1; i >= 0; i--) towers[0].add(i);
6       towers[0].moveDisks(n, towers[2], towers[1]);
7   }
8
9   public class Tower {
10      private Stack<Integer> disks;
11      private int index;
12      public Tower(int i) {
```

```
13        disks = new Stack<Integer>();
14        index = i;
15    }
16
17    public int index() {
18        return index;
19    }
20
21    public void add(int d) {
22        if (!disks.isEmpty() && disks.peek() <= d) {
23            System.out.println("Error placing disk " + d);
24        } else {
25            disks.push(d);
26        }
27    }
28
29    public void moveTopTo(Tower t) {
30        int top = disks.pop();
31        t.add(top);
32        System.out.println("Move disk " + top + " from " + index() +
33                                " to " + t.index());
34    }
35
36    public void print() {
37        System.out.println("Contents of Tower " + index());
38        for (int i = disks.size() - 1; i >= 0; i--) {
39            System.out.println("    " + disks.get(i));
40        }
41    }
42
43    public void moveDisks(int n, Tower destination, Tower buffer) {
44        if (n > 0) {
45            moveDisks(n - 1, buffer, destination);
46            moveTopTo(destination);
47            buffer.moveDisks(n - 1, destination, this);
48        }
49    }
50 }
```

**3.5**    Implement a MyQueue class which implements a queue using two stacks.

pg 52

## SOLUTION

Since the major difference between a queue and a stack is the order (first-in-first-out vs. last-in-first-out), we know that we need to modify peek() and pop() to go in reverse order. We can use our second stack to reverse the order of the elements (by popping s1 and pushing the elements on to s2). In such an implementation, on each peek() and pop() operation, we would pop everything from s1 onto s2, perform the peek / pop operation, and then push everything back.

This will work, but if two pop / peeks are performed back-to-back, we're needlessly moving elements. We can implement a "lazy" approach where we let the elements sit in s2.

s1 will thus be ordered with the newest elements on the top, while s2 will have the oldest elements on the top. We push the new elements onto s1, and peek and pop from s2. When s2 is empty, we'll transfer all the elements from s1 onto s2, in reverse order.

```
1    public class MyQueue<T> {
2        Stack<T> s1, s2;
3        public MyQueue() {
4            s1 = new Stack<T>();
5            s2 = new Stack<T>();
6        }
7
8        public int size() {
9            return s1.size() + s2.size();
10       }
11
12       public void add(T value) {
13           s1.push(value);
14       }
15
16       public T peek() {
17           if (!s2.empty()) return s2.peek();
18           while (!s1.empty()) s2.push(s1.pop());
19           return s2.peek();
20       }
21
22       public T remove() {
23           if (!s2.empty()) return s2.pop();
24           while (!s1.empty()) s2.push(s1.pop());
25           return s2.pop();
26       }
27   }
```

**3.6** Write a program to sort a stack in ascending order. You should not make any assumptions about how the stack is implemented. The following are the only functions that should be used to write this program: push | pop | peek | isEmpty.

pg 52

## SOLUTION

Sorting can be performed with one more stack. The idea is to pull an item from the original stack and push it on the other stack. If pushing this item would violate the sort order of the new stack, we need to remove enough items from it so that it's possible to push the new item. Since the items we removed are on the original stack, we're back where we started. The algorithm is O(N^2) and appears below.

```
1    public static Stack<Integer> sort(Stack<Integer> s) {
2        Stack<Integer> r = new Stack<Integer>();
3        while(!s.isEmpty()) {
4            int tmp = s.pop();
5            while(!r.isEmpty() && r.peek() > tmp) {
6                s.push(r.pop());
7            }
8            r.push(tmp);
9        }
10       return r;
11   }
```

**4.1**    Implement a function to check if a tree is balanced. For the purposes of this question, a balanced tree is defined to be a tree such that no two leaf nodes differ in distance from the root by more than one.

pg 54

## SOLUTION

The idea is very simple: the difference of min depth and max depth should not exceed 1, since the difference of the min and the max depth is the maximum distance difference possible in the tree.

```
1   public static int maxDepth(TreeNode root) {
2       if (root == null) {
3           return 0;
4       }
5       return 1 + Math.max(maxDepth(root.left), maxDepth(root.right));
6   }
7
8   public static int minDepth(TreeNode root) {
9       if (root == null) {
10          return 0;
11      }
12      return 1 + Math.min(minDepth(root.left), minDepth(root.right));
13  }
14
15  public static boolean isBalanced(TreeNode root){
16      return (maxDepth(root) - minDepth(root) <= 1);
17  }
```

**4.2** Given a directed graph, design an algorithm to find out whether there is a route between two nodes.

pg 54

## SOLUTION

This problem can be solved by just simple graph traversal, such as depth first search or breadth first search. We start with one of the two nodes and, during traversal, check if the other node is found. We should mark any node found in the course of the algorithm as 'already visited' to avoid cycles and repetition of the nodes.

```java
1   public enum State {
2       Unvisited, Visited, Visiting;
3   }
4
5   public static boolean search(Graph g, Node start, Node end) {
6       LinkedList<Node> q = new LinkedList<Node>(); // operates as Stack
7       for (Node u : g.getNodes()) {
8           u.state = State.Unvisited;
9       }
10      start.state = State.Visiting;
11      q.add(start);
12      Node u;
13      while(!q.isEmpty()) {
14          u = q.removeFirst(); // i.e., pop()
15          if (u != null) {
16              for (Node v : u.getAdjacent()) {
17                  if (v.state == State.Unvisited) {
18                      if (v == end) {
19                          return true;
20                      } else {
21                          v.state = State.Visiting;
22                          q.add(v);
23                      }
24                  }
25              }
26              u.state = State.Visited;
27          }
28      }
29      return false;
30  }
```

**4.3**   Given a sorted (increasing order) array, write an algorithm to create a binary tree with minimal height.

pg 54

## SOLUTION

We will try to create a binary tree such that for each node, the number of nodes in the left subtree and the right subtree are equal, if possible.

Algorithm:

1.   Insert into the tree the middle element of the array.

2.   Insert (into the left subtree) the left subarray elements

3.   Insert (into the right subtree) the right subarray elements

4.   Recurse

```
1   public static TreeNode addToTree(int arr[], int start, int end){
2       if (end < start) {
3           return null;
4       }
5       int mid = (start + end) / 2;
6       TreeNode n = new TreeNode(arr[mid]);
7       n.left = addToTree(arr, start, mid - 1);
8       n.right = addToTree(arr, mid + 1, end);
9       return n;
10  }
11
12  public static TreeNode createMinimalBST(int array[]) {
13      return addToTree(array, 0, array.length - 1);
14  }
```

**4.4** Given a binary search tree, design an algorithm which creates a linked list of all the nodes at each depth (eg, if you have a tree with depth D, you'll have D linked lists).

pg 54

## SOLUTION

We can do a simple level by level traversal of the tree, with a slight modification of the breath-first traversal of the tree.

In a usual breath first search traversal, we simply traverse the nodes without caring which level we are on. In this case, it is critical to know the level. We thus use a dummy node to indicate when we have finished one level and are starting on the next.

```
1   ArrayList<LinkedList<TreeNode>> findLevelLinkList(TreeNode root) {
2       int level = 0;
3       ArrayList<LinkedList<TreeNode>> result =
4           new ArrayList<LinkedList<TreeNode>>();
5       LinkedList<TreeNode> list = new LinkedList<TreeNode>();
6       list.add(root);
7       result.add(level, list);
8       while (true) {
9           list = new LinkedList<TreeNode>();
10          for (int i = 0; i < result.get(level).size(); i++) {
11              TreeNode n = (TreeNode) result.get(level).get(i);
12              if (n != null) {
13                  if(n.left != null) list.add(n.left);
14                  if(n.right!= null) list.add(n.right);
15              }
16          }
17          if (list.size() > 0) {
18              result.add(level + 1, list);
19          } else {
20              break;
21          }
22          level++;
23      }
24      return result;
25  }
```

**4.5** Write an algorithm to find the 'next' node (e.g., in-order successor) of a given node in a binary search tree where each node has a link to its parent.

pg 54

## SOLUTION

We approach this problem by thinking very, very carefully about what happens on an in-order traversal. On an in-order traversal, we visit X.left, then X, then X.right.

So, if we want to find X.successor(), we do the following:

1. If X has a right child, then the successor must be on the right side of X (because of the order in which we visit nodes). Specifically, the left-most child must be the first node visited in that subtree.

2. Else, we go to X's parent (call it P).

2.a. If X was a left child (P.left = X), then P is the successor of X

2.b. If X was a right child (P.right = X), then we have fully visited P, so we call successor(P).

```
1    public static TreeNode inorderSucc(TreeNode e) {
2        if (e != null) {
3            TreeNode p;
4            // Found right children -> return 1st inorder node on right
5            if (e.parent == null || e.right != null) {
6                p = leftMostChild(e.right);
7            } else {
8                // Go up until we're on left instead of right (case 2b)
9                while ((p = e.parent) != null) {
10                   if (p.left == e) {
11                       break;
12                   }
13                   e = p;
14               }
15           }
16           return p;
17       }
18       return null;
19   }
20
21   public static TreeNode leftMostChild(TreeNode e) {
22       if (e == null) return null;
23       while (e.left != null) e = e.left;
24       return e;
25   }
```

**4.6** Design an algorithm and write code to find the first common ancestor of two nodes in a binary tree. Avoid storing additional nodes in a data structure. NOTE: This is not necessarily a binary search tree.

pg 54

## SOLUTION

If this were a binary search tree, we could do a modified find on the two nodes and see where the paths diverge. Unfortunately, this is not a binary search tree, so we much try other approaches.

*Attempt #1:*

If each node has a link to its parent, we could trace p and q's paths up until they intersect.

*Attempt #2:*

Alternatively, you could follow a chain in which p and q are on the same side. That is, if p and q are both on the left of the node, branch left to look for the common ancestor. When p and q are no longer on the same side, you must have found the first common ancestor.

```
1   public Tree commonAncestor(Tree root, Tree p, Tree q) {
2       if (covers(root.left, p) && covers(root.left, q))
3           return commonAncestor(root.left, p, q);
4       if (covers(root.right, p) && covers(root.right, q))
5           return commonAncestor(root.right, p, q);
6       return root;
7   }
8   private boolean covers(Tree root, Tree p) { /* is p a child of root? */
9       if (root == null) return false;
10      if (root == p) return true;
11      return covers(root.left, p) || covers(root.right, p);
12  }
```

What is the running time of this algorithm? One way of looking at this is to see how many times each node is touched. *Covers* touches every child node, so we know that every single node in the tree must be touched at least once, and many nodes are touched multiple times.

*Attempt #3:*

For any node r, we know the following:

1. If p is on one side and q is on the other, r is the first common ancestor.

2. Else, the first common ancestor is on the left or the right side.

So, we can create a simple recursive algorithm called search that calls search(left side) and search(right side) looking at how many nodes (p or q) are placed from the left side and from the right side of the current node. If there are two nodes on one of the sides, then we have to check if the child node on this side is p or q (because in this case the current node is the common ancestor). If the child node is neither p nor q, we should continue to search further (starting from the child).

If one of the searched nodes (p or q) is located on the right side of the current node, then the other node is located on the other side. Thus the current node is the common ancestor.

```
1    static int TWO_NODES_FOUND = 2;
2    static int ONE_NODE_FOUND = 1;
3    static int NO_NODES_FOUND = 0;
4
5    // Checks how many "special" nodes are located under this root
6    int covers(TreeNode root, TreeNode p, TreeNode q) {
7        int ret = NO_NODES_FOUND;
8        if (root == null) return ret;
9        if (root == p || root == q) ret += 1;
10       ret += covers(root.left, p, q);
11       if(ret == TWO_NODES_FOUND) // Found p and q
12           return ret;
13       return ret + covers(root.right, p, q);
14   }
15
16   TreeNode commonAncestor(TreeNode root, TreeNode p, TreeNode q) {
17       if (q == p && (root.left == q || root.right == q)) return root;
18       int nodesFromLeft = covers(root.left, p, q); // Check left side
19       if (nodesFromLeft == TWO_NODES_FOUND) {
20           if(root.left == p || root.left == q) return root.left;
21           else return commonAncestor(root.left, p, q);
22       } else if (nodesFromLeft == ONE_NODE_FOUND) {
23           if (root == p) return p;
24           else if (root == q) return q;
25       }
26       int nodesFromRight = covers(root.right, p, q); // Check right side
27       if(nodesFromRight == TWO_NODES_FOUND) {
28           if(root.right == p || root.right == q) return root.right;
29           else return commonAncestor(root.right, p, q);
30       } else if (nodesFromRight == ONE_NODE_FOUND) {
31           if (root == p) return p;
32           else if (root == q) return q;
33       }
34       if (nodesFromLeft == ONE_NODE_FOUND &&
35           nodesFromRight == ONE_NODE_FOUND) return root;
36       else return null;
37   }
```

**4.7** You have two very large binary trees: T1, with millions of nodes, and T2, with hundreds of nodes. Create an algorithm to decide if T2 is a subtree of T1.

pg 54

## SOLUTION

Note that the problem here specifies that T1 has millions of nodes—this means that we should be careful of how much space we use. Let's say, for example, T1 has 10 million nodes—this means that the data alone is about 40 mb. We could create a string representing the inorder and preorder traversals. If T2's preorder traversal is a substring of T1's preorder traversal, and T2's inorder traversal is a substring of T1's inorder traversal, then T2 is a substring of T1. We can check this using a suffix tree. However, we may hit memory limitations because suffix trees are extremely memory intensive. If this become an issue, we can use an alternative approach.

*Alternative Approach:* The treeMatch procedure visits each node in the small tree at most once and is called no more than once per node of the large tree. Worst case runtime is at most O(n * m), where n and m are the sizes of trees T1 and T2, respectively. If k is the number of occurrences of T2's root in T1, the worst case runtime can be characterized as O(n + k * m).

```
1   boolean containsTree(TreeNode t1, TreeNode t2) {
2       if (t2 == null) return true; // The empty tree is always a subtree
3       else return subTree(t1, t2);
4   }
5
6   boolean subTree(TreeNode r1, TreeNode r2) {
7       if (r1 == null)
8           return false; // big tree empty & subtree still not found.
9       if (r1.data == r2.data) {
10          if (matchTree(r1,r2)) return true;
11      }
12      return (subTree(r1.left, r2) || subTree(r1.right, r2));
13  }
14
15  boolean matchTree(TreeNode r1, TreeNode r2) {
16      if (r2 == null && r1 == null)
17          return true; // nothing left in the subtree
18      if (r1 == null || r2 == null)
19          return false; // big tree empty & subtree still not found
20      if (r1.data != r2.data)
21          return false;  // data doesn't match
22      return (matchTree(r1.left, r2.left) &&
23              matchTree(r1.right, r2.right));
24  }
25  }
```

**4.8** You are given a binary tree in which each node contains a value. Design an algorithm to print all paths which sum up to that value. Note that it can be any path in the tree - it does not have to start at the root.

pg 54

## SOLUTION

Let's approach this problem by simplifying it. What if the path had to start at the root? In that case, we would have a much easier problem:

Start from the root and branch left and right, computing the sum thus far on each path. When we find the sum, we print the current path. Note that we don't stop just because we found the sum. Why? Because we could have the following path (assume we are looking for the sum 5): 2 + 3 + –4 + 3 + 1 + 2. If we stopped once we hit 2 + 3, we'd miss several paths (2 + 3 + -4 + 3 + 1 and 3 + -4 + 3 + 1 + 2). So, we keep going along every possible path.

Now, what if the path can start anywhere? In that case, we make a small modification. On every node, we look "up" to see if we've found the sum. That is—rather than asking "does this node start a path with the sum?," we ask "does this node complete a path with the sum?"

```
1    void findSum(TreeNode head, int sum, ArrayList<Integer> buffer,
2                 int level) {
3        if (head == null) return;
4        int tmp = sum;
5        buffer.add(head.data);
6        for (int i = level;i >- 1; i--){
7            tmp -= buffer.get(i);
8            if (tmp == 0) print(buffer, i, level);
9        }
10       ArrayList<Integer> c1 = (ArrayList<Integer>) buffer.clone();
11       ArrayList<Integer> c2 = (ArrayList<Integer>) buffer.clone();
12       findSum(head.left, sum, c1, level + 1);
13       findSum(head.right, sum, c2, level + 1);
14   }
15
16   void print(ArrayList<Integer> buffer, int level, int i2) {
17       for (int i = level; i <= i2; i++) {
18           System.out.print(buffer.get(i) + " ");
19       }
20       System.out.println();
21   }
```

What is the time complexity of this algorithm? Well, if a node is at level r, we do r amount of work (that's in the looking "up" step). We can take a guess at O(n lg n) (n nodes, doing an average of lg n amount of work on each step), or we can be super mathematical:

```
There are 2^r nodes at level r.
1*2^1 + 2*2^2 + 3*2^3 + 4*2^4 + ... d * 2^d
    = sum(r * 2^r, r from 0 to depth)
    = 2 (d-1) * 2^d + 2
n = 2^d ==> d = lg n
NOTE: 2^lg(x) = x
O(2 (lg n - 1) * 2^(lg n) + 2) = O(2 (lg n - 1) * n ) = O(n lg n)
```

Following similar logic, our space complexity is O(n lg n).

**5.1**    You are given two 32-bit numbers, N and M, and two bit positions, i and j. Write a method to set all bits between i and j in N equal to M (e.g., M becomes a substring of N located at i and starting at j).

EXAMPLE:

Input: N = 10000000000, M = 10101, i = 2, j = 6

Output: N = 10001010100

pg 58

## SOLUTION

This code operates by clearing all bits in N between position i and j, and then ORing to put M in there.

```
1    public static int updateBits(int n, int m, int i, int j) {
2        int max = ~0; /* All 1's */
3
4        // 1's through position j, then 0's
5        int left = max - ((1 << j) - 1);
6
7        // 1's after position i
8        int right = ((1 << i) - 1);
9
10       // 1's, with 0s between i and j
11       int mask = left | right;
12
13       // Clear i through j, then put m in there
14       return (n & mask) | (m << i);
15   }
```

**5.2** Given a (decimal - e.g. 3.72) number that is passed in as a string, print the binary representation. If the number can not be represented accurately in binary, print "ERROR"

pg 58

## SOLUTION

First, let's start off by asking ourselves what a non-integer number in binary looks like. By analogy to a decimal number, the number $n = 0.101 = 1 * (1/2^1) + 0 * (1/2^2) + 1 * (1/2^3)$.

Printing the int part of n is straight-forward (see below). To print the decimal part, we can multiply by 2 and check if the 2*n is greater than or equal to one. This is essentially "shifting" the fractional sum. That is:

$$r = 2*n = 2*0.101 = 1*(1 / 2^0) + 0*(1 / 2^1) + 1*(1 / 2^2) = 1.01$$

If r >= 1, then we know that n had a 1 right after the decimal point. By doing this continuously, we can check every digit.

```
1   public static String printBinary(String n) {
2       int intPart = Integer.parseInt(n.substring(0, n.indexOf('.')));
3       double decPart = Double.parseDouble(
4                        n.substring(n.indexOf('.'), n.length()));
5       String int_string = "";
6       while (intPart > 0) {
7           int r = intPart % 2;
8           intPart >>= 1;
9           int_string = r + int_string;
10      }
11      StringBuffer dec_string = new StringBuffer();
12      while (decPart > 0) {
13          if (dec_string.length() > 32) return "ERROR";
14          if (decPart == 1) {
15              dec_string.append((int)decPart);
16              break;
17          }
18          double r = decPart * 2;
19          if (r >= 1) {
20              dec_string.append(1);
21              decPart = r - 1;
22          } else {
23              dec_string.append(0);
24              decPart = r;
25          }
26      }
27      return int_string + "." + dec_string.toString();
28  }
```

**5.3** Given an integer, print the next smallest and next largest number that have the same number of 1 bits in their binary representation.

pg 58

## SOLUTION

*The Brute Force Approach:*

An easy approach is simply brute force: count the number of 1's in n, and then increment (or decrement) until you find a number with the same number of 1's. Easy - but not terribly interesting. Can we do something a bit more optimal? Yes!

*Number Properties Approach for Next Number*

Observations:

» If we "turn on" a 0, we need to "turn off" a 1

» If we turn on a 0 at bit i and turn off a 1 at bit j, the number changes by $2^i - 2^j$.

» If we want to get a bigger number with the same number of 1s and 0s, i must be bigger than j.

Solution:

1. Traverse from right to left. Once we've passed a 1, turn on the next 0. We've now increased the number by $2^i$. Yikes! Example: xxxxx011100 becomes xxxxx111100

2. Turn off the one that's just to the right side of that. We're now bigger by $2^i - 2^{(i-1)}$ Example: xxxxx111100 becomes xxxxx101100

3. Make the number as small as possible by rearranging all the 1s to be as far right as possible: Example: xxxxx101100 becomes xxxxx100011

To get the previous number, we do the reverse.

1. Traverse from right to left. Once we've passed a zero, turn off the next 1. Example: xxxxx100011 becomes xxxxx000011.

2. Turn on the 0 that is directly to the right. Example: xxxxx000011 becomes xxxxx010011.

3. Make the number as big as possible by shifting all the ones as far to the left as possible. Example: xxxxx010011 becomes xxxxx011100 .

And now, for the code. Note the emphasis on pulling common code out into a reusable function. Your interviewer will look for "clean code" like this.

```
1    public static boolean GetBit(int n, int index) {
2        return ((n & (1 << index)) > 0);
3    }
4
5    public static int SetBit(int n, int index, boolean b) {
6        if (b) {
7            return n | (1 << index);
8        } else {
9            int mask = ~(1 << index);
10           return n & mask;
11       }
12   }
13
14   public static int GetNext_NP(int n) {
15       if (n <= 0) return -1;
16
17       int index = 0;
18       int countOnes = 0;
19
20       // Find first one.
21       while (!GetBit(n, index)) index++;
22
23       // Turn on next zero.
24       while (GetBit(n, index)) {
25           index++;
26           countOnes++;
27       }
28       n = SetBit(n, index, true);
29
30       // Turn off previous one
31       index--;
32       n = SetBit(n, index, false);
33       countOnes--;
34
35       // Set zeros
36       for (int i = index - 1; i >= countOnes; i--) {
37           n = SetBit(n, i, false);
38       }
39
40       // Set ones
41       for (int i = countOnes - 1; i >= 0; i--) {
42           n = SetBit(n, i, true);
43       }
44
45       return n;
```

```
46  }
47
48      public static int GetPrevious_NP(int n) {
49          if (n <= 0) return -1; // Error
50
51          int index = 0;
52          int countZeros = 0;
53
54          // Find first zero.
55          while (GetBit(n, index)) index++;
56
57          // Turn off next 1.
58          while (!GetBit(n, index)) {
59              index++;
60              countZeros++;
61          }
62          n = SetBit(n, index, false);
63
64          // Turn on previous zero
65          index--;
66          n = SetBit(n, index, true);
67          countZeros--;
68
69          // Set ones
70          for (int i = index - 1; i >= countZeros; i--) {
71              n = SetBit(n, i, true);
72          }
73
74          // Set zeros
75          for (int i = countZeros - 1; i >= 0; i--) {
76              n = SetBit(n, i, false);
77          }
78
79          return n;
80      }
```

**5.4** Explain what the following code does: ((n & (n-1)) == 0).

pg 58

## SOLUTION

We can work backwards to solve this question.

*What does it mean if A & B == 0?*

It means that A and B never have a 1 bit in the same place. So if n & (n-1) == 0, then n and n-1 never share a 1.

*What does n-1 look like (as compared with n)?*

Try doing subtraction by hand (in base 2 or 10). What happens?

```
  1101011000 [base 2]              593100 [base 10]
-          1                  -         1
= 1101010111 [base 2]            = 593099 [base 10]
```

When you subtract 1 from a number, you look at the least significant bit. If it's a 1 you change it to zero and you are done. If it's a zero, you must "borrow" from a larger bit. So, you go to increasingly larger bits, changing each bit from a 0 to a 1, until you find a 1. You flip that one to a 0 and you are done.

Thus, n-1 will look like n, except that n's initial 0s will be 1's in n-1, and n's least significant 1 will be a 0 in (n-1). That is:

```
if      n = abcde1000
then n-1 = abcde0111
```

*So what does n & (n-1) == 0 indicate?*

n and (n-1) must have no 1s in common. Given that they look like this:

```
if      n = abcde1000
then n-1 = abcde0111
```

abcde must be all 0s, which means that n must look like this: 00001000. n is therefore a power of two.

So, we have our answer: ((n & (n-1)) == 0) checks if n is a power of 2 (or 0).

**5.5** Write a function to determine the number of bits required to convert integer A to integer B.

Input: 31, 14

Output: 2

pg 58

## SOLUTION

This seemingly complex problem is actually rather straightforward. To approach this, ask yourself how you would figure out which bits in two numbers are different. Simple: with an xor.

Each 1 in the xor will represent one different bit between A and B. We then simply need to count the number of bits that are 1.

```
1    public static int bitSwapRequired(int a, int b) {
2        int count = 0;
3        for (int c = a ^ b; c != 0; c = c >> 1) {
4            count += c & 1;
5        }
6        return count;
7    }
```

**5.6**     Write a program to swap odd and even bits in an integer with as few instructions as possible (e.g., bit 0 and bit 1 are swapped, bit 2 and bit 3 are swapped, etc).

pg 58

## SOLUTION

Mask all odd bits with 10101010 in binary (which is 0xAA), then shift them left to put them in the even bits. Then, perform a similar operation for even bits. This takes a total 5 instructions.

```
1   public static int swapOddEvenBits(int x) {
2       return ( ((x & 0xaaaaaaaa) >> 1) | ((x & 0x55555555) << 1) );
3   }
```

**5.7**    An array A[1...n] contains all the integers from 0 to n except for one number which is missing. In this problem, we cannot access an entire integer in A with a single operation. The elements of A are represented in binary, and the only operation we can use to access them is "fetch the jth bit of A[i]", which takes constant time. Write code to find the missing integer. Can you do it in O(n) time?

pg 58

## SOLUTION

Picture a list of binary numbers between 0 to n. What will change when we remove one number? We'll get an imbalance of 1s and 0s in the least significant bit. That is, before removing the number k, we have this list of least significant bits (in some order):

```
0 0 0 0 0 1 1 1 1 1            OR              0 0 0 0 0 1 1 1 1
```

Suppose we secretly removed either a 1 or a 0 from this list. Could we tell which one was removed?

```
remove(0 from 0 0 0 0 0 1 1 1 1 1) --> 0 0 0 0 1 1 1 1 1
remove(1 from 0 0 0 0 0 1 1 1 1 1) --> 0 0 0 0 0 1 1 1 1
remove(0 from 0 0 0 0 0 1 1 1 1)   --> 0 0 0 0 1 1 1 1
remove(1 from 0 0 0 0 0 1 1 1 1)   --> 0 0 0 0 0 1 1 1
```

Note that if 0 is removed, we always wind up with count(1) >= count(0). If 1 is removed, we wind up with count(1) < count(0). Therefore, we can look at the least significant bit to figure out in O(N) time whether the missing number has a 0 or a 1 in the least significant bit (LSB). If LSB(missing) == 0, then we can discard all numbers with LSB = 1. If LSB(missing) == 1, we can discard all numbers with LSB = 0.

What about the next iteration, with the second least significant bit (SLSB)? We've discarded all the numbers with LSB = 1, so our list looks something like this (if n = 5, and missing = 3):

| | | | |
|---|---|---|---|
| ~~00000~~ | ~~00100~~ | ~~01000~~ | ~~01100~~ |
| 00001 | 00101 | 01001 | 01101 |
| ~~00010~~ | ~~00110~~ | ~~01010~~ | |
| ----- | 00111 | 01011 | |

Our SLSBs now look like 0 0 1 0 1 0. Using the same logic as we applied for LSB, we can figure out that the missing number must have SLSB = 1. Our number must look like xxxx11.

Third iteration, discarding numbers with SLSB = 0:

| | | | |
|---|---|---|---|
| ~~00000~~ | ~~00100~~ | ~~01000~~ | ~~01100~~ |
| ~~00001~~ | ~~00101~~ | ~~01001~~ | ~~01101~~ |
| ~~00010~~ | ~~00110~~ | ~~01010~~ | |
| ----- | 00111 | 01011 | |

We can now compute that count(TLSB = 1) = 1 and count(TLSB = 1) = 1. Therefore, TLSB = 0. We can recurse repeatedly, building our number bit by bit:

```
1   int findMissing(ArrayList<BitInteger> array) {
2       return findMissing(array, BitInteger.INTEGER_SIZE - 1);
3   }
4
5   int findMissing(ArrayList<BitInteger> input, int column) {
6       if (column < 0) { // Base case and error condition
7           return 0;
8       }
9       ArrayList<BitInteger> oddIndices = new ArrayList<BitInteger>();
10      ArrayList<BitInteger> evenIndices = new ArrayList<BitInteger>();
11      for (BitInteger t : input) {
12          if (t.fetch(column) == 0) {
13              evenIndices.add(t);
14          } else {
15              oddIndices.add(t);
16          }
17      }
18      if (oddIndices.size() >= evenIndices.size()) {
19          return (findMissing(evenIndices, column - 1)) << 1 | 0;
20      } else {
21          return (findMissing(oddIndices, column - 1)) << 1 | 1;
22      }
23  }
24
```

What is the run-time of this algorithm? On the first pass, we look at O(N) bits. On the second pass, we've eliminated N/2 numbers, so we then look at O(N/2) bits. On the third pass, we have eliminated another half of the numbers, so we then look at O(N/4) bits. If we keep going, we get an equation that looks like:

$$O(N) + O(N/2) + O(N/4) + O(N/8) + \ldots = O(2N) = O(N)$$

Our run-time is O(N).

**6.1** Add arithmetic operators (plus, minus, times, divide) to make the following expression true: 3 1 3 6 = 8. You can use any parentheses you'd like.

pg 60

## SOLUTION

An interviewer is asking this problem to see how you think and approach problems—so don't just guess randomly.

Try approaching this the following way: What sorts of operations would get us to 8? I can think of a few:

```
4 * 2 = 8
16 / 2 = 8
4 + 4 = 8
```

Let's start with the first one. Is there any way to make 3 1 3 6 produce 4 * 2? We can easily notice that 3 + 1 = 4 (the first two numbers). We can also notice that 6 / 3 = 2. If we had "3 1 6 3", we'd be done, since (3 + 1)*(6 / 3) = 8. Although it seems a little unconventional to do this, we can, in fact, just flip the 6 and the 3 to get the solution:

```
(( 3 + 1 ) / 3) * 6 = 8
```

**6.2** There is an 8x8 chess board in which two diagonally opposite corners have been cut off. You are given 31 dominos, and a single domino can cover exactly two squares. Can you use the 31 dominos to cover the entire board? Prove your answer (by providing an example, or showing why it's impossible).

pg 60

## SOLUTION

Impossible. Here's why: The chess board initially has 32 black and 32 white squares. By removing opposite corners (which must be the same color), we're left with 30 of one color and 32 of the other color. Let's say, for the sake of argument, that we have 30 black and 32 white squares.

When we lay down each domino, we're taking up one white and one black square. Therefore, 31 dominos will take up 31 white squares and 31 black squares exactly. On this board, however, we must have 30 black squares and 32 white squares. Hence, it is impossible.

**6.3** You have a five quart jug and a three quart jug, and an unlimited supply of water (but no measuring cups). How would you come up with exactly four quarts of water?

NOTE: The jugs are oddly shaped, such that filling up exactly 'half' of the jug would be impossible.

pg 60

## SOLUTION

We can pour water back and forth between the two jugs as follows:

| 5 Quart Contents | 3 Quart Contents | Note |
|:---:|:---:|:---:|
| 5 | 0 | Filled 5 quart jug |
| 2 | 3 | Filled 3Q with 5Q's contents |
| 0 | 2 | Dumped 3Q |
| 5 | 2 | Filled 5Q |
| 4 | 3 | Fill remainder of 3Q with 5Q |
| 4 |  | Done! We have four quarts. |

## OBSERVATIONS AND SUGGESTIONS:

» Many brain teasers have a math / CS root to them—this is one of them! Note that as long as the two jug sizes are relatively prime (i.e., have no common prime factors), you can find a pour sequence for any value between 1 and the sum of the jug sizes.

**6.4** A bunch of men are on an island. A genie comes down and gathers everyone to-gether and places a magical hat on some people's heads (i.e., at least one person has a hat). The hat is magical: it can be seen by other people, but not by the wearer of the hat himself. To remove the hat, those (and only those who have a hat) must dunk themselves underwater at exactly midnight. If there are n people and c hats, how long does it take the men to remove the hats? The men cannot tell each other (in any way) that they have a hat.

FOLLOW UP

Prove that your solution is correct.

pg 60

## SOLUTION

This problem seems hard, so let's simplify it by looking at specific cases.

*Case c = 1:* Exactly one man is wearing a hat.

Assuming all the men are intelligent, the man with the hat should look around and realize that no one else is wearing a hat. Since the genie said that at least one person is wearing a hat, he must conclude that he is wearing a hat. Therefore, he would be able to remove it that night.

*Case c = 2:* Exactly two men are wearing hats.

The two men with hats see one hat, and are unsure whether c = 1 or c = 2. They know, from the previous case, that if c = 1, the hats would be removed on Night #1. Therefore, if the other man still has a hat, he must deduce that c = 2, which means that he has a hat. Both men would then remove the hats on Night #2

*Case General:* If c = 3, then each man is unsure whether c = 2 or 3. If it were 2, the hats would be removed on Night #2. If they are not, they must deduce that c = 3, and therefore they have a hat. We can follow this logic for c = 4, 5, ...

### Proof by Induction

Using induction to prove a statement P(n)

***If (1)*** P(1) = TRUE (e.g., the statement is true when n = 1)

***AND (2)*** if P(n) = TRUE -> P(n+1) = TRUE (e.g., P(n+1) is true whenever P(2) is true).

***THEN*** P(n) = TRUE for all n >= 1.

### Explanation

» Condition 2 sets up an infinite deduction chain: P(1) implies P(2) implies P(3) implies ... P(n) implies P(n+1) implies ...

---

» Condition one (P(1) is true) ignites this chain, with truth cascading off into infinity.

*Base Case: c = 1 (See previous page).*

*Assume true for c hats. i.e., if there are c hats, it will take c nights to remove all of them.*

*Prove true for c+1 hats.*

Each man with a hat sees c hat, and can not be immediately sure whether there are c hats or c+1 hats. However, he knows that if there are c hats, it will take exactly c nights to remove them. Therefore, when c nights have passed and everyone still has a hat, he can only conclude that there are c+1 hats. He must know that he is wearing a hat. Each man makes the same conclusion and simultaneously removes the hats on night c+1.

Therefore, we have met the principles of induction. We have proven that it will take c nights to remove c hats.

**6.5** There is a building of 100 floors. If an egg drops from the Nth floor or above it will break. If it's dropped from any floor below, it will not break. You're given 2 eggs. Find N, while minimizing the number of drops for the worst case.

pg 60

## SOLUTION

*Observation*: Regardless of how we drop Egg1, Egg2 must do a linear search. i.e., if Egg1 breaks between floor 10 and 15, we have to check every floor in between with the Egg2

*The Approach:*

A First Try: Suppose we drop an egg from the 10th floor, then the 20th, ...

» If the first egg breaks on the first drop (Floor 10), then we have at most 10 drops total.

» If the first egg breaks on the last drop (Floor 100), then we have at most 19 drops total (floors 10, 20, ...,90, 100, then 91 through 99).

» That's pretty good, but all we've considered is the absolute worst case. We should do some "load balancing" to make those two cases more even.

Goal: Create a system for dropping Egg1 so that the most drops required is consistent, whether Egg1 breaks on the first drop or the last drop.

1.  A perfectly load balanced system would be one in which Drops of Egg1 + Drops of Egg2 is always the same, regardless of where Egg1 broke.

2.  For that to be the case, since each drop of Egg1 takes one more step, Egg2 is allowed one fewer step.

3.  We must, therefore, reduce the number of steps potentially required by Egg2 by one drop each time. For example, if Egg1 is dropped on Floor 20 and then Floor 30, Egg2 is potentially required to take 9 steps. When we drop Egg1 again, we must reduce potential Egg2 steps to only 8. That is, we must drop Egg1 at floor 39.

4.  We know, therefore, Egg1 must start at Floor X, then go up by X-1 floors, then X-2, ..., until it gets to 100.

5.  Solve for X+(X-1)+(X-2)+...+1 = 100. X(X+1)/2 = 100 -> X = 14

We go to Floor 14, then 27, then 39, ... This takes 14 steps maximum.

**6.6** There are one hundred closed lockers in a hallway. A man begins by opening all one hundred lockers. Next, he closes every second locker. Then he goes to every third locker and closes it if it is open or opens it if it is closed (e.g., he toggles every third locker). After his one hundredth pass in the hallway, in which he toggles only locker number one hundred, how many lockers are open?

*pg 60*

## SOLUTION

*Question: For which rounds is a door toggled (open or closed)?*

A door n is toggled once for each factor of n, including itself and 1. That is, door 15 is toggled on round 1, 3, 5, and 15.

*Question:* When would a door be left open?

*Answer:* A door is left open if the number of factors (x) is odd. You can think about this by pairing factors off as an open and a close. If there's one remaining, the door will be open.

*Question:* When would x be odd?

*Answer:* x is odd if n is a perfect square. Here's why: pair n's factors by their complements. For example, if n is 36, the factors are (1, 36), (2, 18), (3, 12), (4, 9), (6, 6). Note that (6, 6) only contributes 1 factor, thus giving n an odd number of factors.

*Question:* How many perfect squares are there?

*Answer:* There are 10 perfect squares. You could count them (1, 4, 9, 16, 25, 36, 49, 64, 81, 100), or you could simply realize that you can take the numbers 1 through 10 and square them (1*1, 2*2, 3*3, ..., 10*10).

Therefore, there are 10 lockers open.

**7.1** Design the data structures for a generic deck of cards. Explain how you would sub-class it to implement particular card games.

pg 62

## SOLUTION

```
1   public class Card {
2       public enum Suit {
3           CLUBS (1), SPADES (2), HEARTS (3), DIAMONDS (4);
4           int value;
5           private Suit(int v) { value = v; }
6       };
7
8       private int card;
9       private Suit suit;
10
11      public Card(int r, Suit s) {
12          card = r;
13          suit = s;
14      }
15
16      public int value() { return card; }
17      public Suit suit() { return suit; }
18  }
```

Assume that we're building a blackjack game, so we need to know the value of the cards. Face cards are ten and an ace is 11 (most of the time, but that's the job of the Hand class, not the following class).

```
1   public class BlackJackCard extends Card {
2       public BlackJackCard(int r, Suit s) { super(r, s); }
3
4       public int value() {
5           int r = super.value();
6           if (r == 1) return 11; // aces are 11
7           if (r < 10) return r;
8           return 10;
9       }
10
11      boolean isAce() {
12          return super.value() == 1;
13      }
14  }
```

**7.2** Imagine you have a call center with three levels of employees: fresher, technical lead (TL), product manager (PM). There can be multiple employees, but only one TL or PM. An incoming telephone call must be allocated to a fresher who is free. If a fresher can't handle the call, he or she must escalate the call to technical lead. If the TL is not free or not able to handle it, then the call should be escalated to PM. Design the classes and data structures for this problem. Implement a method getCallHandler().

pg 62

## SOLUTION

All three ranks of employees have different work to be done, so those specific functions are profile specific. We should keep these specific things within their respective class.

There are a few things which are common to them, like address, name, job title, age, etc. These things can be kept in one class and can be extended / inherited by others.

Finally, there should be one CallHandler class which would route the calls to the concerned person.

> NOTE: On any object oriented design question, there are many ways to design the objects. Discuss the trade-offs of different solutions with your interviewer. You should usually design for long term code flexibility and maintenance.

```
1    public class CallHandler {
2        static final int LEVELS = 3; // we have 3 levels of employees
3        static final int NUM_FRESHERS = 5; // we have 5 freshers
4        ArrayList<Employee>[] employeeLevels = new ArrayList[LEVELS];
5        // queues for each call's rank
6        Queue<Call>[] callQueues = new LinkedList[LEVELS];
7
8        public CallHandler() { ... }
9
10       Employee getCallHandler(Call call) {
11           for (int level = call.rank; level < LEVELS - 1; level++) {
12               ArrayList<Employee> employeeLevel = employeeLevels[level];
13               for (Employee emp : employeeLevel) {
14                   if (emp.free) {
15                       return emp;
16                   }
17               }
18           }
19           return null;
20       }
21
22       // routes the call to an available employee, or adds to a queue
```

```
23      void dispatchCall(Call call) {
24          // try to route the call to an employee with minimal rank
25          Employee emp = getCallHandler(call);
26          if (emp != null) {
27              emp.ReceiveCall(call);
28          } else {
29              // place the call into queue according to its rank
30              callQueues[call.rank].add(call);
31          }
32      }
33      void getNextCall(Employee e) {...} // look for call for e's rank
34  }
35
36  class Call {
37      int rank = 0; // minimal rank of employee who can handle this call
38      public void reply(String message) { ... }
39      public void disconnect() { ... }
40  }
41
42  class Employee {
43      CallHandler callHandler;
44      int rank; // 0- fresher, 1 - technical lead, 2 - product manager
45      boolean free;
46      Employee(int rank) { this.rank = rank; }
47      void ReceiveCall(Call call) { ... }
48      void CallHandled(Call call) { ... } // call is complete
49      void CannotHandle(Call call) { // escalate call
50          call.rank = rank + 1;
51          callHandler.dispatchCall(call);
52          free = true;
53          callHandler.getNextCall(this); // look for waiting call
54      }
55  }
56
57  class Fresher extends Employee {
58      public Fresher() { super(0); }
59  }
60  class TechLead extends Employee {
61      public TechLead() { super(1); }
62  }
63  class ProductManager extends Employee {
64      public ProductManager() { super(2); }
65  }
```

**7.3** Design a musical juke box using object oriented principles.

pg 62

## SOLUTION

Let's first understand the basic system components:

» CD player

» CD

» Display () (displays length of song, remaining time and playlist)

Now, let's break this down further:

» Playlist creation (includes add, delete, shuffle etc sub functionalities)

» CD selector

» Track selector

» Queueing up a song

» Get next song from playlist

A user also can be introduced:

» Adding

» Deleting

» Credit information

How do we group this functionality based on Objects (data + functions which go together)?

Object oriented design suggests wrapping up data with their operating functions in a single entity class.

```
1   public class CD { }
2   public class CDPlayer {
3       private Playlist p;
4       private CD c;
5       public Playlist getPlaylist() { return p; }
6       public void setPlaylist(Playlist p) { this.p = p; }
7       public CD getCD() { return c; }
8       public void setCD(CD c) { this.c = c; }
9       public CDPlayer(Playlist p) { this.p = p; }
10      public CDPlayer(CD c, Playlist p) { ... }
11      public CDPlayer(CD c) { this.c = c; }
12      public void playTrack(Song s) { ... }
13  }
14
15  public class JukeBox {
```

```
16          private CDPlayer cdPlayer;
17          private User user;
18          private Set<CD> cdCollection;
19          private TrackSelector ts;
20
21          public JukeBox(CDPlayer cdPlayer, User user, Set<CD> cdCollection,
22                        TrackSelector ts) { ... }
23          public Song getCurrentTrack() { return ts.getCurrentSong();   }
24          public void processOneUser(User u) { this.user = u;    }
25   }
26
27   public class Playlist {
28          private Song track;
29          private Queue<Song> queue;
30          public Playlist(Song track, Queue<Song> queue) { ... }
31          public Song getNextTrackToPlay(){ return queue.peek(); }
32          public void queueUpTrack(Song s){ queue.add(s); }
33   }
34
35   public class Song {
36          private String songName;
37   }
38
39   public class TrackSelector {
40          private Song currentSong;
41          public TrackSelector(Song s) { currentSong=s; }
42          public void setTrack(Song s) { currentSong = s;}
43          public Song getCurrentSong() { return currentSong; }
44   }
45
46   public class User {
47          private String name;
48          public String getName() { return name; }
49          public void setName(String name) { this.name = name; }
50          public long getID() { return ID; }
51          public void setID(long iD) { ID = iD; }
52          private long ID;
53          public User(String name, long iD) { ... }
54          public User getUser() { return this; }
55          public static User addUser(String name, long iD) { ... }
56   }
```

**7.4**    Design a chess game using object oriented principles.

pg 62

## SOLUTION

```
1    public class ChessPieceTurn { };
2    public class GameManager {
3        void processTurn(PlayerBase player) { };
4        boolean acceptTurn(ChessPieceTurn turn) { return true; };
5        Position currentPosition;
6    }
7
8    public abstract class PlayerBase {
9        public abstract ChessPieceTurn getTurn(Position p);
10   }
11   class ComputerPlayer extends PlayerBase {
12       public ChessPieceTurn getTurn(Position p) { return null; }
13       public void setDifficulty() { };
14       public PositionEstimator estimater;
15       public PositionBackTracker backtracter;
16   }
17   public class HumanPlayer extends PlayerBase {
18       public ChessPieceTurn getTurn(Position p) { return null; }
19   }
20
21   public abstract class ChessPieceBase {
22       abstract boolean canBeChecked();
23       abstract boolean isSupportCastle();
24   }
25   public class King extends ChessPieceBase { ... }
26   public class Queen extends ChessPieceBase { ... }
27
28   public class Position { // represents chess positions in compact form
29       ArrayList<ChessPieceBase> black;
30       ArrayList<ChessPieceBase> white;
31   }
32
33   public class PositionBackTracker {
34       public static Position getNext(Position p) { return null; }
35   }
36   public class PositionEstimator {
37       public static PositionPotentialValue estimate(Position p) { ... }
38   }
39   public abstract class PositionPotentialValue {
40       abstract boolean lessThan(PositionPotentialValue pv);
41   }
```

**7.5**    Design the data structures for an online book reader system.

pg 62

## SOLUTION

Since the problem doesn't describe much about the functionality, let's assume we want to design a basic online reading system which provides the following functionality:

» User membership creation and extension.

» Searching the database of books

» Reading the books

To implement these we may require many other functions, like get, set, update, etc. Objects required would likely include User, Book, and Library.

The following code / object oriented design describes this functionality:

```
1   public class Book {
2       private long ID;
3       private String details;
4       private static Set<Book> books;
5
6       public Book(long iD, String details) { ... }
7       public static void addBook(long iD, String details){
8           books.add(new Book(iD, details));
9       }
10
11      public void update() { }
12      public static void delete(Book b) { books.remove(b); }
13      public static Book find(long id){
14          for (Book b : books)
15              if(b.getID() == id) return b;
16          return null;
17      }
18  }
19
20  public class User {
21      private long ID;
22      private String details;
23      private int accountType;
24      private static Set<User> users;
25
26      public Book searchLibrary(long id) { return Book.find(id); }
27      public void renewMembership() { ... }
28
29      public static User find(long ID) {
```

```
30              for (User u : users) {
31                  if (u.getID() == ID) return u;
32              }
33              return null;
34          }
35
36          public static void addUser(long ID, String details,
37                                       int accountType) {
38              users.add(new User(ID, details, accountType));
39          }
40
41          public User(long iD, String details, int accountType) { ... }
42  }
43
44  public class OnlineReaderSystem {
45      private Book b;
46      private User u;
47      public OnlineReaderSystem(Book b, User u) { ... }
48      public void listenRequest() { }
49      public Book searchBook(long ID) { return Book.find(ID); }
50      public User searchUser(long ID){ return User.find(ID); }
51      public void display() { }
52  }
```

This design is a very simplistic implementation of such a system. We have a class for User to keep all the information regarding the user, and an identifier to identify each user uniquely. We can add functionality like registering the user, charging a membership amount and monthly / daily quota, etc.

Next, we have book class where we will keep all the book's information. We would also implement functions like add / delete / update books.

Finally, we have a manager class for managing the online book reader system which would have a listen function to listen for any incoming requests to log in. It also provides book search functionality and display functionality. Because the end user interacts through this class, search must be implemented here.

**7.6** Implement a jigsaw puzzle. Design the data structures and explain an algorithm to solve the puzzle.

pg 62

## SOLUTION

```
1   class Edge {
2       enum Type { inner, outer, flat }
3       Piece parent;
4       Type type;
5       bool fitsWith(Edge type) { ... }; // Inners & outer fit together.
6   }
7   class Piece {
8       Edge left, right, top, bottom;
9       Orientation solvedOrientation = ...; // 90, 180, etc
10  }
11  class Puzzle {
12      Piece[][] pieces; /* Remaining pieces left to put away. */
13      Piece[][] solution;
14      Edge[] inners, outers, flats;
15      /* We're going to solve this by working our way in-wards, starting
16       * with the corners. This is a list of the inside edges. */
17      Edge[] exposed_edges;
18
19      void sort() {
20          /* Iterate through all edges, adding each to inners, outers,
21           * etc, as appropriate. Look for the corners—add those to
22           * solution. Add each non-flat edge of the corner to
23           * exposed_edges. */
24      }
25
26      void solve() {
27          foreach edge1 in exposed_edges {
28              /* Look for a match to edge1 */
29              if (edge1.type == Edge.Type.inner) {
30                  foreach edge2 in outers {
31                      if edge1.fitsWith(edge2) {
32                          /* We found a match! Remove edge1 from
33                           * exposed_edges. Add edge2's piece to
34                           * solution. Check which edges of edge2 are
35                           * exposed, and add those to exposed_edges. */
36                      }
37                  }
38                  /* Do the same thing, swapping inner & outer. */
39              }
40          }
```

```
41      }
42  }
```

## Overview:

1.  We grouped the edges by their type. Because inners go with outers, and vice versa, this enables us to go straight to the potential matches.

    We keep track of the inner perimeter of the puzzle (exposed_edges) as we work our way inwards. exposed_edges is initialized to be the corner's edges.

**7.7** Explain how you would design a chat server. In particular, provide details about the various backend components, classes, and methods. What would be the hardest problems to solve?

pg 62

## SOLUTION

*What is our chat server?*

This is something you should discuss with your interviewer, but let's make a couple of assumptions: imagine we're designing a basic chat server that needs to support a small number of users. People have a contact list, they see who is online vs offline, and they can send text-based messages to them. We will not worry about supporting group chat, voice chat, etc. We will also assume that contact lists are mutual: I can only talk to you if you can talk to me. Let's keep it simple.

*What specific actions does it need to support?*

»   User A signs online

»   User A asks for their contact list, with each person's current status.

»   Friends of User A now see User A as online

»   User A adds User B to contact list

»   User A sends text-based message to User B

»   User A changes status message and/or status type

»   User A removes User B

»   User A signs offline

*What can we learn about these requirements?*
We must have a concept of users, add request status, online status, and messages.

*What are the core components?*
We'll need a database to store items and an "always online" application as the server. We might recommend using XML for the communication between the chat server and the clients, as it's easy for a person and a machine to read.

*What are the key objects and methods?*

We have listed the key objects and methods below. Note that we have hidden many of the details, such as how to actually push the data out to a client.

```
1    enum StatusType {
2        online, offline, away;
3    }
4
```

```
5    class Status {
6        StatusType status_type;
7        String status_message;
8    }
9
10   class User {
11       String username;
12       String display_name;
13       User[] contact_list;
14       AddRequest[] requests;
15       boolean updateStatus(StatusType stype, String message) { … };
16       boolean addUserWithUsername(String name);
17       boolean approveRequest(String username);
18       boolean denyRequest(String username);
19       boolean removeContact(String username);
20       boolean sendMessage(String username, String message);
21   }
22   /* Holds data that from_user would like to add to_user */
23   class AddRequest {
24       User from_user;
25       User to_user;
26   }
27   class Server {
28       User getUserByUsername(String username);
29   }
```

*What problems would be the hardest to solve (or the most interesting)?*

**Q1**  *How do we know if someone is online—I mean, really, really know?*

While we would like users to tell us when they sign off, we can't know for sure. A user's connection might have died, for example. To make sure that we know when a user has signed off, we might try regularly pinging the client to make sure it's still there.

**Q2**  *How do we deal with conflicting information?*

We have some information stored in the computer's memory and some in the database. What happens if they get out of sync? Which one is "right"?

**Q3**  *How do we make our server scale?*

While we designed out chat server without worrying—too much– about scalability, in real life this would be a concern. We'd need to split our data across many servers, which would increase our concern about out of sync data.

**Q4**  *How we do prevent denial of service attacks?*

Clients can push data to us—what if they try to DOS us? How do we prevent that?

**7.8** Othello is played as follows: Each Othello piece is white on one side and black on the other. When a piece is surrounded by its opponents on both the left and right sides, or both the top and bottom, it is said to be captured and its color is flipped. On your turn, you must capture at least one of your opponent's pieces. The game ends when either user has no more valid moves, and the win is assigned to the person with the most pieces. Implement the object oriented design for Othello.

pg 62

## SOLUTION

Othello has these major steps:

2. Game () which would be the main function to manage all the activity in the game:

3. Initialize the game which will be done by constructor

4. Get first user input

5. Validate the input

6. Change board configuration

7. Check if someone has won the game

8. Get second user input

9. Validate the input

10. Change the board configuration

11. Check if someone has won the game...

NOTE: The full code for Othello is contained in the code attachment.

```
1    public class Question {
2        private final int white = 1;
3        private final int black = 2;
4        private int[][] board;
5
6        /* Sets up the board in the standard othello starting positions,
7         * and starts the game */
8        public void start () { ... }
9
10       /* Returns the winner, if any. If there are no winners, returns
11        * 0 */
12       private int won() {
13       if (!canGo (white) && !canGo (black)) {
14           int count = 0;
```

```
15          for (int i = 0; i < 8; i++) {
16              for (int j = 0; j < 8; j++) {
17                  if (board [i] [j] == white) {
18                      count++;
19                  }
20                  if (board [i] [j] == black) {
21                      count--;
22                  }
23              }
24          }
25          if (count > 0) return white;
26          if (count < 0) return black;
27          return 3;
28      }
29      return 0;
30  }
31
32  /* Returns whether the player of the specified color has a valid
33   * move in his turn. This will return false when
34   * 1. none of his pieces are present
35   * 2. none of his moves result in him gaining new pieces
36   * 3. the board is filled up
37   */
38  private boolean canGo(int color) { ... }
39
40  /* Returns if a move at coordinate (x,y) is a valid move for the
41   * specified player */
42  private boolean isValid(int color, int x, int y) { ... }
43
44  /* Prompts the player for a move and the coordinates for the move.
45   * Throws an exception if the input is not valid or if the entered
46   * coordinates do not make a valid move. */
47  private void getMove (int color) throws Exception { ... }
48
49  /* Adds the move onto the board, and the pieces gained from that
50   * move. Assumes the move is valid. */
51  private void add (int x, int y, int color) { ... }
52
53  /* The actual game: runs continuously until a player wins */
54  private void game() {
55      printBoard();
56      while (won() == 0) {
57          boolean valid = false;
58          while (!valid) {
59              try {
60                  getMove(black);
```

```
61              valid = true;
62            } catch (Exception e) {
63                System.out.println ("Enter a valid coordinate!");
64            }
65          }
66          valid = false;
67          printBoard();
68          while (!valid) {
69              try {
70                  getMove(white);
71                  valid = true;
72              } catch (Exception e) {
73                  System.out.println ("Enter a valid coordinate!");
74              }
75          }
76          printBoard ();
77      }
78
79      if (won()!=3) {
80          System.out.println (won () == 1 ? "white" : "black" +
81                                  " won!");
82      } else {
83          System.out.println("It's a draw!");
84      }
85    }
86 }
```

**7.9** Explain the data structures and algorithms that you would use to design an in-memory file system. Illustrate with an example in code where possible.

pg 62

## SOLUTION

For data block allocation, we can use bitmask vector and linear search (see "Practical File System Design") or B+ trees (see Wikipedia).

```
1    struct DataBlock { char data[DATA_BLOCK_SIZE]; };
2    DataBlock dataBlocks[NUM_DATA_BLOCKS];
3    struct INode { std::vector<int> datablocks; };
4    struct MetaData {
5        int size;
6        Date last_modifed, created;
7        char extra_attributes;
8    };
9    std::vector<bool> dataBlockUsed(NUM_DATA_BLOCKS);
10   std::map<string, INode *> mapFromName;
11   struct FSBase;
12   struct File : public FSBase {
13    private:
14       std::vector<INode> * nodes;
15       MetaData metaData;
16   };
17
18   struct Directory : pubic FSBase { std::vector<FSBase* > content; };
19   struct FileSystem {
20       init();
21       mount(FileSystem*);
22       unmount(FileSystem*);
23       File createFile(cosnt char* name) { ... }
24       Directory createDirectory(const char* name) { ... }
25       // mapFromName to find INode corresponding to file
26       void openFile(File * file, FileMode mode) { ... }
27       void closeFile(File * file) { ... }
28       void writeToFile(File * file, void * data, int num) { ... }
29       void readFromFile(File* file, void* res, int numbutes,
30                         int position) { ... }
31   };
```

**7.10**    Describe the data structures and algorithms that you would use to implement a garbage collector in C++.

pg 62

## SOLUTION

In C++, garbage collection with reference counting is almost always implemented with smart pointers, which perform reference counting. The main reason for using smart pointers over raw ordinary pointers is the conceptual simplicity of implementation and usage.

With smart pointers, everything related to garbage collection is performed behind the scenes - typically in constructors / destructors / assignment operator / explicit object management functions.

There are two types of functions, both of which are very simple:

```
1    RefCountPointer::type1() {
2        /* implementation depends on reference counting organisation.
3         * There can also be no ref. counter at all (see approach #4) */
4        incrementRefCounter(); }
5
6    RefCountPointer::type2() {
7        /* Implementation depends on reference counting organisation.
8         * There can also be no ref. counter at all (see approach #4). */
9        decrementRefCounter();
10       if (referenceCounterIsZero()) {
11           destructObject();
12       }
13   }
```

There are several approaches for reference counting implementation in C++:

1. Simple reference counting.

```
1    struct Object { };
2    struct RefCount {
3        int count;
4    };
5    struct RefCountPtr {
6        Object * pointee;
7        RefCount * refCount;
8    };
```

Advantages: performance.

Disadvantages: memory overhead because of two pointers.

2. Alternative reference counting.

---

```
1   struct Object { … };
2   struct RefCountPtrImpl {
3       int count;
4       Object * object;
5   };
6   struct RefCountPtr {
7       RefCountPtrImpl * pointee;
8   };
```

Advantages: no memory overhead because of two pointers.

Disadvantages: performance penalty because of extra level of indirection.

3. Intrusive reference counting.

```
1   struct Object { … };
2   struct ObjectIntrusiveReferenceCounting {
3       Object object;
4       int count;
5   };
6   struct RefCountPtr {
7       ObjectIntrusiveReferenceCounting * pointee;
8   };
```

Advantages: no previous disadvantages.

Disadvantages: class for intrusive reference counting should be modified.

4. Ownership list reference counting. It is an alternative for approach 1-3. For 1-3 it is only important to determine that counter is zero—its actual value is not important. This is the main idea of approach # 4.

All Smart-Pointers for given objects are stored in doubly-linked lists. The constructor of a smart pointer adds the new node to a list, and the destructor removes a node from the list and checks if the list is empty or not. If it is empty, the object is deleted.

```
1   struct Object { };
2   struct ListNode {
3       Object * pointee;
4       ListNode * next;
5   }
```

# Solutions to Chapter 8 | Recursion

**8.1**   Write a method to generate the nth Fibonacci number.

pg 64

## SOLUTION

There are three potential approaches: (1) recursive approach (2) iterative approach (3) using matrix math. We have described the recursive and iterative approach below, as you would not be expected to be able to derive the matrix-based approach in an interview. For the interested math-geeks, you may read about the (most efficient) matrix-based algorithm at http://en.wikipedia.org/wiki/Fibonacci_number#Matrix_form.

Recursive Solution:
```
1   int fibo(int n) {
2       if (n == 0) {
3           return 0; // f(0) = 0
4       } else if (n == 1) {
5           return 1; // f(1) = 1
6       } else if (n > 1) {
7           return fibo(n-1) + fibo(n-2); // f(n) = f(n–1) + f(n-2)
8       } else {
9           return -1; // Error condition
10      }
11  }
```

Iterative Solution:
```
1   int fibo(int n)  {
2       if (n < 0) return -1; // Error condition.
3       if (n == 0) return 0;
4       int a = 1, b = 1;
5       for (int i = 3; i <= n; i++) {
6           int c = a + b;
7           a = b;
8           b = c;
9       }
10      return b;
11  }
```

**8.2** Imagine a robot sitting on the upper left hand corner of an NxN grid. The robot can only move in two directions: right and down. How many possible paths are there for the robot?

FOLLOW UP

Imagine certain squares are "off limits", such that the robot can not step on them. Design an algorithm to get all possible paths for the robot.

*pg 64*

## SOLUTION

*Part 1:* (For clarity, we will solve this part assuming an X by Y grid)

Each path has $(X-1)+(Y-1)$ steps. Imagine the following paths:

```
X X Y Y X (move right -> right -> down -> down -> right)
X Y X Y X (move right -> down -> right -> down -> right)
...
```

Each path can be fully represented by the moves at which we move right. That is, if I were to ask you which path you took, you could simply say "I moved right on step 3 and 4."

Since you must always move right X-1 times, and you have X-1 + Y-1 total steps, you have to pick X-1 times to move right out of X-1+Y-1 choices. Thus, there are C(X-1, X-1+Y-1) paths (e.g., X-1+Y-1 choose X-1):

$$(X-1 + Y-1)! / ((X-1)! * (Y-1)!)$$

*Part 2: Code*

We can implement a simple recursive algorithm with backtracking:

```
1   ArrayList<Point> current_path = new ArrayList<Point>();
2   public static boolean getPaths(int x, int y) {
3       Point p = new Point(x, y);
4       current_path.add(p);
5       if (0 == x && 0 == y) return true; // current_path
6       boolean success = false;
7       if (x >= 1 && is_free(x - 1, y)) { // Try right
8           success = getPaths(x - 1, y); // Free!  Go right
9       }
10      if (!success && y >= 1 && is_free(x, y - 1)) { // Try down
11          success = getPaths(x, y - 1); // Free!  Go down
12      }
13      if (!success) {
14          current_path.remove(p); // Wrong way!
15      }
16      return success;
17  }
```

**8.3**    Write a method that returns all subsets of a set.

pg 64

## SOLUTION

We should first have some reasonable expectations of our time and space complexity. How many subsets of a set are there? We can compute this by realizing that when we generate a subset, each element has the "choice" of either being in there or not. That is, for the first element, there are 2 choices. For the second, there are two, etc. So, doing 2 * 2 * ... * 2 n times gives us $2^n$ subsets. We will not be able to do better than this in time or space complexity.

Approach #1: Recursion

This is a great problem to implement with recursion since we can build all subsets of a set using all subsets of a smaller set. Specifically, given a set S, we can do the following recursively:

»    Let first = S[0]. Let smallerSet = S[1, ..., n].

»    Compute all subsets of smallerSet and put them in allsubsets.

»    For each subset in allsubsets, clone it and add first to the subset.

The following code implements this algorithm:

```
1   ArrayList<ArrayList<Integer>> getSubsets(ArrayList<Integer> set,
2                                             int index) {
3       ArrayList<ArrayList<Integer>> allsubsets;
4       if (set.size() == index) {
5           allsubsets = new ArrayList<ArrayList<Integer>>();
6           allsubsets.add(new ArrayList<Integer>()); // Empty set
7       } else {
8           allsubsets = getSubsets(set, index + 1);
9           int item = set.get(index);
10          ArrayList<ArrayList<Integer>> moresubsets =
11              new ArrayList<ArrayList<Integer>>();
12          for (ArrayList<Integer> subset : allsubsets) {
13              ArrayList<Integer> newsubset = new ArrayList<Integer>();
14              newsubset.addAll(subset); //
15              newsubset.add(item);
16              moresubsets.add(newsubset);
17          }
18          allsubsets.addAll(moresubsets);
19      }
20      return allsubsets;
21  }
```

Approach #2: Combinatorics

»    When we're generating a set, we have two choices for each element: (1) the element is

---

in the set (the "yes" state) or (2) the element is not in the set (the "no" state). This means that each subset is a sequence of yesses / nos—e.g., "yes, yes, no, no, yes, no"

» This gives us 2^n possible subsets. How can we iterate through all possible sequences of "yes" / "no" states for all elements? If each "yes" can be treated as a 1 and each "no" can be treated as a 0, then each subset can be represented as a binary string.

» Generating all subsets then really just comes down to generating all binary numbers (that is, all integers). Easy!

```
1   ArrayList<ArrayList<Integer>> getSubsets2(ArrayList<Integer> set) {
2       ArrayList<ArrayList<Integer>> allsubsets =
3           new ArrayList<ArrayList<Integer>>();
4       int max = 1 << set.size();
5       for (int i = 0; i < max; i++) {
6           ArrayList<Integer> subset = new ArrayList<Integer>();
7           int k = i;
8           int index = 0;
9           while (k > 0) {
10              if ((k & 1) > 0) {
11                  subset.add(set.get(index));
12              }
13              k >>= 1;
14              index++;
15          }
16          allsubsets.add(subset);
17      }
18      return allsubsets;
19  }
```

**8.4**    Write a method to compute all permutations of a string

pg 64

## SOLUTION

Let's assume a given string S represented by the letters A1, A2, A3, ..., An

To permute set S, we can select the first character, A1, permute the remainder of the string to get a new list. Then, with that new list, we can "push" A1 into each possible position.

For example, if our string is "abc", we would do the following:

1.  Let first = "a" and let remainder = "bc"

2.  Let list = permute(bc) = {"bc", "cd"}

3.  Push "a" into each location of "bc" (--> "abc", "bac", "bca") and "cb" (--> "acb", "cab", "cba")

4.  Return our new list

Now, the code to do this:

```
1    public static ArrayList<String> getPerms(String s) {
2        ArrayList<String> permutations = new ArrayList<String>();
3        if (s == null) { // error case
4            return null;
5        } else if (s.length() == 0) { // base case
6            permutations.add("");
7            return permutations;
8        }
9
10       char first = s.charAt(0); // get the first character
11       String remainder = s.substring(1); // remove the first character
12       ArrayList<String> words = getPerms(remainder);
13       for (String word : words) {
14           for (int j = 0; j <= word.length(); j++) {
15               permutations.add(insertCharAt(word, first, j));
16           }
17       }
18       return permutations;
19   }
20
21   public static String insertCharAt(String word, char c, int i) {
22       String start = word.substring(0, i);
23       String end = word.substring(i);
24       return start + c + end;
25   }
```

This solution takes O(n!) time, since there are n! permutations.

**8.5** Implement an algorithm to print all valid (e.g., properly opened and closed) combinations of n-pairs of parentheses.

EXAMPLE:

input: 3 (e.g., 3 pairs of parentheses)

output: ()()(), ()(()), (())(), ((()))

pg 64

## SOLUTION

We can solve this problem recursively by recursing through the string. On each iteration, we have the index for a particular character in the string. We need to select either a left or a right paren. When can we use left, and when can we use a right paren?

» Left: As long as we haven't used up all the left parentheses, we can always insert a left paren.

» Right: We can insert a right paren as long as it won't lead to a syntax error. When will we get a syntax error? We will get a syntax error if there are more right parentheses than left.

So, we simply keep track of the number of left and right parentheses allowed. If there are left parens remaining, we'll insert a left paren and recurse. If there are more right parens remaining than left (eg, if there are more left parens used), then we'll insert a right paren and recurse.

```
1   public static void printPar(int l, int r, char[] str, int count) {
2       if (l < 0 || r < l) return; // invalid state
3       if (l == 0 && r == 0) {
4           System.out.println(str); // found one, so print it
5       } else {
6           if (l > 0) { // try a left paren, if there are some available
7               str[count] = '(';
8               printPar(l - 1, r, str, count + 1);
9           }
10          if (r > l) { // try a right paren, if there's a matching left
11              str[count] = ')';
12              printPar(l, r - 1, str, count + 1);
13          }
14      }
15  }
16
17  public static void printPar(int count) {
18      char[] str = new char[count*2];
19      printPar(count, count, str, 0);
20  }
```

**8.6**   Implement the "paint fill" function that one might see on many image editing programs. That is, given a screen (represented by a 2-dimensional array of Colors), a
point, and a new color, fill in the surrounding area until you hit a border of that color.

pg 64

## SOLUTION

First, let's visualize how this method works. When we call Paint Fill (eg, "click" paint fill in the
image editing application) on, say, a green pixel, we want to "bleed" outwards. Pixel by pixel,
we expand outwards calling PaintFill on the surrounding pixel. When we hit a pixel that is
not green, we stop. Surrounding green pixels may still be painted if they are touched by
another Paint Fill operation.

We can implement this algorithm recursively:

```
1    enum Color {
2        Black, White, Red, Yellow, Green
3    }
4    boolean PaintFill(Color[][] screen, int x, int y, Color ocolor,
5                    Color ncolor) {
6        if (x < 0 || x >= screen[0].length ||
7            y < 0 || y >= screen.length) {
8            return false;
9        }
10       if (screen[y][x] == ocolor) {
11           screen[y][x] = ncolor;
12           PaintFill(screen, x - 1, y, ocolor, ncolor); // left
13           PaintFill(screen, x + 1, y, ocolor, ncolor); // right
14           PaintFill(screen, x, y - 1, ocolor, ncolor); // top
15           PaintFill(screen, x, y + 1, ocolor, ncolor); // bottom
16       }
17       return true;
18   }
19
20   boolean PaintFill(Color[][] screen, int x, int y, Color ncolor) {
21       return PaintFill(screen, x, y, screen[y][x], ncolor);
22   }
```

**8.7** Given an infinite number of quarters (25 cents), dimes (10 cents), nickels (5 cents) and pennies (1 cent), write code to calculate the number of ways of representing n cents.

pg 64

## SOLUTION

This is a recursive problem, so let's figure out how to do makeChange(n) using prior solutions (i.e., sub-problems). Let's say n = 100, so we want to compute the number of ways of making change of 100 cents. What's the relationship to its sub-problems?

We know that makeChange(100):

= makeChange(100 using 0 quarters) + makeChange(100 using 1 quarter) + makeChange(100 using 2 quarter) + makeChange(100 using 3 quarter) + makeChange(100 using 4 quarter)

Can we reduce this further? Yes!

= makeChange(100 using 0 quarters) + makeChange(75 using 0 quarter) + makeChange(50 using 0 quarters) + makeChange(25 using 0 quarters) + 1

Now what? We've used up all our quarters, so now we can start applying our next biggest denomination: dimes.

This leads to a recursive algorithm that looks like this:

```
1   public static int makeChange(int n, int denom) {
2       int next_denom = 0;
3       switch (denom) {
4       case 25:
5           next_denom = 10;
6           break;
7       case 10:
8           next_denom = 5;
9           break;
10      case 5:
11          next_denom = 1;
12          break;
13      case 1:
14          return 1;
15      }
16      int ways = 0;
17      for (int i = 0; i * denom <= n; i++) {
18          ways += makeChange(n - i * denom, next_denom);
19      }
20      return ways;
21  }
22
23  System.out.writeln(makeChange(n, 25));
```

**8.8**    Write an algorithm to print all ways of arranging eight queens on a chess board so that none of them share the same row, column or diagonal.

pg 64

## SOLUTION

We will use a backtracking algorithm. For each row, the column where we want to put the queen is based on checking that it does not violate the required condition.

1. For this, we need to store the column of the queen in each row as soon as we have finalized it. Let ColumnForRow[] be the array which stores the column number for each row.

2. The checks that are required for the three given conditions are:

» On same Column :      ColumnForRow[i] == ColumnForRow[j]

» On same Diagonal:    (ColumnForRow[i] - ColumnForRow[j] ) == ( i - j) or
                                       (ColumnForRow[j] - ColumnForRow[i]) == (i - j)

```
1   int columnForRow[] = new int [8];
2   boolean check(int row) {
3       for (int i = 0; i < row; i++) {
4           int diff = Math.abs(columnForRow[i] - columnForRow[row]);
5           if (diff == 0 || diff == row - i) return false;
6       }
7       return true;
8   }
9
10  void PlaceQueen(int row){
11      if (row == 8) {
12          printBoard();
13          return;
14      }
15      for (int i = 0; i < 8; i++) {
16          columnForRow[row]=i;
17          if(check(row)){
18              PlaceQueen(row+1);
19          }
20      }
21  }
```

**9.1**    You are given two sorted arrays, A and B, and A has a large enough buffer at the end
to hold B. Write a method to merge B into A in sorted order.

pg 66

## SOLUTION

This code is a part of the standard merge-sort code. We merge A and B from the back, by
comparing each element.

```
1    public static void merge(int[] a, int[] b, int n, int m) {
2        int k = m + n - 1; // Index of last location of array b
3        int i = n - 1; // Index of last element in array b
4        int j = m - 1; // Index of last element in array a
5
6        // Start comparing from the last element and merge a and b
7        while (i >= 0 && j >= 0) {
8            if (a[i] > b[j]) {
9                a[k--] = a[i--];
10            } else {
11                a[k--] = b[j--];
12            }
13        }
14        while (j >= 0) {
15            a[k--] = b[j--];
16        }
17    }
```

Note: You don't need to copy the contents of a after running out of b's. They are
already in place.

**9.2** Write a method to sort an array of strings so that all the anagrams are next to each other.

pg 66

## SOLUTION

The basic idea is to implement a normal sorting algorithm where you override the compareTo method to compare the "signature" of each string. In this case, the signature is the alphabetically sorted string.

```
1   public class AnagramComparator implements Comparator<String> {
2       public String sortChars(String s) {
3           char[] content = s.toCharArray();
4           Arrays.sort(content);
5           return new String(content);
6       }
7
8       public int compare(String s1, String s2) {
9           return sortChars(s1).compareTo(sortChars(s2));
10      }
11  }
```

Now, just sort the arrays, using this compareTo method instead of the usual one.

```
12  Arrays.sort(array, new AnagramComparator());
```

**9.3**   Given a sorted array of n integers that has been rotated an unknown number of times, give an O(log n) algorithm that finds an element in the array. You may assume that the array was originally sorted in increasing order.

EXAMPLE:

Input: find 5 in array (15 16 19 20 25 1 3 4 5 7 10 14)

Output: 8 (the index of 5 in the array)

pg 66

## SOLUTION

We can do this with a modification of binary search.

```
1    public static int search(int a[], int l, int u, int x) {
2        while (l <= u) {
3            int m = (l + u) / 2;
4            if (x == a[m]) {
5                return m;
6            } else if (a[l] <= a[m]) {
7                if (x > a[m]) {
8                    l = m+1;
9                } else if (x >=a [l]) {
10                   u = m-1;
11               } else {
12                   l = m+1;
13               }
14           }
15           else if (x < a[m]) u = m-1;
16           else if (x <= a[u]) l = m+1;
17           else u = m - 1;
18       }
19       return -1;
20   }
21
22   public static int search(int a[], int x) {
23       return search(a, 0, a.length - 1, x);
24   }
```

What about duplicates? You may observe that the above function doesn't give you an efficient result in case of duplicate elements. However, if your array has duplicate entries then we can't do better than O(n) which is as good as linear search.

For example, if the array is [2,2,2,2,2,2,2,2,3,2,2,2,2,2,2,2,2,2,2], there is no way to find element 3 until you do a linear search.

**9.4** If you have a 2 GB file with one string per line, which sorting algorithm would you use to sort the file and why?

pg 66

## SOLUTION

When an interviewer gives a size limit of 2GB, it should tell you something - in this case, it suggests that they don't want you to bring all the data into memory.

So what do we do? We only bring part of the data into memory..

*Algorithm:*

How much memory do we have available? Let's assume we have X MB of memory available.

1. Divide the file into K chunks, where X * K = 2 GB. Bring each chunk into memory and sort the lines as usual using any O(n log n) algorithm. Save the lines back to the file.

2. Now bring the next chunk into memory and sort.

3. Once we're done, merge them one by one.

The above algorithm is also known as external sort. Step 3 is known as N-way merge

The rationale behind using external sort is the size of data. Since the data is too huge and we can't bring it all into memory, we need to go for a disk based sorting algorithm.

**9.5** Given a sorted array of strings which is interspersed with empty strings, write a method to find the location of a given string.

Example: find "ball" in ["at", "", "", "", "ball", "", "", "car", "", "", "dad", "", ""] will return 4

Example: find "ballcar" in ["at", "", "", "", "", "ball", "car", "", "", "dad", "", ""] will return -1

*pg 66*

## SOLUTION

Use ordinary binary search, but when you hit an empty string, advance to the next non-empty string; if there is no next non-empty string, search the left half.

```
1    public int search(String[] strings, String str, int first, int last) {
2        while (first <= last) {
3            // Ensure there is something at the end
4            while (first <= last && strings[last] == "") {
5                --last;
6            }
7            if (last < first) {
8                return -1; // this block was empty, so fail
9            }
10           int mid = (last + first) >> 1;
11           while (strings[mid] == "") {
12               ++mid; // will always find one
13           }
14           int r = strings[mid].compareTo(str);
15           if (r == 0) return mid;
16           if (r < 0) {
17               first = mid + 1;
18           } else {
19               last = mid - 1;
20           }
21       }
22       return -1;
23   }
24
25   public int search(String[] strings, String str) {
26       if (strings == null || str == null) return -1;
27       if (str == "") {
28           for (int i = 0; i < strings.length; i++) {
29               if (strings[i] == "") return i;
30           }
31           return -1;
32       }
33       return search(strings, str, 0, strings.length - 1);
34   }
```

**9.6** Given a matrix in which each row and each column is sorted, write a method to find an element in it.

pg 66

## SOLUTION

Assumptions:

» Rows are sorted left to right in ascending order. Columns are sorted top to bottom in ascending order.

» Matrix is of size MxN.

This algorithm works by elimination. Every move to the left (--col) eliminates all the elements below the current cell in that column. Likewise, every move down eliminates all the elements to the left of the cell in that row.

```
1   boolean FindElem(int[][] mat, int elem, int M, int N) {
2       int row = 0;
3       int col = N-1;
4       while (row < M && col >= 0) {
5           if (mat[row][col] == elem) {
6               return true;
7           } else if (mat[row][col] > elem) {
8               col--;
9           } else {
10              row++;
11          }
12      }
13      return false;
14  }
```

**9.7** A circus is designing a tower routine consisting of people standing atop one anoth-er's shoulders. For practical and aesthetic reasons, each person must be both shorter and lighter than the person below him or her. Given the heights and weights of each person in the circus, write a method to compute the largest possible number of peo-ple in such a tower.

EXAMPLE:

Input (ht, wt): (65, 100) (70, 150) (56, 90) (75, 190) (60, 95) (68, 110)

Output: The longest tower is length 6 and includes from top to bottom: (56, 90) (60,95) (65,100) (68,110) (70,150) (75,190)

pg 66

## SOLUTION

Step 1. Sort all items by height first, and then by weight. This means that if all the heights are unique, then the items will be sorted by their height. If heights are the same, items will be sorted by their weight.

Example:

» Before sorting: (60, 100) (70, 150) (56, 90) (75, 190) (60, 95) (68,110).

» After sorting: (56, 90), (60, 95), (60,100), (68, 110), (70,150), (75,190).

Step 2. Find the longest sequence which contains increasing heights and increasing weights.

To do this, we:
a) Start at the beginning of the sequence. Currently, max_sequence is empty.
b) If, for the next item, the height and the weight is not greater than those of the previous item, we mark this item as "unfit".

| (60,95) | (65,100) | (75,80) | (80, 100) |
|---------|----------|---------|-----------|
|         |          | (unfit item) |      |

c) If the sequence found has more items than "max sequence", it becomes "max sequence".
d) After that the search is repeated from the "unfit item", until we reach the end of the origi-nal sequence.

```
1   public class Question {
2       ArrayList<HtWt> items;
3       ArrayList<HtWt> lastFoundSeq;
4       ArrayList<HtWt> maxSeq;
5
```

```
6        // Returns longer sequence
7        ArrayList<HtWt> seqWithMaxLength(ArrayList<HtWt> seq1,
8                                         ArrayList<HtWt> seq2) {
9            return seq1.size() > seq2.size() ? seq1 : seq2;
10       }
11
12       // Fills next seq w decreased wts&returns index of 1st unfit item.
13       int fillNextSeq(int startFrom, ArrayList<HtWt> seq) {
14           int firstUnfitItem = startFrom;
15           if (startFrom < items.size()) {
16               for (int i = 0; i < items.size(); i++) {
17                   HtWt item = items.get(i);
18                   if (i == 0 || items.get(i-1).isBefore(item)) {
19                       seq.add(item);
20                   } else {
21                       firstUnfitItem = i;
22                   }
23               }
24           }
25           return firstUnfitItem;
26       }
27
28       // Find the maximum length sequence
29       void findMaxSeq() {
30           Collections.sort(items);
31           int currentUnfit = 0;
32           while (currentUnfit < items.size()) {
33               ArrayList<HtWt> nextSeq = new ArrayList<HtWt>();
34               int nextUnfit = fillNextSeq(currentUnfit, nextSeq);
35               maxSeq = seqWithMaxLength(maxSeq, nextSeq);
36               if (nextUnfit == currentUnfit) break;
37               else currentUnfit = nextUnfit;
38           }
39       }
40   }
```

**10.1** You have a basketball hoop and someone says that you can play 1 of 2 games.

Game #1: You get one shot to make the hoop.

Game #2: You get three shots and you have to make 2 of 3 shots.

If p is the probability of making a particular shot, for which values of p should you pick one game or the other?

pg 68

## SOLUTION

*Probability of winning Game 1: p*

*Probability of winning Game 2:*

Let s(k,n) be the probability of making exactly k shots out of n. The probability of winning game 2 is s(2, 3)+s(3, 3). Since, s(k, n) = C(n, k) ( 1- p)^(n - k) p^k, the probability of winning is 3 * (1 - p) * p^2 + p^3.

Simplified, it becomes 3 * p^2 - 2 * p^3.

You should play Game1 if P(Game1) > P(Game2):

```
p > 3*p^2 - 2*p^3.
1 > 3*p - 2*p^2
2*p^2 - 3*p + 1 > 0
(2p - 1)(p - 1) > 0
```

Both terms must be positive or both must be negative.  But we know p < 1, so (p - 1) < 0. This means both terms must be negative.

```
(2p - 1) < 0
2p < 1
p < .5
```

So, we should play Game1 if p < .5.

**10.2** There are three ants on different vertices of a triangle. What is the probability of collision (between any two or all of them) if they start walking on the sides of the triangle?

Similarly find the probability of collision with 'n' ants on an 'n' vertex polygon.

pg 68

## SOLUTION

None of the three ants will collide if all three are moving in clockwise direction, or all three are moving in a counter-clockwise direction. Otherwise, there will definitely be a collision.

How many ways are there for the three ants to move? Each ant can move in 2 directions, so there are $2^3$ ways the ant can move. There are only two ways which will avoid a collision, therefore the probability of collision is $(2^3 - 2) / (2^3) = 6 / 8 = 3 / 4$.

To generalize this to an n-vertex polygon: there are still only 2 ways in which the ants can move to avoid a collision, but there are $2^n$ ways they can move total. Therefore, in general, probability of collision is $(2^n - 2) / 2^n = 1 - 1/2^{(n-1)}$.

**10.3**   Given two lines on a Cartesian plane, determine whether the two lines would intersect.

*pg 68*

## SOLUTION

There are a lot of unknowns in this problem (what format are the lines in? What if they are the same line?), but let's assume:

» If two lines are the same (same line = same slope and y-intercept), they are considered to intersect.

» We get to decide the data structure.

```
1    public class Line {
2        static double epsilon = 0.000001;
3        public double slope;
4        public double yintercept;
5
6        public Line(double s, double y) {
7            slope = s;
8            yintercept = y;
9        }
10
11       public boolean intersect(Line line2) {
12           return Math.abs(slope - line2.slope) > epsilon ||
13                  Math.abs(yintercept - line2.yintercept) < epsilon;
14       }
15   }
```

## OBSERVATIONS AND SUGGESTIONS:

» Ask questions. This question has a lot of unknowns—ask questions to clarify them. Many interviewers intentionally ask vague questions to see if you'll clarify your assumptions.

» When possible, design and use data structures. It shows that you understand and care about object oriented design.

» Think through which data structures you design to represent a line. There are a lot of options, with lots of trade offs. Pick one and explain your choice.

» Don't assume that the slope and y-intercept are integers.

» Understand limitations of floating point representations. Never check for equality with ==.

**10.4** Write a method to implement *, - , / operations. You should use only the + operator.

pg 68

## SOLUTION

With an understanding of what each operation (minus, times, divide) does, this problem can be approached logically.

» Subtraction should be relatively straightforward, as we all know that a - b is the same thing as a + (-1)*b.

» Multiplication: we have to go back to what we learned in grade school: 21 * 3 = 21 + 21 + 21.  It's slow, but it works.

» Division is the trickiest, because we usually think of 21 / 3 as something like "if you divide a 21 foot board into 3 pieces, how big is each piece?" If we think about it the other way around, it's a little easier: "I divided a 21 foot board in x pieces and got pieces of 3 feet each, how many pieces were there?" From here, we can see that if we continuously subtract 3 feet from 21 feet, we'll know how many pieces there are.  That is, we continuously subtract b from a and count how many times we can do that.

```
1    /* Flip a positive sign to negative, or a negative sign to pos */
2    public static int FnNegate(int a) {
3        int neg = 0;
4        int d = a < 0 ? 1 : -1;
5        while (a != 0) {
6            neg += d;
7            a += d;
8        }
9        return neg;
10   }
11
12   /* Subtract two numbers by negating b and adding them */
13   public static int FnMinus(int a, int b) {
14       return a + FnNegate(b);
15   }
16
17   /* Check if a and b are different signs */
18   public static boolean DifferentSigns(int a, int b) {
19       return ((a < 0 && b > 0) || (a > 0 && b < 0)) ? true : false;
20   }
21
22   /* Return absolute value */
23   public static int abs(int a) {
24       if (a < 0) return FnNegate(a);
25       else return a;
26   }
```

```
27
28  /* Multiply a by b by adding a to itself b times */
29  public static int FnTimes(int a, int b) {
30      if (a < b) return FnTimes(b, a); // algo is faster if b < a
31      int sum = 0;
32      for (int iter = abs(b); iter > 0; --iter) sum += a;
33      if (b < 0) sum = FnNegate(sum);
34      return sum;
35  }
36
37  /* Divide a by b by literally counting how many times does b go into
38   * a. That is, count how many times you can subtract b from a until
39   * you hit 0. */
40  public static int FnDivide(int a, int b) throws
41          java.lang.ArithmeticException {
42      if (b == 0) {
43          throw new java.lang.ArithmeticException("Divide by 0.");
44      }
45      int quotient = 0;
46      int divisor = FnNegate(abs(b));
47      int divend; /* dividend */
48      for (divend = abs(a); divend >= abs(divisor); divend += divisor) {
49          ++quotient;
50      }
51      if (DifferentSigns(a, b)) quotient = FnNegate(quotient);
52      return quotient;
53  }
```

## OBSERVATIONS AND SUGGESTIONS

» A logical approach of going back to what exactly multiplication and division do comes in handy. Remember that. All (good) interview problems can be approached in a logical, methodical way!

» The interviewer is looking for this sort of logical work-your-way-through-it approach.

» This is a great problem to demonstrate your ability to write clean code—specifically, to show your ability to re-use code. For example, if you were writing this solution and didn't put FnNegate in its own method, you should move it out once you see that you'll use it multiple times.

» Be careful about making assumptions while coding. Don't assume that the numbers are all positive, or that a is bigger than b.

**10.5** Given two squares on a two dimensional plane, find a line that would cut these two squares in half.

pg 68

## SOLUTION

Any line that goes through the center of a rectangle must cut it in half. Therefore, if you drew a line connecting the centers of the two squares, it would cut both in half.

```
1   public class Square {
2       public double left;
3       public double top;
4       public double bottom;
5       public double right;
6       public Square(double left, double top, double size) {
7           this.left = left;
8           this.top = top;
9           this.bottom = top + size;
10          this.right = left + size;
11      }
12
13      public Point middle() {
14          return new Point((this.left + this.right) / 2,
15                           (this.top + this.bottom) / 2);
16      }
17
18      public Line cut(Square other) {
19          Point middle_s = this.middle();
20          Point middle_t = other.middle();
21          if (middle_s == middle_t) {
22              return new Line(new Point(left, top),
23                  new Point(right, bottom));
24          } else {
25              return new Line(middle_s, middle_t);
26          }
27      }
28  }
```

## SUGGESTIONS AND OBSERVATIONS

The main point of this problem is to see how careful you are about coding. It's easy to glance over the special cases (e.g., the two squares having the same middle). Make a list of these special cases *before* you start the problem and make sure to handle them appropriately.

**10.6** Given a two dimensional graph with points on it, find a line which passes the most number of points.

pg 68

## SOLUTION

If we draw a line between every two points, we can check to see which line is the most common. A brute force approach would be to simply iterate through each line segment (formed by pairs of points) and count how many points fall on it. This would take O(N^3) time.

Before we discuss if we can do better, let's figure out how we can represent a line. A line can be represented in (at least) two different ways: (1) as a pairing of points or (2) as a slope and a y-intercept.

Because our line is infinite, the slope and y-intercept approach seems more appropriate. The slope and y-intercept approach has an additional advantage: every line segment on the same greater line will have identical slopes and y-intercepts.

Let's re-think our solution. We have a bunch of line segments, represented as a slope and y-intercept, and we want to find the most common slope and y-intercept. How can we find the most common one?

This is really no different than the old "find the most common number in a list of numbers" problem. We just iterate through the lines segments and use a hash table to count the number of times we've seen each line.

```
1   public static Line findBestLine(GraphPoint[] points) {
2       Line bestLine = null;
3       HashMap<Line, Integer> line_count = new HashMap<Line, Integer>();
4       for (int i = 0; i < points.length; i++) {
5           for (int j = i + 1; j < points.length; j++) {
6               Line line = new Line(points[i], points[j]);
7               if (!line_count.containsKey(line)) {
8                   line_count.put(line, 0);
9               }
10              line_count.put(line, line_count.get(line) + 1);
11              if (bestLine == null ||
12                  line_count.get(line) > line_count.get(bestLine)) {
13                  bestLine = line;
14              }
15          }
16      }
17      return bestLine;
18  }
19
20  public class Line {
21      private static double epsilon = .0001;
```

```
22      public double slope;
23      public double intercept;
24      private boolean infinite_slope = false;
25      public Line(GraphPoint p, GraphPoint q) {
26          if (Math.abs(p.x - q.x) > epsilon) { // if x's are different
27              slope = (p.y - q.y) / (p.x - q.x); // compute slope
28              intercept = p.y - slope * p.x; // y intercept from y=mx+b
29          } else {
30              infinite_slope = true;
31              intercept = p.x; // x-intercept, since slope is infinite
32          }
33      }
34
35      public boolean isEqual(double a, double b) {
36          return (Math.abs(a - b) < epsilon);
37      }
38
39      @Override
40      public int hashCode()  {
41          int sl = (int)(slope * 1000);
42          int in = (int)(intercept * 1000);
43          return sl | in;
44      }
45
46      @Override
47      public boolean equals(Object o) {
48          Line l = (Line) o;
49          if (isEqual(l.slope, slope) && isEqual(l.intercept, intercept)
50              && (infinite_slope == l.infinite_slope)) {
51              return true;
52          }
53          return false;
54      }
55  }
```

## OBSERVATIONS AND SUGGESTIONS

» Be careful about the calculation of the slope of a line. The line might be completely vertical. We can keep track of this in a separate flag (infinite_slope). We need to check this condition in the equals method.

» Remember that when we perform division to calculate the slope, division is not exact. Therefore, rather than checking to see if two slopes are exactly equal, we need to check if they're different by greater than epsilon.

**10.7** Design an algorithm to find the kth number such that the only prime factors are 3, 5, and 7.

pg 68

## SOLUTION

Any such number will look like $(3^i)*(5^j)*(7^k)$.  Here are the first 13 numbers:

| 1  | -     | 3^0 * 5^0 * 7 ^ 0 |
|----|-------|-------------------|
| 3  | 3     | 3^1 * 5^0 * 7 ^ 0 |
| 5  | 5     | 3^0 * 5^1 * 7 ^ 0 |
| 7  | 7     | 3^0 * 5^0 * 7 ^ 1 |
| 9  | 3*3   | 3^2 * 5^0 * 7 ^ 0 |
| 15 | 3*5   | 3^1 * 5^1 * 7 ^ 0 |
| 21 | 3*7   | 3^1 * 5^0 * 7 ^ 1 |
| 25 | 5*5   | 3^0 * 5^2 * 7 ^ 0 |
| 27 | 3*9   | 3^3 * 5^0 * 7 ^ 0 |
| 35 | 5*7   | 3^0 * 5^1 * 7 ^1  |
| 45 | 5*9   | 3^2 * 5^1 * 7 ^0  |
| 49 | 7*7   | 3^0 * 5^0 * 7 ^2  |
| 63 | 3*21  | 3^2 * 5^0 * 7 ^1  |

» 3 * (previous number in list)

» 5 * (previous number in list)

» 7 * (previous number in list)

How would we find the next number in the list? Well, we could multiply 3, 5 and 7 times each number in the list and find the smallest element that has not yet been added to our list. This solution is O(n^2). Not bad, but I think we can do better.

In our current algorithm, we're doing 3*1, 3*3, 3*5, 3*7, 3*9, 3*15, 3*21, 3*25 ..., and the same for 5 and 7. We've already done almost all this work before—why are we doing it again?

We can fix this by multiplying each number we add to our list by 3, 5, 7 and putting the re-sults in one of the three first-in-first-out queues. To look for the next "magic" number, we pick the smallest element in the three queues.  Here is the algorithm:

1. Initialize array magic and queues Q3, Q5 and Q7
2. Insert 1 into magic.
3. Insert 1*3, 1*5 and 1*7 into Q3, Q5 and Q7 respectively.
4. Let x be the minimum element in Q3, Q5 and Q7.  Append x to magic.
5. If x was found in:

Q3 -> append x*3, x*5 and x*7 to Q3, Q5 and Q7. Remove x from Q3.

Q5 -> append x*5 and x*7 to Q5 and Q7. Remove x from Q5.

Q7 -> only append x*7 to Q7. Remove x from Q7.

Note: we do not need to append x*3 and x*5 to all lists because they will already be found in another list.

6. Repeat steps 4 - 6 until we've found k elements.

```
1   public static int getKthMagicNumber(int k) {
2       if (k <= 0) return 0;
3       int val = 1;
4       Queue<Integer> Q3 = new LinkedList<Integer>();
5       Queue<Integer> Q5 = new LinkedList<Integer>();
6       Queue<Integer> Q7 = new LinkedList<Integer>();
7       Q3.add(3);
8       Q5.add(5);
9       Q7.add(7);
10      for (--k; k > 0; --k) { // We've done one iteration already.
11          val = Math.min(Q3.peek().intValue(),
12              Math.min(Q5.peek().inValue(), Q7.peek().intValue()));
13          if (val == Q7.peek()) {
14              Q7.remove();
15          } else {
16              if (val == Q5.peek()) {
17                  Q5.remove();
18              } else { // must be from Q3
19                  Q3.remove();
20                  Q3.add(val * 3);
21              }
22              Q5.add(val * 5);
23          }
24          Q7.add(val * 7);
25      }
26      return val;
27  }
```

## OBSERVATIONS AND SUGGESTIONS:

When you get this question, do your best to solve it—even though it's really difficult. Explain a brute force approach (not as tricky) and then start thinking about how you can optimize it. Or, try to find a pattern in the numbers.

Chances are, your interviewer will help you along when you get stuck. Whatever you do, don't give up! Think out loud, wonder aloud, explain your thought process. Your interviewer will probably jump in to guide you.

**11.1** Find the mistake(s) in the following code:

```
1   unsigned int i;
2   for (i = 100; i <= 0; --i)
3       printf("%d\n", i);
```

pg 70

## SOLUTION

The printf will never get executed, as "i" is initialized to 100, so condition check "i <= 0" will fail.

Suppose the code is changed to "i >= 0." Then, it will become an infinite loop, because "i" is an unsigned int which can't be negative.

The correct code to print all numbers from 100 to 1, is "i > 0".

```
1   unsigned int i;
2   for (i = 100; i > 0; --i)
3       printf("%d\n", i);
```

One additional correction is to use %u in place of %d, as we are printing unsigned int.

```
1   unsigned int i;
2   for (i = 100; i > 0; --i)
3       printf("%u\n", i);
```

**11.2** You are given the source to an application which crashes when it is run. After running it ten times in a debugger, you find it never crashes in the same place. The application is single threaded, and uses only the C standard library. What programming errors could be causing this crash? How would you test each one?

pg 70

## SOLUTION

The question largely depends on the type of application being diagnosed. However, we can give some general causes of random crashes.

1.  Random variable: The application uses some random number or variable component which may not be fixed for every execution of the program. Examples include: user input, a random number generated by the program, or the time of day.

2.  Memory Leak: The program may have run out of memory. Other culprits are totally random for each run since it depends on the number of processes running at that particular time. This also includes heap overflow or corruption of data on the stack.

It is also possible that the program depends on another application / external module that could lead to the crash. If our application, for example, depends on some system attributes and they are modified by another program, then this interference may lead to a crash. Programs which interact with hardware are more prone to these errors.

In an interview, we should ask about which kind of application is being run. This information may give you some idea about the kind of error the interviewer is looking for. For example, a web server is more prone to memory leakage, whereas a program that runs close to the system level is more prone to crashes due to system dependencies.

**11.3** We have the following method used in a chess game: boolean canMoveTo(int x, int y) x and y are the coordinates of the chess board and it returns whether or not the piece can move to that position. Explain how you would test this method.

pg 70

## SOLUTION

There are two primary types of testing we should do:

*Validation of input/output:*

We should validate both the input and output to make sure that each are valid. This might entail:

1.  Checking whether input is within the board limit.

    »   Attempt to pass in negative numbers

    »   Attempt to pass in x which is larger than the width

    »   Attempt to pass in y which is larger than the width

    Depending on the implementation, these should either return false or throw an exception.

2.  Checking if output is within the valid set of return values. (Not an issue in this case, since there are no "invalid" boolean values.)

*Functional testing:*

Ideally, we would like to test every possible board, but this is far too big. We can do a reasonable coverage of boards however. There are 6 pieces in chess, so we need to do something like this:

```
1   foreach piece a:
2       for each other type of piece b (6 types + empty space)
3           foreach direction d
4               Create a board with piece a.
5               Place piece b in direction d.
6               Try to move - check return value.
```

**11.4** How would you load test a webpage without using any test tools?

pg 70

## SOLUTION

Load testing helps to identify a web application's maximum operating capacity, as well as any bottlenecks that may interfere with its performance. Similarly, it can check how an application responds to variations in load.

To perform load testing, we must first identify the performance-critical scenarios and the metrics which fulfill our performance objectives. Typical criteria include:

» response time

» throughput

» resource utilization

» maximum load that the system can bear.

Then, we design tests to simulate the load, taking care to measure each of these criteria.

In the absence of formal testing tools, we can basically create our own. For example, we could simulate concurrent users by creating thousands of virtual users. We would write a multi-threaded program with thousands of threads, where each thread acts as a real-world user loading the page. For each user, we would programmatically measure response time, data I/O, etc.

We would then analyze the results based on the data gathered during the tests and compare it with the accepted values.

**11.5** How would you test a pen?

pg 70

## SOLUTION

This problem is largely about understand the constraints: what exactly is the pen? You should ask a lot of questions to understand what exactly you are trying to test. To illustrate the technique in this problem, let us guide you through a mock-conversation.

**Interviewer:** How would you test a pen?

**Candidate:** Let me find out a bit about the pen. Who is going to use the pen?

**Interviewer:** Probably children.

**Candidate:** Ok, that's interesting. What will they be doing with it? Will they be writing, drawing, or doing something else with it?

**Interviewer:** Drawing.

**Candidate:** Ok, great. On what? Paper? Clothing? Walls?

**Interviewer:** On clothing.

**Candidate:** Great. What kind of tip does the pen have? Felt? Ball point? Is it intended to wash off, or is it intended to be permanent?

**Interviewer:** It's intended to wash off.

…. many questions later …

**Candidate:** Ok, so as I understand it, we have a pen that is being targeted at 5—10 year olds. The pen has a felt tip and comes in red, green, blue and black. It's intended to wash off clothing. Is that correct?

…

The candidate now has a problem that is significantly different from what it initially seemed to be. Thus, the candidate might now want to test:

1.  Does the pen wash off with warm water, cold water, and luke warm water?

2.  Does the pen wash off after staying on the clothing for several weeks? What happens if you wash the clothing while the pen is still wet?

3.  Is the pen safe (e.g.—non-toxic) for children?

and so on...

**11.6** How would you test an ATM in a distributed banking system?

pg 70

## SOLUTION

The first thing to do on this question is to clarify assumptions. Ask the following questions:

» Who is going to use the ATM? Answers might be "anyone," or it might be "blind people" - or any number of other answers.

» What are they going to use it for? Answers might be "withdrawing money," "transferring money," "checking their balance," or many other answers.

» What tools do we have to test? Do we have access to the code, or just the ATM machine?

Remember: a good tester makes sure she knows what she's testing!

Here are a few test cases for how to test just the withdrawing functionality:

» Withdrawing money less than the account balance

» Withdrawing money greater than the account balance

» Withdrawing money equal to the account balance

» Withdrawing money from an ATM and from the internet at the same time

» Withdrawing money when the connection to the bank's network is lost

» Withdrawing money from multiple ATMs simultaneously

**12.1** If you were integrating a feed of end of day stock price information (open, high, low, and closing price) for 5,000 companies, how would you do it? You are responsible for the development, rollout and ongoing monitoring and maintenance of the feed. Describe the different methods you considered and why you would recommend your approach. The feed is delivered once per trading day in a comma-separated format via an FTP site. The feed will be used by 1000 daily users in a web application.

pg 72

## SOLUTION

Let's assume we have some scripts which are scheduled to get the data via FTP at the end of the day. Where do we store the data? How do we store the data in such a way that we can do various analyses of it?

### Proposal #1

Keep the data in text files. This would be very difficult to manage and update, as well as very hard to query. Keeping unorganized text files would lead to a very inefficient data model.

### Proposal #2

We could use a database. This provides the following benefits:

» Logical storage of data.

» Facilitates an easy way of doing query processing over the data.

Example: return all stocks having open > N AND closing price < M

Advantages:

» Makes the maintenance easy once installed properly.

» Roll back, backing up data, and security could be provided using standard database features. We don't have to "reinvent the wheel."

### Proposal #3

If requirements are not that broad and we just want to do a simple analysis and distribute the data, then XML could be another good option.

Our data has fixed format and fixed size: company_name, open, high, low, closing price. The XML could look like this:

```
<root>
<date value="2008-10-12">
    <company name="foo">
        <open>126.23</open>
        <high>130.27</high>
        <low>122.83</low>
```

```
                <closingPrice>127.30</closingPrice>
            </company>
            <company name="bar">
                <open>52.73</open>
                <high>60.27</high>
                <low>50.29</low>
                <closingPrice>54.91</closingPrice>
            </company>
        </date>
        <date value="2008-10-11"> . . . </date>
    </root>
```

**Benefits:**

»   Very easy to distribute. This is one reason that XML is a standard data model to share / distribute data.

»   Efficient parsers are available to parse the data and extract out only desired data.

»   We can add new data to the XML file by carefully appending data. We would not have to re-query the database.

However, querying the data could be difficult.

**12.2** How would you design the data structures for a very large social network (Facebook, LinkedIn, etc)? Describe how you would design an algorithm to show the connection, or path, between two people (e.g., Me -> Bob -> Susan -> Jason -> You).

pg 72

## SOLUTION

*Approach:*

Forget that we're dealing with millions of users at first. Design this for the simple case.

We can construct a graph by assuming every person is a node and if there is an edge between two nodes, then the two people are friends with each other.

```
class Person {
    Person[] friends;
    // Other info
}
```

If I want to find the connection between two people, I would start with one person and do a simple breadth first search.

*But... oh no! Millions of users!*

When we deal with a service the size of Orkut or Facebook, we cannot possibly keep all of our data on one machine. That means that our simple Person data structure from above doesn't quite work—our friends may not live on the same machine as us. Instead, we can replace our list of friends with a list of their IDs, and traverse as follows:

1.  For each friend ID: int machine_index = lookupMachineForUserID(id);

2.  Go to machine machine_index

3.  Person friend = lookupFriend(machine_index);

There are more optimizations and follow up questions here than we could possibly discuss, but here are just a few thoughts.

*Optimization: Reduce Machine Jumps*

Jumping from one machine to another is expensive. Instead of randomly jumping from machine to machine with each friend, try to batch these jumps—e.g., if 5 of my friends live on one machine, I should look them up all at once.

*Optimization: Smart Division of People and Machines*

People are much more likely to be friends with people who live in the same country as them. Rather than randomly dividing people up across machines, try to divvy them up by country, city, state, etc. This will reduce the number of jumps.

*Question: Breadth First Search usually requires "marking" a node as visited. How do you do that in this case?*

Usually, in BFS, we mark a node as visited by setting a flag visited in its node class. Here, we don't want to do that (there could be multiple searches going on at the same time, so it's bad to just edit our data). In this case, we could mimic the marking of nodes with a hash table to lookup a node id and whether or not it's been visited.

Other Follow-Up Questions:

» In the real world, servers fail. How does this affect you?

» How could you take advantage of caching?

» Do you search until the end of the graph (infinite)? How do you decide when to give up?

» In real life, some people have more friends of friends than others, and are therefore more likely to make a path between you and someone else. How could you use this data to pick where you start traversing?

The following code demonstrates our algorithm:

```
1   public class Server {
2       ArrayList<Machine> machines = new ArrayList<Machine>();
3   }
4
5   public class Machine {
6       public ArrayList<Person> persons = new ArrayList<Person>();
7       public int machineID;
8   }
9
10  public class Person {
11      private ArrayList<Integer> friends;
12      private int ID;
13      private int machineID;
14      private String info;
15      private Server server = new Server();
16
17      public String getInfo() { return info; }
18      public void setInfo(String info) {
19          this.info = info;
20      }
21
22      public int[] getFriends() {
23          int[] temp = new int[friends.size()];
24          for (int i = 0; i < temp.length; i++) {
25              temp[i] = friends.get(i);
26          }
27          return temp;
28      }
```

```
29      public int getID() { return ID; }
30      public int getMachineID() { return machineID; }
31      public void addFriend(int id) { friends.add(id); }
32
33      // Look up a person given their ID and Machine ID
34      public Person lookUpFriend(int machineID, int ID) {
35          for (Machine m : server.machines) {
36              if (m.machineID == machineID) {
37                  for (Person p : m.persons) {
38                      if (p.ID == ID){
39                          return p;
40                      }
41                  }
42              }
43          }
44          return null;
45      }
46
47      // Look up a machine given the machine ID
48      public Machine lookUpMachine(int machineID) {
49          for (Machine m:server.machines) {
50              if (m.machineID == machineID)
51                  return m;
52          }
53          return null;
54      }
55
56      public Person(int iD, int machineID) {
57          ID = iD;
58          this.machineID = machineID;
59      }
60  }
```

**12.3** Given an input file with four billion integers, provide an algorithm to generate an integer which is not contained in the file. Assume you have 1 GB of memory.

FOLLOW UP

What if you have only 10 MB of memory?

pg 72

## SOLUTION

There are a total of 2^32, or 4 billion, distinct integers possible. We have 1 GB of memory, or 8 billion bits.

Thus, with 8 billion bits, we can map all possible integers to a distinct bit with the available memory. The logic is as follows:

1. Create a bit vector (BV) of size 4 billion.

2. Initialize BV with all 0's

3. Scan all numbers (num) from the file and write BV[num] = 1;

4. Now scan again BV from 0th index

5. Return the first index which has 0 value.

```
1  byte[] bitfield = new byte [0xFFFFFFF/8];
2  void findOpenNumber2() throws FileNotFoundException {
3      Scanner in = new Scanner(new FileReader("input_file_q11_4.txt"));
4      while (in.hasNextInt()) {
5          int n = in.nextInt ();
6          /* Finds the corresponding number in the bitfield by using the
7           * OR operator to set the nth bit of a byte (e.g.. 10 would
8           * correspond to the 2nd bit of index 2 in the byte array). */
9          bitfield [n / 8] |= 1 << (n % 8);
10     }
11
12     for (int i = 0 ; i < bitfield.length; i++) {
13         for (int j = 0; j < 8; j++) {
14             /* Retrieves the individual bits of each byte. When 0 bit
15              * is found, finds the corresponding value. */
16             if ((bitfield[i] & (1 << j)) == 0) {
17                 System.out.println (i * 8 + j);
18                 return;
19             }
20         }
21     }
22 }
```

*Follow Up: What if we have only 10 MB memory?*

It's possible to find a missing integer with just two passes of the data set. We can divide up the integers into blocks of some size (we'll discuss how to decide on a size later). Let's just assume that we divide up the integers into blocks of 1000. So, block 0 represents the numbers 0 through 999, block 1 represents blocks 1000 - 1999, etc. Since the range of ints is finite, we know that the number of blocks needed is finite.

In the first pass, we count how many ints are in each block. That is, if we see 552, we know that that is in block 0, we increment counter[0]. If we see 1425, we know that that is in block 1, so we increment counter[1].

At the end of the first pass, we'll be able to quickly spot a block that is missing a number. If our block size is 1000, then any block which has fewer than 1000 numbers must be missing a number. Pick any one of those blocks.

In the second pass, we'll actually look for which number is missing. We can do this by creating a simple bit vector of size 1000. We iterate through the file, and for each number that should be in our block, we set the appropriate bit in the bit vector. By the end, we'll know which number (or numbers) is missing.

Now we just have to decide what the block size is.

A quick answer is $2^{20}$ values per block. We will need an array with $2^{12}$ block counters and a bit vector in $2^{17}$ bytes. Both of these can comfortably fit in $10*2^{20}$ bytes.

What's the smallest footprint? When the array of block counters occupies the same memory as the bit vector. Let $N = 2^{32}$.

```
counters (bytes): blocks * 4
bit vector (bytes): (N / blocks) / 8

blocks * 4 = (N / blocks) / 8
blocks^2 = N / 32

blocks = sqrt(N/2)/4
```

It's possible to find a missing integer with just under 65KB (or, more exactly, $sqrt(2)*2^{15}$ bytes).

```
1    int bitsize = 1048576; // 2^20 bits (2^17 bytes)
2    int blockNum = 4096; // 2^12
3    byte[] bitfield = new byte[bitsize/8];
4    int[] blocks = new int[blockNum];
5
6    void findOpenNumber() throws FileNotFoundException {
7        int starting = -1;
8        Scanner in = new Scanner (new FileReader ("input_file_q11_4.txt"));
```

```
9       while (in.hasNextInt()) {
10          int n = in.nextInt();
11          blocks[n / (bitfield.length * 8)]++;
12      }
13
14      for (int i = 0; i < blocks.length; i++) {
15          if (blocks[i] < bitfield.length * 8){
16              /* if value < 2^20, then at least 1 number is missing in
17               * that section. */
18              starting = i * bitfield.length * 8;
19              break;
20          }
21      }
22
23      in = new Scanner(new FileReader("input_file_q11_4.txt"));
24      while (in.hasNextInt()) {
25          int n = in.nextInt();
26          /* If the number is inside the block that's missing numbers,
27           * we record it */
28          if( n >= starting && n < starting + bitfield.length * 8){
29              bitfield [(n-starting) / 8] |= 1 << ((n - starting) % 8);
30          }
31      }
32
33      for (int i = 0 ; i < bitfield.length; i++) {
34          for (int j = 0; j < 8; j++) {
35              /* Retrieves the individual bits of each byte. When 0 bit
36               * is found, finds the corresponding value. */
37              if ((bitfield[i] & (1 << j)) == 0) {
38                  System.out.println(i * 8 + j + starting);
39                  return;
40              }
41          }
42      }
43  }
```

**12.4** You have an array with all the numbers from 1 to N, where N is at most 32,000. The array may have duplicate entries and you do not know what N is. With only 4KB of memory available, how would you print all duplicate elements in the array?

pg 72

## SOLUTION

We have 4KB of memory which means we can address up to 8 * 4 * (2^10) bits. Note that 32* (2^10) bits is greater than 32000. We can create a bit vector with 32000 bits, where each bit represents one integer.

NOTE: While this isn't an especially difficult problem, it's important to implement this cleanly. We will define our own bit vector class to hold a large bit vector.

```
1    public static void checkDuplicates(int[] array) {
2        BitSet bs = new BitSet(32000);
3        for (int i = 0; i < array.length; i++) {
4            int num = array[i];
5            int num0 = num - 1; // bitset starts at 0, numbers start at 1
6            if (bs.get(num0)) {
7                System.out.println(num);
8            } else {
9                bs.set(num0);
10           }
11       }
12   }
13
14   class BitSet {
15       int[] bitset;
16
17       public BitSet(int size) {
18           bitset = new int[size >> 5]; // divide by 32
19       }
20
21       boolean get(int pos) {
22           int wordNumber = (pos >> 5); // divide by 32
23           int bitNumber = (pos & 0x1F); // mod 32
24           return (bitset[wordNumber] & (1 << bitNumber)) != 0;
25       }
26
27       void set(int pos) {
28           int wordNumber = (pos >> 5); // divide by 32
29           int bitNumber = (pos & 0x1F); // mod 32
30           bitset[wordNumber] |= 1 << bitNumber;
31       }
32   }
```

**12.5**    If you were designing a web crawler, how would you avoid getting into infinite loops?

pg 72

## SOLUTION

First, how does the crawler get into a loop? The answer is very simple: when we re-parse an already parsed page. This would mean that we revisit all the links found in that page, and this would continue in a circular fashion.

Be careful about what the interviewer considers the "same" page. Is it URL or content? One could easily get redirected to a previously crawled page.

So how do we stop visiting an already visited page? The web is a graph-based structure, and we commonly use DFS (depth first search) and BFS (breadth first search) for traversing graphs. We can mark already visited pages the same way that we would in a BFS/DFS.

We can easily prove that this algorithm will terminate in any case. We know that each step of the algorithm will parse only new pages, not already visited pages. So, if we assume that we have N number of unvisited pages, then at every step we are reducing N (N-1) by 1. That proves that our algorithm will continue until they are only N steps.

## SUGGESTIONS AND OBSERVATIONS

»    This question has a lot of ambiguity.  Ask clarifying questions!

»    Be prepared to answer questions about coverage.

»    What kind of pages will you hit with a DFS versus a BFS?

»    What will you do when your crawler runs into a honey pot that generates an infinite subgraph for you to wander about?

**12.6** You have a billion urls, where each is a huge page. How do you detect the duplicate documents?

pg 72

## SOLUTION

Observations:

1. Pages are huge, so bringing all of them in memory is a costly affair. We need a shorter representation of pages in memory. A hash is an obvious choice for this.

2. Billions of urls exist so we don't want to compare every page with every other page (that would be O(n^2)).

Based on the above two observations we can derive an algorithm which is as follows:

1. Iterate through the pages and compute the hash table of each one.

2. Check if the hash value is in the hash table. If it is, throw out the url as a duplicate. If it is not, then keep the url and insert it in into the hash table.

This algorithm will provide us a list of unique urls. But wait, can this fit on one computer?

» How much space does each page take up in the hash table?

  » Each page hashes to a four byte value.

  » Each url is an average of 30 characters, so that's another 30 bytes at least.

  » Each url takes up roughly 34 bytes.

» 34 bytes * 1 billion = 31.6 gigabytes. We're going to have trouble holding that all in memory!

What do we do?

» We could split this up into files. We'll have to deal with the file loading / unloading—ugh.

» We could hash to disk. Size wouldn't be a problem, but access time might. A hash table on disk would require a random access read for each check and write to store a viewed url. This could take msecs waiting for seek and rotational latencies. Elevator algorithms could elimate random bouncing from track to track.

» Or, we could split this up across machines, and deal with network latency. Let's go with this solution, and assume we have n machines.

  » First, we hash the document to get a hash value v

  » v%n tells us which machine this document's hash table can be found on.

  » v / n is the value in the hash table that is located on its machine.

---

**12.7** You have to design a database that can store terabytes of data. It should support efficient range queries. How would you do it?

pg 72

## SOLUTION

Construct an index for each field that requires range queries. Use a B+ tree to implement the index. A B+ tree organizes sorted data for efficient insertion, retrieval and removal of records. Each record is identified by a key (for this problem, it is the field value). Since it is a dynamic, multilevel index, finding the beginning of the range depends only on the height of the tree, which is usually quite small. Record references are stored in the leaves, sorted by the key. Additional records can be found by following a next block reference. Records will be sequentially available until the key value reaches the maximum value specified in the query. Thus, runtimes will be dominated by the number of elements in a range.

Avoid using trees that store data at interior nodes, as traversing the tree will be expensive since it won't be resident in memory.

# Solutions to Chapter 13 | C++

**13.1**   Write a method to print the last K lines of an input file using C++.

pg 76

## SOLUTION

One brute force way could be to count the number of lines (N) and then print from N-10 to Nth line. But, this requires two reads of the file – potentially very costly if the file is large.

We need a solution which allows us to read just once and be able to print the last K lines. We can create extra space for K lines and then store each set of K lines in the array. So, initially, our array has lines 0 through 9, then 1 through 10, then 2 through 11, etc (if K = 10). Each time that we read a new line, we purge the oldest line from the array. Instead of shifting the array each time (very inefficient), we will use a circular array. This will allow us to always find the oldest element in O(1) time.

Example of inserting elements into a circular array:

```
step 1 (initially):  array = {a, b, c, d, e, f}. p = 0
step 2 (insert g):   array = {g, b, c, d, e, f}. p = 1
step 3 (insert h):   array = {g, h, c, d, e, f}. p = 2
step 4 (insert i):   array = {g, h, i, d, e, f}. p = 3
```

Code:

```
1   string L[K];
2   int lines = 0;
3   while (file.good()) {
4       getline(file, L[lines % K]); // read file line by line
5       ++lines;
6   }
7   // if less than K lines were read, print them all
8   int start, count;
9   if (lines < K) {
10      start = 0;
11      count = lines;
12  } else {
13      start = lines % K;
14      count = K;
15  }
16  for (int i = 0; i < count; ++i) {
17      cout << L[(start + i) % K] << endl;
18  }
```

## OBSERVATIONS AND SUGGESTIONS:

»   Note, if you do printf(L[(index + i) % K]) when there are %'s in the string, bad things will happen.

---

**13.2** Compare and contrast a hash table vs. an STL map. How is a hash table implemented? If the number of inputs is small, what data structure options can be used instead of a hash table?

pg 76

## SOLUTION

*Compare and contrast Hash Table vs. STL map*

In a hash table, a value is stored by applying hash function on a key. Thus, values are not stored in a hash table in sorted order. Additionally, since hash tables use the key to find the index that will store the value, an insert/lookup can be done in amortised O(1) time (assuming only a few collisions in the hashtable). One must also handle potential collisions in a hashtable.

In an STL map, insertion of key/value pair is in sorted order of key. It uses a tree to store values, which is why an O(log N) insert/lookup is required. There is also no need to handle collisions. An STL map works well for things like:

» find min element

» find max element

» print elements in sorted order

» find the exact element or, if the element is not found, find the next smallest number

*How is a hash table implemented?*

1. A good hash function is required (e.g.: operation % prime number) to ensure that the hash values are uniformly distributed.

2. A collision resolving method is also needed: chaining (good for dense table entries), probing (good for sparse table entries), etc.

3. Implement methods to dynamically increase or decrease the hash table size on a given criterion. For example, when the [number of elements] by [table size] ratio is greater than the fixed threshold, increase the hash table size by creating a new hash table and transfer the entries from the old table to the new table by computing the index using new hash function.

*What can be used instead of a hash table, if the number of inputs is small?*

You can use an STL map. Although this takes O(log n) time, since the number of inputs is small, this time is negligible.

**13.3** How do virtual functions work in C++?

pg 76

## SOLUTION

A virtual function depends on a "vtable" or "Virtual Table". If any function of a class is declared as virtual, a v-table is constructed which stores addresses of the virtual functions of this class. The compiler also adds a hidden vptr variable in all such classes which points to the vtable of that class. If a virtual function is not overridden in the derived class, the vtable of the derived class stores the address of the function in his parent class. The v-table is used to resolve the address of the function, for whenever the virtual function is called. Dynamic binding in C++ is therefore performed through the vtable mechanism.

Thus, when we assign the derived class object to the base class pointer, the vptr points to the vtable of the derived class. This assignment ensures that the most derived virtual function gets called.

```
1   class Shape {
2     public:
3         int edge_length;
4         virtual int circumference () {
5             cout << "Circumference of Base Class\n";
6             return 0;
7         }
8   };
9   class Triangle: public Shape {
10    public:
11        int circumference () {
12            cout<< "Circumference of Triangle Class\n";
13            return 3 * edge_length;
14        }
15  };
16  void main() {
17      Shape * x = new Shape();
18      x->circumference(); // prints "Circumference of Base Class"
19      Shape *y = new Triangle();
20      y->circumference(); // prints "Circumference of Triangle Class"
21  }
```

In the above example, circumference is a virtual function in shape class, so it becomes virtual in each of the derived classes (triangle, rectangle). C++ non-virtual function calls are resolved at compile time with static binding, while virtual function calls are resolved at run time with dynamic binding.

**13.4** What is the difference between deep copy and shallow copy? Explain how you would use each.

pg 76

## SOLUTION

```
1    struct Test {
2        char * ptr;
3    };
4    void shallow_copy(Test & src, Test & dest) {
5        dest.ptr = src.ptr;
6    }
7    void deep_copy(Test & src, Test & dest) {
8        dest.ptr = malloc(strlen(src.ptr) + 1);
9        memcpy(dest.ptr, src.ptr);
10   }
```

Note that shallow_copy may cause a lot of programming run-time errors, especially with the creation and deletion of objects. Shallow copy should be used very carefully and only when a programmer really understands what he wants to do. In most cases shallow copy is used when there is a need to pass information about a complex structure without actual duplication of data (e.g., call by reference). One must also be careful with destruction of shallow copy.

In real life, shallow copy is rarely used. There is an important programming concept called "smart pointer" that, in some sense, is an enhancement of the shallow copy concept.

Deep copy should be used in most cases, especially when the size of the copied structure is small.

# Solutions to Chapter 13 | C++

**13.5** What is the significance of the keyword "volatile" in C?

pg 76

## SOLUTION

Volatile informs the compiler that the value of the variable can change from the outside, without any update done by the code.

Declaring a simple volatile variable:

```
volatile int x;
int volatile x;
```

Declaring a pointer variable for a volatile memory (only the pointer address is volatile):

```
volatile int * x;
int volatile * x;
```

Declaring a volatile pointer variable for a non-volatile memory (only memory contained is volatile):

```
int * volatile x;
```

Declaring a volatile variable pointer for a volatile memory (both pointer address and memory contained are volatile):

```
volatile int * volatile x;
int volatile * volatile x;
```

Volatile variables are not optimized, but this can actually be useful. Imagine this function:

```
1    int opt = 1;
2    void Fn(void) {
3        start:
4            if (opt == 1) goto start;
5            else break;
6    }
```

At first glance, our code appears to loop infinitely. The compiler will try to optimize it to:

```
1    void Fn(void) {
2        start:
3            int opt = 1;
4            if (true)
5            goto start;
6    }
```

This becomes an infinite loop. However, an external program might write '0' to the location of variable opt. Volatile variables are also useful when multi-threaded programs have global variables and any thread can modify these shared variables. Of course, we don't want optimization on them.

**13.6**    What is name hiding in C++?

pg 76

## SOLUTION

Let us explain through an example.  In C++, when you have a class with an overloaded method, and you then extend and override that method, you must override all of the overloaded methods.

For example:

```
1   class FirstClass {
2   public:
3       virtual void MethodA (int);
4       virtual void MethodA (int, int);
5   };
6   void FirstClass::MethodA (int i) {
7       std::cout << "ONE!!\n";
8   }
9   void FirstClass::MethodA (int i, int j) {
10      std::cout << "TWO!!\n";
11  }
```

This is a simple class with two methods (or one overloaded method). If you want to override the one-parameter version, you can do the following:

```
1   class SecondClass : public FirstClass {
2    public:
3       void MethodA (int);
4   };
5   void SecondClass::MethodA (int i) {
6       std::cout << "THREE!!\n";
7   }
8   void main () {
9       SecondClass a;
10      a.MethodA (1);
11      a.MethodA (1, 1);
12  }
```

However, the second call won't work, since the two-parameter MethodA is not visible. That is name hiding.

**13.7**   Why does a destructor in base class need to be declared virtual?

pg 76

## SOLUTION

Calling a method with an object pointer always invokes:

»   the most derived class function, if a method is virtual.

»   the function implementation corresponding to the object pointer type (used to call the method), if a method is non-virtual.

A virtual destructor works in the same way. A destructor gets called when an object goes out of scope or when we call delete on an object pointer.

When any derived class object goes out of scope, the destructor of that derived class gets called first. It then calls its parent class destructor so memory allocated to the object is properly released.

But, if we call delete on a base pointer which points to a derived class object, the base class destructor gets called first (for non-virtual function). For example:

```
1   class Base {
2     public:
3         Base() { cout << "Base Constructor " << endl; }
4         ~Base() { cout << "Base Destructor " << endl; } /* see below */
5   };
6   class Derived: public Base {
7     public:
8         Derived() { cout << "Derived Constructor " << endl; }
9         ~Derived() { cout << "Derived Destructor " << endl; }
10  };
11  void main() {
12      Base *p = new Derived();
13      delete p;
14  }
```

**Output:**

```
Base Constructor
Derived Constructor
Base Destructor
```

If we declare the base class destructor as virtual, this makes all the derived class destructors virtual as well.

If we replace the above destructor with:

```
1   virtual ~Base() {
2       cout << "Base Destructor" << endl;
3   }
```

Then the output becomes:

```
Base Constructor
Derived Constructor
Derived Destructor
Base Destructor
```

So we should use virtual destructors if we call delete on a base class pointer which points to a derived class.

**13.8** Write a method that takes a pointer to a Node structure as a parameter and returns a complete copy of the passed-in data structure. The Node structure contains two pointers to other Node structures.

pg 76

## SOLUTION

The algorithm will maintain a mapping from a node address in the original structure to the corresponding node in the new structure. This mapping will allow us to discover previously copied nodes during a traditional depth first traversal of the structure. (Traversals often mark visited nodes--the mark can take many forms and does not necessarily need to be stored in the node.) Thus, we have a simple recursive algorithm:

```
1   typedef map<Node*, Node*> NodeMap;
2
3   Node * copy_recursive(Node * cur, NodeMap & nodeMap) {
4       if(cur == NULL) {
5           return NULL;
6       }
7       NodeMap::iterator i = nodeMap.find(cur);
8       if (i != nodeMap.end()) {
9           // we've been here before, return the copy
10          return i->second;
11      }
12      Node * node = new Node;
13      nodeMap[cur] = node; // map current node before traversing links
14      node->ptr1 = copy_recursive(cur->ptr1, nodeMap);
15      node->ptr2 = copy_recursive(cur->ptr2, nodeMap);
16      return node;
17  }
18  Node * copy_structure(Node * root) {
19      NodeMap nodeMap; // we will need an empty map
20      return copy_recursive(root, nodeMap);
21  }
22
```

**13.9** Write a smart pointer (smart_ptr) class.

pg 76

## SOLUTION

Smart_ptr is the same as a normal pointer, but it provides safety via automatic memory. It avoids dangling pointers, memory leaks, allocation failures etc. The smart pointer must maintain a single reference count for all instances.

```
1   template <class T> class SmartPointer {
2   public:
3       SmartPointer(T * ptr) {
4           ref = ptr;
5           ref_count = (unsigned*)malloc(sizeof(unsigned));
6           *ref_count = 1;
7       }
8       SmartPointer(SmartPointer<T> & sptr) {
9           ref = sptr.ref;
10          ref_count = sptr.ref_count;
11          ++*ref_count;
12      }
13      SmartPointer<T> & operator=(SmartPointer<T> & sptr) {
14          if (this != &sptr) {
15              ref = sptr.ref;
16              ref_count = sptr.ref_count;
17              ++*ref_count;
18          }
19          return *this;
20      }
21      ~SmartPointer() {
22          --*ref_count;
23          if (*ref_count == 0) {
24              delete ref;
25              free(ref_count);
26              ref = NULL;
27              ref_count = NULL;
28          }
29      }
30      T getValue() { return *ref; }
31  protected:
32      T * ref;
33      unsigned * ref_count;
34  };
```

**14.1** In terms of inheritance, what is the effect of keeping a constructor private?

pg 78

## SOLUTION

Declaring the constructor private will ensure that no one outside of the class can directly instantiate the class. In this case, the only way to create an instance of the class is by providing a static public method, as is done when using the Factory Method Pattern.

Additionally, because the constructor is private, the class also cannot be inherited.

**14.2**   In Java, does the finally block gets executed if we insert a return statement inside the try block of a try-catch-finally?

pg 78

## SOLUTION

Yes, it will get executed.

The finally block gets executed when the try block exists.  However, even when we attempt to exit within the try block (normal exit, return, continue, break or any exception), the finally block will still be executed.

Note: There are some cases in which the finally block will not get executed: if the virtual machine exits in between try/catch block execution, or the thread which is executing try/catch block gets killed.

**14.3** What is the difference between final, finally, and finalize?

pg 78

## SOLUTIONS

*Final*

When applied to a variable (primitive): The value of the variable cannot change.

When applied to a variable (reference): The reference variable cannot point to any other object on the heap.

When applied to a method: The method cannot be overridden.

When applied to a class: The class cannot be subclassed.

*Finally*

There is an optional finally block after the try block or after the catch block. Statements in the finally block will always be executed (except if JVM exits from the try block). The finally block is used to write the clean up code.

*Finalize*

This is the method that the JVM runs before running the garbage collector.

**14.4** Explain the difference between templates in C++ and generics in Java.

pg 78

## SOLUTION

| C++ Templates | Java Generics |
|---|---|
| Classes and functions can be templated. | Classes and methods can be genericized. |
| Parameters can be any type or integral value. | Parameters can only be reference types (not primitive types). |
| Separate copies of the class or function are likely to be generated for each type parameter when compiled. | One version of the class or function is compiled, works for all type parameters. |
| Objects of a class with different type parameters are different types at run time. | Type parameters are erased when compiled; objects of a class with different type parameters are the same type at run time. |
| Implementation source code of the templated class or function must be included in order to use it (declaration insufficient). | Signature of the class or function from a compiled class file is sufficient to use it. |
| Templates can be specialized - a separate implementation could be provided for a particular template parameter. | Generics cannot be specialized. |
| Does not support wildcards. Instead, return types are often available as nested typedefs. | Supports wildcard as type parameter if it is only used once. |
| Does not directly support bounding of type parameters, but metaprogramming provides this. | Supports bounding of type parameters with "extends" and "super" for upper and lower bounds, respectively; allows enforcement of relationships between type parameters. |
| Allows instantiation of class of type parameter type. | Does not allow instantiation of class of type parameter type. |
| Type parameter of templated class can be used for static methods and variables. | Type parameter of templated class cannot be used for static methods and variables. |
| Static variables are not shared between classes of different type parameters. | Static variables are shared between instances of a classes of different type parameters. |

From http://en.wikipedia.org/wiki/Comparison_of_Java_and_C%2B%2B#Templates_vs._Generics

**14.5**   Explain what object reflection is in Java and why it is useful.

pg 78

## SOLUTION

Object Reflection is a feature in Java which provides a way to get reflective information about Java classes and objects, such as:

1.   Getting information about methods and fields present inside the class at run time.

2.   Creating a new instance of a class.

3.   Getting and setting the object fields directly by getting field reference, regardless of what the access modifier is.

```
1    import java.lang.reflect.*;
2
3    public class Sample {
4        public static void main(String args[]) {
5            try {
6                Class c = Class.forName("java.sql.Connection");
7                Method m[] = c.getDeclaredMethods();
8                for (int i = 0; i < 3; i++) {
9                    System.out.println(m[i].toString());
10               }
11           } catch (Throwable e) {
12               System.err.println(e);
13           }
14       }
15   }
```

This code's output is the names of the first 3 methods inside the "java.sql.Connection" class (with fully qualified parameters).

*Why it is useful:*

1.   Helps in observing or manipulating the runtime behavior of applications.

2.   Useful while debugging and testing applications, as it allows direct access to methods, constructors, fields, etc.

**14.6** Suppose you are using a map in your program, how would you count the number of times the program calls the put() and get() functions?

pg 78

## SOLUTION

One simple solution is to put count variables for get() and put() methods and, whenever they are called, increment the count. We can also achieve this by extending the existing library map and overriding the get() and put() functions.

At first glance, this seems to work. However, what if we created multiple instances of the map? How would you sum up the total count for each map object?

The simplest solution for this is to keep the count variables static. We know static variables have only one copy for all objects of the class so the total count would be reflected in count variables.

**15.1** Write a method to find the number of employees in each department.

pg 80

## SOLUTION

This problem uses a straight-forward join of Departments and Employees. Note that we use a left join instead of an inner join because we want to include Departments with 0 employees.

```
1   select Dept_Name, Departments.Dept_ID, count(*) as 'num_employees'
2   from Departments
3   left join Employees
4   on Employees.Dept_ID = Departments.Dept_ID
5   group by Departments.Dept_ID, Dept_Name
```

**15.2** What are the different types of joins? Please explain how they differ and why certain types are better in certain situations.

pg 80

## SOLUTION

JOIN is used to combine the results of two tables. To perform a join, each of the tables must have at least one field which will be used to find matching records from the other table. The join type defines which records will go into the result set.

Let's take for example two tables: one table lists "regular" beverages, and another lists the calorie-free beverages. Each table has two fields: the beverage name and its product code. The "code" field will be used to perform the record matching.

*Regular Beverages:*

| Name | Code |
| --- | --- |
| Budweiser | BUDWEISER |
| Coca-Cola | COCACOLA |
| Pepsi | PEPSI |

*Calorie-Free Beverages:*

| Code | Name |
| --- | --- |
| COCACOLA | Diet Coca-Cola |
| FRESCA | Fresca |
| PEPSI | Diet Pepsi |
| PEPSI | Pepsi Light |
| Water | Purified Water |

Let's join this table by the code field. Whereas the order of the joined tables makes sense in some cases, we will consider the following statement:

```
[Beverage] JOIN [Calorie-Free Beverage]
```

i.e. [Beverage] is from the left of the join operator, and [Calorie-Free Beverage] is from the right.

**1. INNER JOIN:** Result set will contain only those data where the criteria match. In our example we will get 3 records: 1 with COCACOLA and 2 with PEPSI codes.

**2. OUTER JOIN:** OUTER JOIN will always contain the results of INNER JOIN, however it can contain some records that have no matching record in other table. OUTER JOINs are divided to following subtypes:

**2.1. LEFT OUTER JOIN**, or simply **LEFT JOIN**: The result will contain all records from the left table. If no matching records were found in the right table, then its fields will contain the NULL values. In our example, we would get 4 records. In addition to INNER JOIN results, BUDWEISER will be listed, because it was in the left table.

**2.2. RIGHT OUTER JOIN**, or simply **RIGHT JOIN**: This type of join is the opposite of LEFT JOIN; it will contain all records from the right table, and missing fields from the left table will contain NULL. If we have two tables A and B, then we can say that statement A LEFT JOIN B is equivalent to statement B RIGHT JOIN A.

In our example, we will get 5 records. In addition to INNER JOIN results, FRESCA and WATER records will be listed.

**2.3. FULL OUTER JOIN**

This type of join combines the results of LEFT and RIGHT joins. All records from both tables will be part of the result set, whether the matching record exists in the other table or not. If no matching record was found then the corresponding result fields will have a NULL value.

In our example, we will get 6 records.

**15.3** What is denormalization? Explain the pros and cons.

pg 80

## SOLUTION

Denormalization is the process of attempting to optimize the performance of a database by adding redundant data or by grouping data. In some cases, denormalization helps cover up the inefficiencies inherent in relational database software. A relational normalized database imposes a heavy access load over physical storage of data even if it is well tuned for high performance.

A normalized design will often store different but related pieces of information in separate logical tables (called relations). If these relations are stored physically as separate disk files, completing a database query that draws information from several relations (a join operation) can be slow. If many relations are joined, it may be prohibitively slow. There are two strategies for dealing with this. The preferred method is to keep the logical design normalized, but allow the database management system (DBMS) to store additional redundant information on disk to optimize query response. In this case, it is the DBMS software's responsibility to ensure that any redundant copies are kept consistent. This method is often implemented in SQL as indexed views (Microsoft SQL Server) or materialized views (Oracle). A view represents information in a format convenient for querying, and the index ensures that queries against the view are optimized.

The more usual approach is to denormalize the logical data design. With care, this can achieve a similar improvement in query response, but at a cost—it is now the database designer's responsibility to ensure that the denormalized database does not become inconsistent. This is done by creating rules in the database called constraints, that specify how the redundant copies of information must be kept synchronized. It is the increase in logical complexity of the database design and the added complexity of the additional constraints that make this approach hazardous. Moreover, constraints introduce a trade-off, speeding up reads (SELECT in SQL) while slowing down writes (INSERT, UPDATE, and DELETE). This means a denormalized database under heavy write load may actually offer worse performance than its functionally equivalent normalized counterpart.

A denormalized data model is not the same as a data model that has not been normalized, and denormalization should only take place after a satisfactory level of normalization has taken place and that any required constraints and/or rules have been created to deal with the inherent anomalies in the design. For example, all the relations are in third normal form and any relations with join and multivalued dependencies are handled appropriately.

From *http://en.wikipedia.org/wiki/Denormalization*

**15.4** Draw an entity-relationship diagram for a database with companies, people, and professionals (people who work for companies).

pg 80

## SOLUTION

People who work for companies are Professionals. So there is an ISA (is a) relationship between People and Professionals (or we could say that a Professional is derived from People).

Each Professional has additional information such as degree, work experiences, etc, in addition to the properties derived from People.

A Professional works for one company at a time, but Companies can hire many Professionals, so there is a Many to One relationship between Professionals and Companies. This "Works For" relationship can store attributes such as date of joining the company, salary, etc. These attributes are only defined when we relate a Professional with a Company.

A Person can have multiple phone numbers, which is why Phone is a multi-valued attribute.

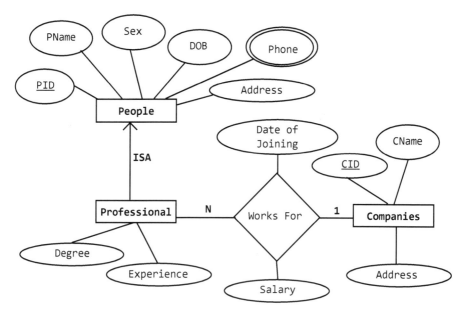

---

**15.5** Imagine a simple database storing information for students' grades. Design what this database might look like, and provide a SQL query to return a list of the honor roll students (top 10%), sorted by their grade point average.

pg 80

## SOLUTION

In a simplistic database, we'll have at least these three objects: Students, Courses, and CourseEnrollment. Students will have at least the student name and ID, and will likely have other personal information. Courses will contain the course name and ID, and will likely contain the course description, professor, etc. CourseEnrollment will pair Students and Courses, and will also contain a field for CourseGrade. We will assume that CourseGrade is an integer.

Our SQL query to get the list of honor roll students might look like this:

```
1   SELECT StudentName, GPA
2   FROM (
3          SELECT  top 10 percent Avg(CourseEnrollment.Grade) AS GPA,
4                  CourseEnrollment.StudentID
5          FROM CourseEnrollment
6          GROUP BY CourseEnrollment.StudentID
7          ORDER BY Avg(CourseEnrollment.Grade)) Honors
8   INNER JOIN Students ON Honors.StudentID = Students.StudentID
```

This database could get arbitrarily more complicated if we wanted to add in professor information, billing, etc.

**16.1** Explain the following terms: virtual memory, page fault, thrashing.

pg 82

## SOLUTION

*Virtual memory* is a computer system technique which gives an application program the impression that it has contiguous working memory (an address space), while in fact it may be physically fragmented and may even overflow on to disk storage. Systems that use this technique make programming of large applications easier and use real physical memory (e.g. RAM) more efficiently than those without virtual memory.

*http://en.wikipedia.org/wiki/Virtual_memory*

*Page Fault:* A page is a fixed-length block of memory that is used as a unit of transfer between physical memory and external storage like a disk, and a page fault is an interrupt (or exception) to the software raised by the hardware, when a program accesses a page that is mapped in address space, but not loaded in physical memory.

*http://en.wikipedia.org/wiki/Page_fault*

Thrash is the term used to describe a degenerate situation on a computer where increasing resources are used to do a decreasing amount of work. In this situation the system is said to be thrashing. Usually it refers to two or more processes accessing a shared resource repeatedly such that serious system performance degradation occurs because the system is spending a disproportionate amount of time just accessing the shared resource. Resource access time may generally be considered as wasted, since it does not contribute to the advancement of any process. In modern computers, thrashing may occur in the paging system (if there is not 'sufficient' physical memory or the disk access time is overly long), or in the communications system (especially in conflicts over internal bus access), etc.

*http://en.wikipedia.org/wiki/Thrash_(computer_science)*

**16.2** What is a Branch Target buffer? Explain how it can be used in reducing bubble cycles in cases of branch misprediction.

pg 82

## SOLUTION

Branch misprediction occurs when the CPU mispredicts the next instruction to be executed.

The CPU uses pipelining which allows several instructions to be processed simultaneously. But during a conditional jump, the next instruction to be executed depends on the result of the condition. Branch Prediction tries to guess the next instruction. However, if the guess is wrong, we are penalized because the instruction which was executed must be discarded.

Branch Target Buffer (BTB) reduces the penalty by predicting the path of the branch, computing the target of the branch and caching the information used by the branch. There will be no stalls if the branch entry found on BTB and the prediction is correct, otherwise the penalty will be at least two cycles.

**16.3** Describe direct memory access (DMA). Can a user level buffer / pointer be used by kernel or drivers?

pg 82

## SOLUTION

Direct Memory is a feature which provides direct access (read/write) to system memory without interaction from the CPU. The "DMA Controller" manages this by requesting the System bus access (DMA request) from CPU. CPU completes its current task and grants access by asserting DMA acknowledgement signal. Once it gets the access, it reads/writes the data and returns back the system bus to the CPU by asserting the bus release signal. This transfer is faster than the usual transfer by CPU. Between this time CPU is involved with processing task which doesn't require memory access.

By using DMA, drivers can access the memory allocated to the user level buffer / pointer.

**16.4** Write a step by step execution of things that happen after a user presses a key on the keyboard. Use as much detail as possible.

pg 82

## SOLUTION

1. The keyboard sends a scan code of the key to the keyboard controller (Scan code for key pressed and key released is different).

2. The keyboard controller interprets the scan code and stores it in a buffer.

3. The keyboard controller sends a hardware interrupt to the processor. This is done by putting signal on "interrupt request line": IRQ 1.

4. The interrupt controller maps IRQ 1 into INT 9.

5. An interrupt is a signal which tells the processor to stop what it was doing currently and do some special task.

6. The processor invokes the "Interrupt handler". CPU fetches the address of "Interrupt Service Routine" (ISR) from "Interrupt Vector Table" maintained by the OS (Processor use the IRQ number for this).

7. The ISR reads the scan code from port 60h and decides whether to process it or pass the control to program for taking action.

**16.5**    Write a program to find whether a machine is big endian or little endian.

pg 82

## SOLUTION

```
1   #define BIG_ENDIAN 0
2   #define LITTLE_ENDIAN 1
3   int TestByteOrder() {
4       short int word = 0x0001;
5       char *byte = (char *) &word;
6       return (byte[0] ? LITTLE_ENDIAN : BIG_ENDIAN);
7   }
```

**16.6** Discuss how would you make sure that a process doesn't access an unauthorized part of the stack.

pg 82

## SOLUTION

As with any ambiguously worded interview question, it may help to probe the interviewer to understand what specifically you're intended to solve. Are you trying to prevent code that has overflowed a buffer from compromising the execution by overwriting stack values? Are you trying to maintain some form of thread-specific isolation between threads? Is the code of interest native code like C++ or running under a virtual machine like Java?

Remember that, in a multi-threaded environment, there can be multiple stacks in a process.

*NATIVE CODE*

One threat to the stack is malicious program input, which can overflow a buffer and over-write stack pointers, thus circumventing the intended execution of the program.

If the interviewer is looking for a simple method to reduce the risk of buffer overflows in native code, modern compilers provide this sort of stack protection through a command line option. With Microsoft's CL, you just pass /GS to the compiler. With GCC, you can use -fstack-protector-all.

For more complex schemes, you could set individual permissions on the range of memory pages representing the stack section you care about. In the Win32 API, you'd use the VirtualProtect API to mark the page PAGE_READONLY or PAGE_NOACCESS. This will cause the code accessing the region to go through an exception on access to the specific section of the stack.

Alternately, you could use the HW Debug Registers (DRs) to set a read or write breakpoint on the specific memory addresses of interest. A separate process could be used to debug the process of interest, catch the HW exception that would be generated if this section of the stack were accessed.

However, it's very important to note that under normal circumstances, threads and processes are not means of access control. Nothing can prevent native code from writing anywhere within the address space of its process, including to the stack. Specifically, there is nothing to prevent malicious code in the process from calling VirtualProtect and marking the stack sections of interest PAGE_EXECUTE_READWRITE. Equally so, nothing prevents code from zeroing out the HW debug registers, eliminating your breakpoints. In summary, nothing can fully prevent native code from accessing memory addresses, including the stack, within its own process space.

*MANAGED CODE*

A final option is to consider requiring this code that should be "sandboxed" to run in a managed language like Java or C# / .NET. By default, the virtual machines running managed code in these languages make it impossible to gain complete access to the stack from within the process.

One can use further security features of the runtimes to prevent the code from spawning additional processes or running "unsafe" code to inspect the stack. With .NET, for example, you can use Code Access Security (CAS) or appdomain permissions to control such execution.

**16.7** What are the best practices to prevent reverse engineering of DLLs?

pg 82

## SOLUTION

Best practices include the following:

» Use obfuscators.

» Do not store any data (string, etc) in open form. Always compress or encode it.

» Use a static link so there is no DLL to attack.

» Strip all symbols.

» Use a .DEF file and an import library to have anonymous exports known only by their export ids.

» Keep the DLL in a resource and expose it in the file system (under a suitably obscure name, perhaps even generated at run time) only when running.

» Hide all real functions behind a factory method that exchanges a secret (better, proof of knowledge of a secret) for a table of function pointers to the real methods.

» Use anti-debugging techniques borrowed from the malware world to prevent reverse engineering. (Note that this will likely get you false positives from AV tools.)

» Use protectors.

**16.8** A device boots with an empty FIFO queue. In the first 400 ns period after startup, and in each subsequent 400 ns period, a maximum of 80 words will be written to the queue. Each write takes 4 ns. A worker thread requires 3 ns to read a word, and 2 ns to process it before reading the next word. What is the shortest depth of the FIFO such that no data is lost?

pg 82

## SOLUTION

While a perfectly optimal solution is complex, an interviewer is most interested in how you approach the problem.

*THEORY*

First, note that writes do not have to be evenly distributed within a period. Thus a likely worst case is 80 words are written at the end of the first period, followed by 80 more at the start of the next.

Note that the maximum write rate for a full period is exactly matched by a full period of processing (400 ns / ((3 ns + 2 ns)/process) = 80 processed words/period).

As the 2nd period in our example is fully saturated, adding writes from a 3rd period would not add additional stress, and this example is a true worst case for the conditions.

*A SAFE QUEUE DEPTH*

For an estimate of maximum queue size, notice that these 160 writes take 640 ns (160 writes * 4 ns / write = 640 ns), during which time only 128 words have been read (640 ns / ((3 ns + 2 ns) / word) = 128 words). However, the first read cannot start until the first write has finished, which fills an extra slot in the queue.

Also, depending on the interactions between read and write timing, a second additional slot may be necessary to ensure a write does not trash the contents of a concurrently occurring read. Thus, a safe estimate is that the queue must be at least 34 words deep (160 - 128 + 1 + 1 = 34) to accommodate the unread words.

*FINDING AN OPTIMAL (MINIMAL) QUEUE DEPTH*

Depending on the specifics of the problem, it's possible that the final queue spot could be safely removed. In many cases, the time required to do an edge case analysis to determine safety is not worth the effort. However, if the interviewer is interested, the full analysis follows.

We are interested in the exact queue load during the final (160th) consecutive write to the queue. We can approach this by graphing the queue load from time = 0 ns, observing the pattern, and extending it to time = 716 ns, the time of the final consecutive write.

The graph below shows that the queue load increases as each write begins, and decreases

---

3 ns after a read begins. Uninteresting time segments are surrounded by [brackets]. Each character represents 1 ns.

| | 0 - 79 ns | 80 - 99 ns | 100 - 707 ns | 708 - 723 ns | >= 724 ns |
|---|---|---|---|---|---|
| Writer | | AAAABBBBCCCCDDDDEEEE | | XXXXYYYYZZZZ____ | |
| Worker | | ____aaaaabbbbbccccccd | | opppppqqqqqrrrrr | |
| Queue Load | | 11112221222222223222 | | 3333333343333322 * | |

```
Y = Writing word 159 @ 712 ns
Z = Writing word 160 @ 716 ns
q = Processing word 127 @ 714 ns
r = Processing word 128
* = Between 708 and 723 ns, the queue load is shown as 30 plus the
    digit shown at each ns.
```

Note that the queue load does in fact reach a maximum of 34 at time = 716 ns.

As an interesting note, if the problem had required only 2 ns of the 5 ns processing time to complete a read, the optimal queue depth would decrease to 33.

The below graphs are unnecessary, but show empirically that adding writes from the 3rd period does not change the queue depth required.

| | < 796 ns | 797 - 807 ns | 808 - 873 ns | 874 - 885 ns |
|---|---|---|---|---|
| Writer | | ____AAAABBBB | | !!@@@@####$$ |
| Worker | | ^^^&&&&&**** | | yyyyyzzzzzaa |
| Queue Load | | 877788778887 | | 112111221122 * |

```
A = Writing word 161
& = Processing word 144
# = Writing word 181
z = Processing word 160 @ 779 ns
* = Between 874 and 885 ns, the queue load is shown as 20 plus the
    digit shown at each ns.
```

| | < 1112 ns | 1112 - 1123 ns |
|---|---|---|
| Writer | | YYYYZZZZ____ |
| Worker | | ^^&&&&&%%%%% |
| Queue Load | | 333343333322 * |

```
Z = Writing word 240 @ 1116 ns
& = Processing word 207 @ 1114 ns
* = Between 1112 and 1123 ns, the queue load is shown as 30 plus the
    digit shown at each ns.
```

**16.9** Write an aligned malloc & free function that takes number of bytes and aligned byte (which is always power of 2)

EXAMPLE

align_malloc (1000,128) will return a memory address that is a multiple of 128 and that points to memory of size 1000 bytes.

aligned_free() will free memory allocated by align_malloc.

*pg 82*

## SOLUTION

1.  We will use malloc routine provided by C to implement the functionality.

    Allocate memory of size (bytes required + alignment – 1 + sizeof(void*)) using malloc.

    alignment: malloc can give us any address and we need to find a multiple of alignment.

    (Therefore, at maximum multiple of alignment, we will be alignment-1 bytes away from any location.)

    sizeof(size_t): We are returning a modified memory pointer to user, which is different from the one that would be returned by malloc. We also need to extra space to store the address given by malloc, so that we can free memory in aligned_free by calling free routine provided by C.

2.  If it returns NULL, then aligned_malloc will fail and we return NULL.

3.  Else, find the aligned memory address which is a multiple of alignment (call this p2).

4.  Store the address returned by malloc (e.g., p1 is just size_t bytes ahead of p2), which will be required by aligned_free.

5.  Return p2.

```
1   void* aligned_malloc(size_t required_bytes, size_t alignment) {
2       void* p1; // original block
3       void** p2; // aligned block
4       int offset = alignment - 1 + sizeof(void*);
5       if ((p1 = (void*)malloc(required_bytes + offset)) == NULL) {
6           return NULL;
7       }
8       p2 = (void**)(((size_t)(p1) + offset) & ~(alignment - 1));
9       p2[-1] = p1;
10      return p2;
11  }
12  void aligned_free(void *p) {
13      free(((void**)p)[-1]);
14  }
```

**16.10** Write a function called my2DAlloc which allocates a two dimensional array. Minimize the number of calls to malloc and make sure that the memory is accessible by the notation arr[i][j].

pg 82

## SOLUTION

We will use one call to malloc.

Allocate one block of memory to hold the row vector and the array data. The row vector will reside in rows * sizeof(int*) bytes. The integers in the array will take up another rows * cols * sizeof(int) bytes.

Constructing the array in a single malloc has the added benefit of allowing disposal of the array with a single free call rather than using a special function to free the subsidiary data blocks.

```
1   #include <malloc.h>
2
3   int** My2DAlloc(int rows, int cols) {
4       int header = rows * sizeof(int*);
5       int data = rows * cols * sizeof(int);
6       int** rowptr = (int**)malloc(header + data);
7       int* buf = (int*)(rowptr + rows);
8       int k;
9       for (k = 0; k < rows; ++k) {
10          rowptr[k] = buf + k*cols;
11      }
12      return rowptr;
13  }
```

**17.1** Explain what happens, step by step, after you type a URL into a browser. Use as much detail as possible.

pg 84

## SOLUTION

There's no right, or even complete, answer for this question. This question allows you to go into arbitrary amounts of detail depending on what you're comfortable with. Here's a start though:

1. Browser contacts the DNS server to find the IP address of URL.

2. DNS returns back the IP address of the site.

3. Browser opens TCP connection to the web server at port 80.

4. Browser fetches the html code of the page requested.

5. Browser renders the HTML in the display window.

6. Browser terminates the connection when window is closed.

One of the most interesting steps is Step 1 and 2 - "Domain Name Resolution." The web addresses we type are nothing but an alias to an IP address in human readable form. Mapping of domain names and their associated Internet Protocol (IP) addresses is managed by the Domain Name System (DNS), which is a distributed but hierarchical entity.

Each domain name server is divided into zones. A single server may only be responsible for knowing the host names and IP addresses for a small subset of a zone, but DNS servers can work together to map all domain names to their IP addresses. That means if one domain name server is unable to find the IP addresses of a requested domain then it requests the information from other domain name servers.

**17.2** Explain any common routing protocol in detail. For example: BGP, OSPF, RIP.

pg 84

## SOLUTION

Depending on the reader's level of understanding, knowledge, interest or career aspirations, he or she may wish to explore beyond what is included here. Wikipedia and other websites are great places to look for a deeper understanding. We will provide only a short summary.

*BGP: Border Gateway Protocol*

BGP is the core routing protocol of the Internet. "When a BGP router first comes up on the Internet, either for the first time or after being turned off, it establishes connections with the other BGP routers with which it directly communicates. The first thing it does is download the entire routing table of each neighboring router. After that it only exchanges much shorter update messages with other routers.

BGP routers send and receive update messages to indicate a change in the preferred path to reach a computer with a given IP address. If the router decides to update its own routing tables because this new path is better, then it will subsequently propagate this information to all of the other neighboring BGP routers to which it is connected, and they will in turn decide whether to update their own tables and propagate the information further."

Borrowed from http://www.livinginternet.com/i/iw_route_egp_bgp.htm.

*RIP: Routing Information Protocol*

"RIP provides the standard IGP protocol for local area networks, and provides great network stability, guaranteeing that if one network connection goes down the network can quickly adapt to send packets through another connection. "

"What makes RIP work is a routing database that stores information on the fastest route from computer to computer, an update process that enables each router to tell other routers which route is the fastest from its point of view, and an update algorithm that enables each router to update its database with the fastest route communicated from neighboring routers."

Borrowing from http://www.livinginternet.com/i/iw_route_igp_rip.htm.

*OSPF: Open Shortest Path First*

"Open Shortest Path First (OSPF) is a particularly efficient IGP routing protocol that is faster than RIP, but also more complex."

The main difference between OSPF and RIP is that RIP only keeps track of the closest router for each destination address, while OSPF keeps track of a complete topological database of all connections in the local network. The OSPF algorithm works as described below.

»   Startup. When a router is turned on it sends Hello packets to all of its neighbors, receives their Hello packets in return, and establishes routing connections by synchronizing databases with adjacent routers that agree to synchronize.

»   Update. At regular intervals each router sends an update message called its "link state" describing its routing database to all the other routers, so that all routers have the same description of the topology of the local network.

»   Shortest path tree. Each router then calculates a mathematical data structure called a "shortest path tree" that describes the shortest path to each destination address and therefore indicates the closest router to send to for each communication; in other words -- "open shortest path first".

See http://www.livinginternet.com/i/iw_route_igp_ospf.htm.

**17.3**   Compare and contrast the IPv4 and IPv6 protocols.

pg 84

## SOLUTION

IPv4 and IPv6 are the internet protocols applied at the network layer. IPv4 is the most widely used protocol right now and IPv6 is the next generation protocol for internet.

» IPv4 is the fourth version of Internet protocol which uses 32 bit addressing whereas IPv6 is a next generation internet protocol which uses 128 bits addressing.

» IPv4 allows 4,294,967,296 unique addresses where as IPv6 can hold 340-undecillion (34, 000, 000, 000, 000, 000, 000, 000, 000, 000, 000, 000, 000) unique IP addresses.

» IPv4 has different class types: A,B,C,D and E.  Class A, Class B, and Class C are the three classes of addresses used on IP networks in common practice.  Class D addresses are reserved for multicast.  Class E addresses are simply reserved, meaning they should not be used on IP networks (used on a limited basis by some research organizations for experimental purposes).

» IPv6 addresses are broadly classified into three categories:

1.   Unicast addresses: A Unicast address acts as an identifier for a single interface.  An IPv6 packet sent to a Unicast address is delivered to the interface identified by that address.

2.   Multicast addresses: A Multicast address acts as an identifier for a group / set of interfaces that may belong to the different nodes.  An IPv6 packet delivered to a multicast address is delivered to the multiple interfaces.

3.   Anycast addresses: Anycast addresses act as identifiers for a set of interfaces that may belong to the different nodes.  An IPv6 packet destined for an Anycast address is delivered to one of the interfaces identified by the address.

» IPv4 address notation: 239.255.255.255, 255.255.255.0

» IPv6 addresses are denoted by eight groups of hexadecimal quartets separated by colons in between them.

» An example of a valid IPv6 address: 2001:cdba:0000:0000:0000:0000:3257:9652

Because of the increase in the population, there is a need of Ipv6 protocol which can provide solution for:

1.   Increased address space

2.   More efficient routing

3.   Reduced management requirement

4.  Improved methods to change ISP

5.  Better mobility support

6.  Multi-homing

7.  Security

8.  Scoped address: link-local, site-local and global-address space

**17.4** What is a network / subnet mask? Explain how host A sends a message / packet to host B when: (a) both are on same network and (b) both are on different networks. Explain which layer makes the routing decision and how.

pg 84

## SOLUTION

A mask is a bit pattern used to identify the network/subnet address. The IP address consists of two components: the network address and the host address.

The IP addresses are categorized into different classes which are used to identify the network address.

*Example*: Consider IP address 152.210.011.002. This address belongs to Class B, so:

```
Network Mask: 11111111.11111111.00000000.00000000
Given Address: 10011000.11010101.00001011.00000010
```

By ANDing Network Mask and IP Address, we get the following network address:

```
10011000.11010101.00000000.00000000 (152.210.0.0)
Host address: 00001011.00000010
```

Similarly, a network administrator can divide any network into sub-networks by using subnet mask. To do this, we further divide the host address into two or more subnets.

For example, if the above network is divided into 18 subnets (requiring a minimum of 5 bits to represent 18 subnets), the first 5 bits will be used to identify the subnet address.

Subnet Mask: 11111111.11111111.11111000.00000000 (255.255.248.0)

Given Address: 10011000.11010101.00001011.00000010

So, by ANDing the subnet mask and the given address, we get the following subnet address: 10011000.11010101.00001000.00000000 (152.210.1.0)

*How Host A sends a message/packet to Host B:*

When both are on same network: the host address bits are used to identify the host within the network.

Both are on different networks: the router uses the network mask to identify the network and route the packet. The host can be identified using the network host address.

The network layer is responsible for making routing decisions. A routing table is used to store the path information and the cost involved with that path, while a routing algorithm uses the routing table to decide the path on which to route the packets.

Routing is broadly classified into Static and Dynamic Routing based on whether the table is fixed or it changes based on the current network condition.

**17.5** What are the differences between TCP and UDP? Explain how TCP handles reliable delivery (explain ACK mechanism), flow control (explain TCP sender's / receiver's window) and congestion control.

pg 84

## SOLUTION

*TCP (Transmission Control Protocol):* TCP is a connection-oriented protocol. A connection can be made from client to server, and from then on any data can be sent along that connection.

»   Reliable - when you send a message along a TCP socket, you know it will get there unless the connection fails completely. If it gets lost along the way, the server will re-request the lost part. This means complete integrity; data will not get corrupted.

»   Ordered - if you send two messages along a connection, one after the other, you know the first message will get there first. You don't have to worry about data arriving in the wrong order.

»   Heavyweight - when the low level parts of the TCP "stream" arrive in the wrong order, re-send requests have to be sent. All the out of sequence parts must be put back together, which requires a bit of work.

*UDP(User Datagram Protocol):* UDP is connectionless protocol. With UDP you send messages (packets) across the network in chunks.

»   Unreliable - When you send a message, you don't know if it'll get there; it could get lost on the way.

»   Not ordered - If you send two messages out, you don't know what order they'll arrive in.

»   Lightweight - No ordering of messages, no tracking connections, etc. It's just fire and forget! This means it's a lot quicker, and the network card / OS have to do very little work to translate the data back from the packets.

*Explain how TCP handles reliable delivery (explain ACK mechanism), flow control (explain TCP sender's/receiver's window).*

For each TCP packet, the receiver of a packet must acknowledge that the packet is received. If there is no acknowledgement, the packet is sent again. These guarantee that every single packet is delivered. ACK is a packet used in TCP to acknowledge receipt of a packet. A TCP window is the amount of outstanding (unacknowledged by the recipient) data a sender can send on a particular connection before it gets an acknowledgment back from the receiver that it has gotten some of it.

For example, if a pair of hosts are talking over a TCP connection that has a TCP window with a size of 64 KB, the sender can only send 64 KB of data and then it must wait for an acknowledgment from the receiver that some or all of the data has been received. If the receiver acknowledges that all the data has been received, then the sender is free to send another 64 KB. If the sender gets back an acknowledgment from the receiver that it received the first 32 KB (which could happen if the second 32 KB was still in transit or it could happen if the second 32 KB got lost), then the sender can only send another additional 32 KB since it can't have more than 64 KB of unacknowledged data outstanding (the second 32 KB of data plus the third).

*Congestion Control*

The TCP uses a network congestion avoidance algorithm that includes various aspects of an additive-increase-multiplicative-decrease scheme, with other schemes such as slow-start in order to achieve congestion avoidance.

There are different algorithms to solve the problem; Tahoe and Reno are the most well known. To avoid congestion collapse, TCP uses a multi-faceted congestion control strategy. For each connection, TCP maintains a congestion window, limiting the total number of unacknowledged packets that may be in transit end-to-end. This is somewhat analogous to TCP's sliding window used for flow control. TCP uses a mechanism called slow start to increase the congestion window after a connection is initialized and after a timeout. It starts with a window of two times the maximum segment size (MSS). Although the initial rate is low, the rate of increase is very rapid: for every packet acknowledged, the congestion window increases by 1 MSS so that for every round trip time (RTT), the congestion window has doubled. When the congestion window exceeds a threshold ssthresh the algorithm enters a new state, called congestion avoidance. In some implementations (i.e., Linux), the initial ssthresh is large, and so the first slow start usually ends after a loss. However, ssthresh is updated at the end of each slow start, and will often affect subsequent slow starts triggered by timeouts.

**18.1** What's the difference between a thread and a process?

pg 86

## SOLUTION

Processes and threads are related to each other but are fundamentally different.

A process can be thought of as an instance of a program in execution. Each process is an independent entity to which system resources (CPU time, memory, etc.) are allocated and each process is executed in a separate address space. One process cannot access the variables and data structures of another process. If you wish to access another process' resources, inter-process communications have to be used such as pipes, files, sockets etc.

A thread uses the same stack space of a process. A process can have multiple threads. A key difference between processes and threads is that multiple threads share parts of their state. Typically, one allows multiple threads to read and write the same memory (no processes can directly access the memory of another process). However, each thread still has its own registers and its own stack, but other threads can read and write the stack memory.

A thread is a particular execution path of a process; when one thread modifies a process resource, the change is immediately visible to sibling threads.

**18.2**   How can you measure the time spent in a context switch?

pg 86

## SOLUTION

This is a tricky question, but let's start with a possible solution.

A context switch is the time spent switching between two processes (e.g., bringing a wait-ing process into execution and sending an executing process into waiting/terminated state). This happens in multitasking. The operating system must bring the state information of waiting processes into memory and save the state information of the running process.

In order to solve this problem, we would like to record timestamps of the last and first in-struction of the swapping processes. The context switching time would be the difference in the timestamps between the two processes.

Let's take an easy example: Assume there are only two processes, P1 and P2.

P1 is executing and P2 is waiting for execution. At some point, the OS must swap P1 and P2—let's assume it happens at the Nth instruction of P1. So, the context switch time for this would be Time_Stamp(P2_1) – Time_Stamp(P2_N)

Easy enough. The tricky part is this: how do we know when this swapping occurs? Swap-ping is governed by the scheduling algorithm of the OS. We can not, of course, record the timestamp of every instruction in the process.

Another issue: there are many kernel level threads which are also doing context switches, and the user does not have any control over them.

Overall, we can say that this is mostly an approximate calculation which depends on the underlying OS. One approximation could be to record the end instruction timestamp of a process and start timestamp of a process and waiting time in queue.

If the total timeof execution of all the processes was T, then the context switch time = T – (SUM for all processes (waiting time + execution time)).

**18.3** Implement a singleton design pattern as a template such that, for any given class Foo, you can call Singleton::instance() and get a pointer to an instance of a singleton of type Foo. Assume the existence of a class Lock which has acquire() and release() methods. How could you make your implementation thread safe and exception safe?

pg 86

## SOLUTION

```
1   using namespace std;
2   /* Place holder for thread synchronization lock */
3   class Lock {
4   public:
5       Lock() { /* placeholder code to create the lock */ }
6       ~Lock() { /* placeholder code to deallocate the lock */ }
7       void AcquireLock() { /* placeholder to acquire the lock */ }
8       void ReleaseLock() { /* placeholder to release the lock */ }
9   };
10
11  /* Singleton class with a method that creates a new instance of the
12   * class of the type of the passed in template if it does not
13   * already exist. */
14  template <class T> class Singleton {
15  private:
16      static Lock lock;
17      static T* object;
18  protected:
19      Singleton() { };
20  public:
21      static T * instance();
22  };
23  Lock Singleton::lock;
24
25  T * Singleton::Instance() {
26      /* if object is not initialized, acquire lock */
27      if (object == 0) {
28          lock.AcquireLock();
29          /* If two threads simultaneously check and pass the first "if"
30           * condition, then only the one who acquired the lock first
31           * should create the instance */
32          if (object == 0) {
33              object = new T;
34          }
35          lock.ReleaseLock();
36      }
37      return object;
38  }
```

```
39
40  int main() {
41      /* foo is any class defined for which we want singleton access */
42      Foo* singleton_foo = Singleton<Foo>::Instance();
43      return 0;
44  }
```

The general method to make a program thread safe is to lock shared resources whenever write permission is given. This way, if one thread is modifying the resource, other threads can not modify it.

**18.4**    Design a class which provides a lock only if there are no possible deadlocks.

pg 86

## SOLUTION

For our solution, we implement a wait / die deadlock prevention scheme.

```
1   class MyThread extends Thread {
2       long time;
3       ArrayList<Resource> res = new ArrayList<Resource>();
4       public ArrayList<Resource> getRes() { return res; }
5
6       public void run() {
7           /* Run infinitely */
8           time = System.currentTimeMillis();
9           int count = 0;
10          while (true) {
11              if (count < 4) {
12                  if (Question.canAcquireResource(this,
13                                              Question.r[count])) {
14                      res.add(Question.r[count]);
15                      count++;
16                      System.out.println("Resource: [" +
17                          Question.r[count - 1].getId() + "] acquired by
18                          thread: [" + this.getName() + "]");
19                      try {
20                          sleep(1000);
21                      } catch (InterruptedException e) {
22                          e.printStackTrace();
23                      }
24                  }
25              }
26              else {
27                  this.stop();
28              }
29          }
30      }
31
32      public long getTime() { return time; }
33      public void setRes(ArrayList<Resource> res) { this.res = res; }
34      MyThread(String name) {
35          super(name);
36      }
37  }
```

**18.5**   Suppose we have the following code:

```
class Foo {
public:
    A(.....); /* If A is called, a new thread will be created and
             * the corresponding function will be executed. */
    B(.....); /* same as above */
    C(.....); /* same as above */
}
Foo f;
f.A(.....);
f.B(.....);
f.C(.....);
```

i) Can you design a mechanism to make sure that B is executed after A, and C is executed after B?

iii) Suppose we have the following code to use class Foo. We do not know how the threads will be scheduled in the OS.

```
Foo f;
f.A(.....); f.B(.....); f.C(.....);
f.A(.....); f.B(.....); f.C(.....);
```

Can you design a mechanism to make sure that all the methods will be executed in sequence?

pg 86

## SOLUTION

---

*i) Can you design a mechanism to make sure that B is executed after A, and C is executed after B?*

```
1   Semaphore s_a(0);
2   Semaphore s_b(0);
3   A {
4       /***/
5       s_a.release(1);
6   }
7   B {
8       s_a.acquire(1);
9       /****/
10      s_b.release(1);
11  }
12  C {
13      s_b.acquire(1);
14      /******/
15  }
```

*ii) Can you design a mechanism to make sure that all the methods will be executed in sequence?*

```
1   Semaphore s_a(0);
```

```
2   Semaphore s_b(0);
3   Semaphore s_c(1);
4   A {
5       s_c.acquire(1);
6       /***/
7       s_a.release(1);
8   }
9   B {
10      s_a.acquire(1);
11      /****/
12      s_b.release(1);
13  }
14  C {
15      s_b.acquire(1);
16      /******/
17      s_c.release(1);
18  }
```

**18.6** You are given a class with synchronized method A, and a normal method C. If you have two threads in one instance of a program, can they call A at the same time? Can they call A and C at the same time?

pg 86

## SOLUTION

Java provides two ways to achieve synchronization: synchronized method and synchronized statement.

Synchronized method: Methods of a class which need to be synchronized are declared with "synchronized" keyword. If one thread is executing a synchronized method, all other threads which want to execute any of the synchronized methods on the same objects get blocked.

Syntax: method1 and method2 need to be synchronized

```
1   public class SynchronizedMethod {
2       // Variables declaration
3       public synchronized returntype Method1() {
4           // Statements
5       }
6       public synchronized returntype method2() {
7           // Statements
8       }
9       // Other methods
10  }
```

Synchronized statement: It provides the synchronization for a group of statements rather than a method as a whole. It needs to provide the object on which these synchronized statements will be applied, unlike in a synchronized method.

Syntax: synchronized statements on "this" object

```
1   synchronized(this) {
2       /* statement 1
3        *  ...
4        * statement N */
5   }
```

*i) If you have two threads in one instance of a program, can they call A at the same time?*

Not possible; read the above paragraph.

*ii) Can they call A and C at the same time?*

Yes. Only methods of the same object which are declared with the keyword synchronized can't be interleaved.

# Solutions to Chapter 19 | Moderate

**19.1**  Write a function to swap a number in place without temporary variables.

pg 89

## SOLUTION

This is a classic interview problem. If you haven't heard this problem before, you can approach it by taking the difference between a and b:

```
1   public static void swap(int a, int b) {
2       a = b - a; // 9 - 5 = 4
3       b = b - a; // 9 - 4 = 5
4       a = a + b; // 4 + 5 = 9
5
6       System.out.println("a: " + a);
7       System.out.println("b: " + b);
8   }
```

You can then optimize it as follows:

```
1   public static void swap_opt(int a, int b) {
2       a = a^b;
3       b = a^b;
4       a = a^b;
5
6       System.out.println("a: " + a);
7       System.out.println("b: " + b);
8   }
```

**19.2** Design an algorithm to figure out if someone has won in a game of tic-tac-toe.

pg 89

## SOLUTION

The first thing to ask your interviewer is whether the hasWon function will be called just once, or multiple times. If it will be called multiple times, you can get a very fast algorithm by amortizing the cost (especially if you can design your own data storage system for the tic-tac-toe board).

Approach #1: If hasWon is called many times

There are only 3^9, or about twenty thousand tic-tac-toe boards. We can thus represent our tic-tac-toe board as an int, with each digit representing a piece (0 means Empty, 1 means Red, 2 means Blue). We set up a hashtable or array in advance with all possible boards as keys, and the values are 0, 1, and 2. Our function then is simply this:

```
int hasWon(int board) {
    return winnerHashtable[board];
}
```

Easy!

Approach #2: If hasWon is only called once

```
1    enum Piece { Empty, Red, Blue };
2    enum Check { Row, Column, Diagonal, ReverseDiagonal }
3
4    Piece getIthColor(Piece[][] board, int index, int var, Check check) {
5        if (check == Check.Row) return board[index][var];
6        else if (check == Check.Column) return board[var][index];
7        else if (check == Check.Diagonal) return board[var][var];
8        else if (check == Check.ReverseDiagonal)
9            return board[board.length - 1 - var][var];
10       return Piece.Empty;
11   }
12
13   Piece getWinner(Piece[][] board, int fixed_index, Check check) {
14       Piece color = getIthColor(board, fixed_index, 0, check);
15       if (color == Piece.Empty) return Piece.Empty;
16       for (int var = 1; var < board.length; var++) {
17           if (color != getIthColor(board, fixed_index, var, check)) {
18               return Piece.Empty;
19           }
20       }
21       return color;
22   }
23
```

```
24   Piece hasWon(Piece[][] board) {
25       int N = board.length;
26       Piece winner = Piece.Empty;
27
28       // Check rows and columns
29       for (int i = 0; i < N; i++) {
30           winner = getWinner(board, i, Check.Row);
31           if (winner != Piece.Empty) {
32               return winner;
33           }
34
35           winner = getWinner(board, i, Check.Column);
36           if (winner != Piece.Empty) {
37               return winner;
38           }
39       }
40
41       winner = getWinner(board, -1, Check.Diagonal);
42       if (winner != Piece.Empty) {
43           return winner;
44       }
45
46       // Check diagonal
47       winner = getWinner(board, -1, Check.ReverseDiagonal);
48       if (winner != Piece.Empty) {
49           return winner;
50       }
51
52       return Piece.Empty;
53   }
```

## SUGGESTIONS AND OBSERVATIONS:

» Note that the runtime could be reduced to O(N) with the addition of row and column count arrays (and two sums for the diagonals)

» A common follow up (or tweak) to this question is to write this code for an NxN board.

**19.3**   Write an algorithm which computes the number of trailing zeros in n factorial.

pg 89

## SOLUTION

Trailing zeros are contributed by pairs of 5 and 2, because 5*2 = 10. To count the number of pairs, we just have to count the number of multiples of 5. Note that while 5 contributes to one multiple of 10, 25 contributes two (because 25 = 5*5).

```
1    public static int numZeros(int num) {
2        int count = 0;
3        if (num < 0) {
4            System.out.println("Factorial is not defined for < 0");
5            return 0;
6        }
7        for (int i = 5; num / i > 0; i *= 5) {
8            count += num / i;
9        }
10       return count;
11   }
```

Let's walk through an example to see how this works: Suppose num = 26. In the first loop, we count how many multiples of five there are by doing 26 / 5 = 5 (these multiples are 5, 10, 15, 20, and 25). In the next loop, we count how many multiples of 25 there are: 26 / 25 = 1 (this multiple is 25). Thus, we see that we get one zero from 5, 10, 15 and 20, and two zeros from 25 (note how it was counted twice in the loops). Therefore, 26! has six zeros.

## OBSERVATIONS AND SUGGESTIONS:

»   This is a bit of a brain teaser, but it can be approached logically (as shown above). By thinking through what exactly will contribute a zero, and what doesn't matter, you can come up with a solution. Again, be very clear in your rules up front so that you can implement this correctly.

**19.4**  Write a method which finds the maximum of two numbers. You should not use if-else or any other comparison operator.

EXAMPLE

Input: 5, 10

Output: 10

pg 89

## SOLUTION

Let's try to solve this by "re-wording" the problem. We will re-word the problem until we get something that has removed all if statements.

Rewording 1: If a > b, return a; else, return b.

Rewording 2: If (a - b) is negative, return b; else, return a.

Rewording 3: If (a - b) is negative, let k = 1; else, let k = 0. Return a - k * (a - b).

Rewording 4: Let c = a - b. Let k = the most significant bit of c. Return a - k * c.

We have now reworded the problem into something that fits the requirements. The code for this is below.

```
1   int getMax(int a, int b) {
2       int c = a - b;
3       int k = (c >> 31) & 0x1;
4       int max = a - k * c;
5       return max;
6   }
```

**19.5** The Game of Master Mind is played as follows:

The computer has four slots containing balls that are red (R), yellow (Y), green (G) or blue (B). For example, the computer might have RGGB (e.g., Slot #1 is red, Slots #2 and #3 are green, Slot #4 is blue).

You, the user, are trying to guess the solution. You might, for example, guess YRGB.

When you guess the correct color for the correct slot, you get a "hit". If you guess a color that exists but is in the wrong slot, you get a "pseudo-hit". For example, the guess YRGB has 2 hits and one pseudo hit.

For each guess, you are told the number of hits and pseudo-hits.

Write a method that, given a guess and a solution, returns the number of hits and pseudo hits.

pg 89

## SOLUTION

This problem is straight-forward. We simply check the number of hits and pseudo-hits. We will store the number of each in a class. To do a quick lookup to see it an element is a pseudo-hit, we will use a bit mask.

```
1   public static class Result {
2       public int hits;
3       public int pseudoHits;
4   };
5
6   public static Result estimate(String guess, String solution) {
7       Result res = new Result();
8       int solution_mask = 0;
9       for (int i = 0; i < 4; ++i) {
10          solution_mask |= 1 << (1 + solution.charAt(i) - 'A');
11      }
12      for (int i = 0; i < 4; ++i) {
13          if (guess.charAt(i) == solution.charAt(i)) {
14              ++res.hits;
15          } else if ((solution_mask &
16                      (1 << (1 + guess.charAt(i) - 'A'))) >= 1) {
17              ++res.pseudoHits;
18          }
19      }
20      return res;
21  }
```

**19.6** Given an integer between 0 and 999,999, print an English phrase that describes the integer (eg, "One Thousand, Two Hundred and Thirty Four").

pg 89

## SOLUTION

This is not an especially challenging problem, but it is a long and tedious one. Your interviewer is unlikely to ask to see every detail, but he / she will be interested in how you approach the problem.

```
1   public static String numtostring(int num) {
2       StringBuilder sb = new StringBuilder();
3
4       // Count number of digits in num.
5       int len = 1;
6       while (Math.pow((double)10, (double)len ) < num) {
7           len++;
8       }
9
10      String[] wordarr1 = {"","One ", "Two ", "Three ", "Four ",
11                           "Five ", "Six ", "Seven ", "Eight ","Nine "};
12      String[] wordarr11 = {"", "Eleven ", "Twelve ", "Thirteen ",
13                           "Fourteen ", "Fifteen ", "Sixteen ",
14                           "Seventeen ", "Eighteen ", "Nineteen "};
15      String[] wordarr10 = {"","Ten ", "Twenty ", "Thirty ", "Forty ",
16                           "Fifty ", "Sixty ", "Seventy ", "Eighty ",
17                           "Ninety "};
18      String[] wordarr100 = {"", "Hundred ", "Thousand "};
19      int tmp;
20      if (num == 0) {
21          sb.append("Zero");
22      } else {
23          if (len > 3 && len % 2 == 0) {
24              len++;
25          }
26          do {
27              // Number greater than 999
28              if (len > 3) {
29                  tmp = (num / (int)Math.pow((double)10,(double)len-2));
30                  // If tmp is 2 digit number and not a multiple of 10
31                  if (tmp / 10 == 1 && tmp%10 != 0) {
32                      sb.append(wordarr11[tmp % 10]) ;
33                  } else {
34                      sb.append(wordarr10[tmp / 10]);
35                      sb.append(wordarr1[tmp % 10]);
36                  }
```

```
37                    if (tmp > 0) {
38                        sb.append(wordarr100[len / 2]);
39                    }
40                    num = num % (int)(Math.pow((double)10,(double)len-2));
41                    len = len-2;
42                } else { // Number is less than 1000
43                    tmp = num / 100;
44                    if (tmp != 0) {
45                        sb.append(wordarr1[tmp]);
46                        sb.append(wordarr100[len / 2]);
47                    }
48                    tmp = num % 100 ;
49                    if(tmp / 10 == 1 && tmp % 10 != 0) {
50                        sb.append(wordarr11[tmp % 10]) ;
51                    } else {
52                        sb.append(wordarr10[tmp / 10]);
53                        sb.append(wordarr1[tmp % 10]);
54                    }
55                    len = 0;
56                }
57            } while(len > 0);
58        }
59        return sb.toString();
60    }
```

**19.7** You are given an array of integers (both positive and negative). Find the continuous sequence with the largest sum. Return the sum.

EXAMPLE

Input: {2, -8, 3, -2, 4, -10}

Output: 5 (i.e., {3, -2, 4} )

pg 89

## SOLUTION

A simple linear algorithm will work by keeping track of the current subsequence sum. If that sum ever drops below zero, that subsequence will not contribute to the subsequent maximal subsequence since it would reduce it by adding the negative sum.

```
1   public static int getMaxSum(int[] a) {
2       int maxsum = 0;
3       int sum = 0;
4       for (int i = 0; i < a.length; i++) {
5           sum += a[i];
6           if (maxsum < sum) {
7               maxsum = sum;
8           } else if (sum < 0) {
9               sum = 0;
10          }
11      }
12      return maxsum;
13  }
```

NOTE: If the array is all negative numbers, what is the correct behavior? Consider this simple array {-3, -10, -5}. You could make a good argument that the maximum sum is either: (A) -3 (if you assume the subsequence can't be empty) (B) 0 (the subsequence has length 0) or (C) MINIMUM_INT (essentially the error case). We went with option B (max sum = 0), but there's no "correct" answer. This is a great thing to discuss with your interviewer to show how careful you are.

**19.8** Design a method to find the frequency of occurrences of any given word in a book.

pg 89

## SOLUTION

The first question – which you should ask your interviewer – is if you're just asking for a single word ("single query") or if you might, eventually, use the same method for many different words ("repetitive queries")? That is, are you simply asking for the frequency of "dog", or might you ask for "dog," and then "cat," "mouse," etc?

*Solution: Single Query*

In this case, we simply go through the book, word by word, and count the number of times that a word appears. This will take O(n) time. We know we can't do better than that, as we must look at every word in the book.

*Solution: Repetitive Queries*

In this case, we create a hash table which maps from a word to a frequency. Our code is then like this:

```
1   Hashtable<String, Integer> setupDictionary(String[] book) {
2       Hashtable<String, Integer> table =
3           new Hashtable<String, Integer>();
4       for (String word : book) {
5           word = word.toLowerCase();
6           if (word.trim() != "") {
7               if (!table.containsKey(word)) table.put(word, 0);
8               table.put(word, table.get(word) + 1);
9           }
10      }
11      return table;
12  }
13
14  int getFrequency(Hashtable<String, Integer> table, String word) {
15      if (table == null || word == null) return -1;
16      word = word.toLowerCase();
17      if (table.containsKey(word)) {
18          return table.get(word);
19      }
20      return 0;
21  }
```

Note: a problem like this is relatively easy. Thus, the interviewer is going to be looking heavily at how careful you are. Did you check for error conditions?

**19.9**   Since XML is very verbose, you are given a way of encoding it where each tag gets mapped to a pre-defined integer value. The language/grammar is as follows:

> Element --> Element Attr* END Element END [aka, encode the element tag, then its attributes, then tack on an END character, then encode its children, then another end tag]
> Attr --> Tag Value [assume all values are strings]
> END --> 01
> Tag --> some predefined mapping to int
> Value --> string value END

Write code to print the encoded version of an xml element (passed in as string).

FOLLOW UP

Is there anything else you could do to (in many cases) compress this even further?

pg 90

## SOLUTION

*Part 1: Solution*

This solution tokenizes the input and then encodes the items, element by element.

> NOTE: See code attachment for full, executable code. We have included an abbreviated section here.

```
1    private Map<String, Byte> tagMap;
2    private static final Byte[] END = { 0, 1 };
3    private List<String> tokens;
4    private int currentTokenIndex;
5
6    byte[] encode(char[] input) throws IOException {
7        tokenize(input);
8        currentTokenIndex = 0;
9        ByteArrayOutputStream outputStream = new ByteArrayOutputStream();
10       encodeTokens(outputStream);
11       return outputStream.toByteArray();
12   }
13
14   void encodeTokens(ByteArrayOutputStream output) {
15       nextToken("<");
16
17       // read tag name
18       String tagName = nextToken();
19       output.write(getTagCode(tagName));
20
21       // read attributes
```

```
22      while (!hasNextToken(">") && !hasNextTokens("/", ">")) {
23          // read next attribute
24          String key = nextToken();
25          nextToken("=");
26          String value = nextToken();
27          output.write(getTagCode(key));
28          for (char c : value.toCharArray()) {
29              output.write(c);
30          }
31          output.write(END[0]);
32          output.write(END[1]);
33      }
34      // end of attributes
35      output.write(END[0]);
36      output.write(END[1]);
37      // finish this element
38      if (hasNextTokens("/", ">")) {
39          nextToken("/");
40          nextToken(">");
41      } else {
42          nextToken(">");
43          // while not the end tag
44          while (!hasNextTokens("<", "/")) {
45              encodeTokens(output); // encode child
46          }
47          // ending tag
48          nextToken("<");
49          nextToken("/");
50          nextToken(tagName);
51          nextToken(">");
52      }
53      output.write(END[0]);
54      output.write(END[1]);
55  }
```

*Part 2: Is there anything you can do to compress this further?*

You can treat the file as a general stream of characters and use any number of compression techniques: Shannon–Fano coding, Huffman coding or Arithmetic coding.

**19.10** Write a method to generate a random number between 1 and 7, given a method that generates a random number between 1 and 5 (i.e., implement rand7() using rand5()).

pg 90

## SOLUTION

First, observe that we cannot do this in a guaranteed finite amount of time. Why? Let's see by a parallel example: How would you use rand2() to create rand3()?

Observe that each call of rand2() and the corresponding decision you make can be represented by a decision tree. On each node, you have two branches. You take the left one when rand2() equals 0 (which happens with 1/2 probability). You take the right one when rand2() equals 1 (which happens with 1/2 probability). You continue branching left and right as you continue to call 1/2. When you reach a leaf, you return a result of 1, 2 or 3 (your rand3() results).

» What's the probability of taking each branch? 1/2.

» What's the probability to reach a particular leaf node? $1/2^j$ (for some j).

» What the probability of returning 3 (for example)? We could compute this by summing up the probabilities of reaching each leaf node with value 3. Each of these paths has probability $1/2^j$, so we know that the total probability of returning 3 must be a series of terms of reciprocal powers of 2 (e.g., $1/2^x + 1/2^y + 1/2^z + \ldots$).

We also know, however, that the probability of returning 3 must be 1/3 (because rand3() should be perfectly random). Can you find a series of reciprocal powers of 2 that sum to 1/3? No, because 3 and 2 are relatively prime.

We can similarly conclude that to solve this problem, we will need to accept a small (infinitesimally small) chance that this process will repeat forever. That's ok.

So, how do we solve this?

In order to generate a random number between 1 and 7, we just need to uniformly generate a larger range than we are looking for and then repeatedly sample until we get a number that is good for us. We will generate a base 5 number with two places with two calls to the RNG.

```
public static int rand7() {
    while (true) {
        int num = 5 * (rand5() - 1) + (rand5() - 1);
        if (num < 21) return (num % 7 + 1);
    }
}
```

**19.11** Design an algorithm to find all pairs of integers within an array which sum to a specified value.

pg 90

## SOLUTION

One easy and (time) efficient solution involves a hash map from integers to integers. This algorithm works by iterating through the array. On each element x, look up sum - x in the hash table and, if it exists, print (x, sum - x). Add x to the hash table, and go to the next element.

### Alternate Solution

*Definition of Complement:* If we're trying to find a pair of numbers that sums to z, the complement of x will be z - x (that is, the number that can be added to x to make z). For example, if we're trying to find a pair of numbers that sum to 12, the complement of –5 would be 17.

*The Algorithm:* Imagine we have the following sorted array: {-2 -1 0 3 5 6 7 9 13 14 }. Let *first* point to the head of the array and *last* point to the end of the array. To find the complement of *first*, we just move *last* backwards until we find it. If *first* + *last* < *sum*, then there is no complement for *first*. We can therefore move *first* forward. We stop when *first* is greater than *last*.

Why must this find all complements for *first*? Because the array is sorted and we're trying progressively smaller numbers. When the sum of *first* and *last* is less than the sum, we know that trying even smaller numbers (as *last*) won't help us find a complement.

Why must this find all complements for *last*? Because all pairs must be made up of a *first* and a *last*. We've found all complements for *first*, therefore we've found all complements of *last*.

```
1    public static void printPairSums(int[] array, int sum) {
2        Arrays.sort(array);
3        int first = 0;
4        int last = array.length - 1;
5        while (first < last) {
6            int s = array[first] + array[last];
7            if (s == sum) {
8                System.out.println(array[first] + " " + array[last]);
9                ++first;
10               --last;
11           } else {
12               if (s < sum) ++first;
13               else --last;
14           }
15       }
16   }
```

**20.1** Write a function that adds two numbers. You should not use + or any arithmetic operators.

pg 91

## SOLUTION

To investigate this problem, let's start off by gaining a deeper understanding of how we add numbers. We'll work in Base 10 so that it's easier to see. To add 759 + 674, I would usually add digit[0] from each number, carry the one, add digit[1] from each number, carry the one, etc. You could take the same approach in binary: add each digit, and carry the one as necessary.

Can we make this a little easier? Yes! Imagine I decided to split apart the "addition" and "carry" steps. That is, I do the following:

1. Add 759 + 674, but "forget" to carry. I then get 323.

2. Add 759 + 674 but only do the carrying, rather than the addition of each digit. I then get 1110.

3. Add the result of the first two operations (recursively, using the same process described in step 1 and 2): 1110 + 323 = 1433.

Now, how would we do this in binary?

1. If I add two binary numbers together but forget to carry, bit[i] will be 0 if bit[i] in a and b are both 0 or both 1. This is an XOR.

2. If I add two numbers together but only carry, I will have a 1 in bit[i] if bit[i-1] in a and b are both 1's. This is an AND, shifted.

3. Now, recurse until there's nothing to carry.

```
1   int add_no_arithm(int a, int b) {
2       if (b == 0) return a;
3       int sum = a ^ b; // add without carrying
4       int carry = (a & b) << 1; // carry, but don't add
5       return add_no_arithm(sum, carry); // recurse
6   }
```

## OBSERVATIONS AND SUGGESTIONS:

The Approach: There are a couple of suggestions for figuring out this problem:

1. Our first instinct in problems like these should be that we're going to have to work with bits. Why? Because when you take away the + sign, what other choice do we have? Plus, that's how computers do it.

2. Our next thought in problems like these should be to really, really understand how you add. Walk through an addition problem to see if you can understand something new—some pattern—and then see if you can replicate that with code.

Your interviewer is looking for two things in this problem:

1. Can you break down a problem and solve it?

2. Do you understand how to work with bits?

**20.2** Write a method to shuffle a deck of cards. It must be a perfect shuffle - in other words, each 52! permutations of the deck has to be equally likely. Assume that you are given a random number generator which is perfect.

pg 91

## SOLUTION

This is a very well known interview question, and a well known algorithm. If you aren't one of the lucky few to have already know this algorithm, read on.

Let's start with a brute force approach: we could randomly selecting items and put them into a new array. We must make sure that we don't pick the same item twice though by somehow marking the node as dead.

```
Array:                 [1] [2] [3] [4] [5]
Randomly select 4:     [4] [?] [?] [?] [?]
Mark element as dead:  [1] [2] [3] [X] [5]
```

The tricky part is, how do we mark [4] as dead such that we prevent that element from being picked again? One way to do it is to swap the now-dead [4] with the first element in the array:

```
Array:                 [1] [2] [3] [4] [5]
Randomly select 4:     [4] [?] [?] [?] [?]
Swap dead element:     [X] [2] [3] [1] [5]


Array:                 [X] [2] [3] [1] [5]
Randomly select 3:     [4] [3] [?] [?] [?]
Swap dead element:     [X] [X] [2] [1] [5]
```

By doing it this way, it's much easier for the algorithm to "know" that the first k elements are dead than that the third, fourth, nineth, etc elements are dead. We can also optimize this by merging the shuffled array and the original array.

```
Randomly select 4:     [4] [2] [3] [1] [5]
Randomly select 3:     [4] [3] [2] [1] [5]
```

This is an easy algorithm to implement iteratively:

```
1   public static void shuffleArray(int[] cards) {
2       int temp, index;
3       for (int i = 0; i < cards.length; i++){
4           index = (int) (Math.random() * (cards.length - i)) + i;
5           temp = cards[i];
6           cards[i] = cards[index];
7           cards[index] = temp;
8       }
9   }
```

**20.3** Write a method to randomly generate a set of m integers from an array of size n. Each element must have equal probability of being chosen.

pg 91

## SOLUTION

Our first instinct on this problem might be to randomly pick elements from the array and put them into our new subset array. But then, what if we pick the same element twice? Ideally, we'd want to somehow "shrink" the array to no longer contain that element. Shrinking is expensive though because of all the shifting required.

Instead of shrinking / shifting, we can swap the element with an element at the beginning of the array and then "remember" that the array now only includes elements j and greater. That is, when we pick subset[0] to be array[k], we replace array[k] with the first element in the array. When we pick subset[1], we consider array[0] to be "dead" and we pick a random element y between 1 and array.size(). We then set subset[1] equal to array[y], and set array[y] equal to array[1]. Elements 0 and 1 are now "dead." Subset[2] is now chosen from array[2] through array[array.size()], and so on.

```
1   /* Random number between lower and higher, inclusive */
2   public static int rand(int lower, int higher) {
3       return lower + (int)(Math.random() * (higher - lower + 1));
4   }
5
6   /* pick M elements from original array.  Clone original array so that
7    * we don't destroy the input. */
8   public static int[] pickMRandomly(int[] original, int m) {
9       int[] subset = new int[m];
10      int[] array = original.clone();
11      for (int j = 0; j < m; j++) {
12          int index = rand(j, array.length - 1);
13          subset[j] = array[index];
14          array[index] = array[j]; // array[j] is now "dead"
15      }
16      return subset;
17  }
```

**20.4** Write a method to count the number of 2s between 0 and n.

pg 91

## SOLUTION

Picture a sequence of numbers:

```
 0   1   2   3   4   5   6   7   8   9
10  11  12  13  14  15  16  17  18  19
20  21  22  23  24  25  26  27  28  29
...
110 111 112 113 114 115 116 117 118 119
```

The last digit will be repeated every 10 numbers, the last two digits will be repeated every 10^2 numbers, the last 3 digits will be repeated every 10^3 numbers, etc.

So, if there are X 2s between 0 and 99, then we know there are 2x twos between 0 and 199. Between 0 and 299, we have 3x twos from the last two digits, and another 100 2s from the first digit.

In other words, we can look at a number like this:

```
f(513) = 5 * f(99) + f(13) + 100
```

To break this down individually:

» The sequence of the last two digits are repeated 5 times, so add 5 * f(99)

» We need to account for the last two digits in 500 -> 513, so add f(13)

» We need to account for the first digit being two between 200 -> 299, so add 100

Of course, if n is, say, 279, we'll need to account for this slightly differently:

```
f(279) = 2 * f(99) + f(79) + 79 + 1
```

To break this down individually:

» The sequence of the last two digits are repeated 2 times, so add 2 * f(99)

» We need to account for the last two digits in 200 -> 279, so add f(79)

» We need to account for the first digit being two between 200 -> 279, so add 79 + 1

Recursive Code:

```
1   public static int count2sR(int n) {
2       // Base case
3       if (n == 0) return 0;
4
5       // 513 into 5 * 100 + 13. [Power = 100; First = 5; Remainder = 13]
6       int power = 1;
7       while (10 * power < n) power *= 10;
8       int first = n / power;
9       int remainder = n % power;
```

```
10
11          // Counts 2s from first digit
12          int nTwosFirst = 0;
13          if (first > 2) nTwosFirst += power;
14          else if (first == 2) nTwosFirst += remainder + 1;
15
16          // Count 2s from all other digits
17          int nTwosOther = first * count2sR(power - 1) + count2sR(remainder);
18
19          return nTwosFirst + nTwosOther;
20      }
```

We can also implement this algorithm iteratively:

```
1   public static int count2sI(int num) {
2       int countof2s = 0, digit = 0;
3       int j = num, seendigits=0, position=0, pow10_pos = 1;
4       /* maintaining this value instead of calling pow() is an 6x perf
5        * gain (48s -> 8s) pow10_posMinus1. maintaining this value
6        * instead of calling Numof2s is an 2x perf gain (8s -> 4s).
7        * overall > 10x speedup */
8       while (j > 0) {
9           digit = j % 10;
10          int pow10_posMinus1 = pow10_pos / 10;
11          countof2s += digit * position * pow10_posMinus1;
12          /* we do this if digit <, >, or = 2
13           * Digit < 2 implies there are no 2s contributed by this
14           * digit.
15           * Digit == 2 implies there are 2 * numof2s contributed by
16           * the previous position + num of 2s contributed by the
17           * presence of this 2 */
18          if (digit == 2) {
19              countof2s += seendigits + 1;
20          }
21          /* Digit > 2 implies there are digit * num of 2s by the prev.
22           * position + 10^position */
23          else if(digit > 2) {
24              countof2s += pow10_pos;
25          }
26          seendigits = seendigits + pow10_pos * digit;
27          pow10_pos *= 10;
28          position++;
29          j = j / 10;
30      }
31      return(countof2s);
32  }
```

**20.5** You have a large text file containing words. Given any two words, find the shortest distance (in terms of number of words) between them in the file. Can you make the searching operation in O(1) time? What about the space complexity for your solution?

pg 91

## SOLUTION

We will assume for this question that the word order does not matter. This is a question you should ask your interviewer. If the word order does matter, we can make the small modification shown in the code below.

To solve this problem, simply traverse the file and for every occurrence of word1 and word2, compare difference of positions and update the current minimum.

```
1    int shortest(String[] words, String word1, String word2) {
2        int pos = 0;
3        int min = Integer.MAX_VALUE / 2;
4        int word1_pos = -min;
5        int word2_pos = -min;
6        for (int i = 0; i < words.length; i++) {
7            String current_word = words[i];
8            if (current_word.equals(word1)) {
9                word1_pos = pos;
10               // Comment following 3 lines if word order matters
11               int distance = word1_pos - word2_pos;
12               if (min > distance)
13                   min = distance;
14           } else if (current_word.equals(word2)) {
15               word2_pos = pos;
16               int distance = word2_pos - word1_pos;
17               if (min > distance) min = distance;
18           }
19           ++pos;
20       }
21       return min;
22   }
```

To solve this problem in less time (but more space), we can create a hash table with each word and the locations where it occurs. We then just need to find the minimum (arithmetic) difference in the locations (e.g., abs(word0.loc[1] - word1.loc[5])).

To find the minimum arithmetic difference, we take each location for word1 (e.g.: 0, 3) and do a modified binary search for it in word2's location list, returning the closest number. Our search for 3, for example, in {2, 7, 9} would return 1. The minimum of all these binary searches is the shortest distance.

---

**20.6** Describe an algorithm to find the largest 1 million numbers in 1 billion numbers. Assume that the computer memory can hold all one billion numbers.

pg 91

## SOLUTION

*Approach 1: Sorting*

Sort the elements and then take the first million numbers from that. Complexity is O(n log n).

*Approach 2: Max Heap*

1.  Create a Min Heap with the first million numbers.

2.  For each remaining number, insert it in the Min Heap and then delete the minimum value from the heap.

3.  The heap now contains the largest million numbers.

4.  This algorithm is O(n log m), where m is the number of values we are looking for.

*Approach 3: Selection Rank Algorithm (if you can modify the original array)*

Selection Rank is a well known algorithm in computer science to find the ith smallest (or largest) element in an array in expected linear time. The basic algorithm for finding the ith smallest elements goes like this:

»   Pick a random element in the array and use it as a 'pivot'. Move all elements smaller than that element to one side of the array, and all elements larger to the other side.

»   If there are exactly i elements on the right, then you just find the smallest element on that side.

»   Otherwise, if the right side is bigger than i, repeat the algorithm on the right. If the right side is smaller than i, repeat the algorithm on the left for i – right.size().

Given this algorithm, you can either:

»   Tweak it to use the existing partitions to find the largest i elements (where i = one million).

»   Or, once you find the ith largest element, run through the array again to return all elements greater than or equal to it.

This algorithm has expected O(n) time.

**20.7** Write a program to find the longest word made of other words.

pg 91

## SOLUTION

The solution below does the following:

1. Sort the array by size, putting the longest word at the front

2. For each word, split it in all possible ways. That is, for "test", split it into {"t", "est"}, {"te", "st"} and {"tes", "t"}.

3. Then, for each pairing, check if the first half and the second both exist elsewhere in the array.

4. "Short circuit" by returning the first string we find that fits condition #3.

What is the time complexity of this?

» Time to sort array: O(n log n)

» Time to check if first / second half of word exists: O(d) per word, where d is the average length of a word.

» Total complexity: O(n log n + n * d). Note that d is fixed (probably around 5—10 characters). Thus, we can guess that for short arrays, the time is estimated by O(n * d), which also equals O(number of characters in the array). For longer arrays, the time will be better estimated by O(n log n).

» Space complexity: O(n).

Optimizations: If we didn't want to use additional space, we could cut out the hash table. This would mean:

» Sorting the array in alphabetical order

» Rather than looking up the word in a hash table, we would use binary search in the array

» We would no longer be able to short circuit.

```
1   class LengthComparator implements Comparator<String> {
2       @Override
3       public int compare(String o1, String o2) {
4           if (o1.length() < o2.length()) return 1;
5           if (o1.length() > o2.length()) return -1;
6           return 0;
7       }
8   }
```

**20.8**   Given a string s and an array of smaller strings T, design a method to search s for each
small string in T.

pg 91

## SOLUTION

First, create a suffix tree for s.  For example, if your word were bibs, you would create the following tree:

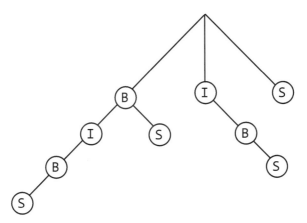

Then, all you need to do is search for each string in T in the suffix tree. Note that if "B" were a
word, you would come up with two locations.

```
1    public class SuffixTree {
2        SuffixTreeNode root = new SuffixTreeNode();
3        public SuffixTree(String s) {
4            for (int i = 0; i < s.length(); i++) {
5                String suffix = s.substring(i);
6                root.insertString(suffix, i);
7            }
8        }
9
10       public ArrayList<Integer> getIndexes(String s) {
11           return root.getIndexes(s);
12       }
13   }
14
15   public class SuffixTreeNode {
16       HashMap<Character, SuffixTreeNode> children = new
17                           HashMap<Character, SuffixTreeNode>();
18       char value;
19       ArrayList<Integer> indexes = new ArrayList<Integer>();
```

```
20        public SuffixTreeNode() { }
21
22        public void insertString(String s, int index) {
23            indexes.add(index);
24            if (s != null && s.length() > 0) {
25                value = s.charAt(0);
26                SuffixTreeNode child = null;
27                if (children.containsKey(value)) {
28                    child = children.get(value);
29                } else {
30                    child = new SuffixTreeNode();
31                    children.put(value, child);
32                }
33                String remainder = s.substring(1);
34                child.insertString(remainder, index);
35            }
36        }
37
38        public ArrayList<Integer> getIndexes(String s) {
39            if (s == null || s.length() == 0) {
40                return indexes;
41            } else {
42                char first = s.charAt(0);
43                if (children.containsKey(first)) {
44                    String remainder = s.substring(1);
45                    return children.get(first).getIndexes(remainder);
46                }
47            }
48            return null;
49        }
50    }
51
52    public class Question {
53        public static void main(String[] args) {
54            String testString = "mississippi";
55            String[] stringList = {"is", "sip", "hi", "sis"};
56            SuffixTree tree = new SuffixTree(testString);
57            for (String s : stringList) {
58                ArrayList<Integer> list = tree.getIndexes(s);
59                if (list != null) {
60                    System.out.println(s + ": " + list.toString());
61                }
62            }
63        }
64    }
```

**20.9**   Numbers are randomly generated and passed to a method. Write a program to find and maintain the median value as new values are generated.

pg 91

## SOLUTIONS

One solution is to use two priority heaps: a max heap for the values below the median, and a min heap for the values above the median. The median will be largest value of the max heap. When a new value arrives it is placed in the below heap if the value is less than or equal to the median, otherwise it is placed into the above heap. The heap sizes can be equal or the below heap has one extra. This constraint can easily be restored by shifting an element from one heap to the other. The median is available in constant time, so updates are O(lg n).

```
1    private Comparator<Integer> maxHeapComparator, minHeapComparator;
2    private PriorityQueue<Integer> maxHeap, minHeap;
3    public void addNewNumber(int randomNumber) {
4        if (maxHeap.size() == minHeap.size()) {
5            if ((minHeap.peek() != null) &&
6                    randomNumber > minHeap.peek()) {
7                maxHeap.offer(minHeap.poll());
8                minHeap.offer(randomNumber);
9            } else {
10                maxHeap.offer(randomNumber);
11            }
12        }
13        else {
14            if(randomNumber < maxHeap.peek()){
15                minHeap.offer(maxHeap.poll());
16                maxHeap.offer(randomNumber);
17            }
18            else {
19                minHeap.offer(randomNumber);
20            }
21        }
22    }
23    public static double getMedian() {
24        if (maxHeap.isEmpty()) return minHeap.peek();
25        else if (minHeap.isEmpty()) return maxHeap.peek();
26        if (maxHeap.size() == minHeap.size()) {
27            return (minHeap.peek() + maxHeap.peek()) / 2;
28        } else if (maxHeap.size() > minHeap.size()) {
29            return maxHeap.peek();
30        } else {
31            return minHeap.peek();
32        }
33    }
```

**20.10** Given two words of equal length that are in a dictionary, write a method to transform one word into another word by changing only one letter at a time. The new word you get in each step must be in the dictionary.

EXAMPLE:

Input: DAMP, LIKE

Output: DAMP -> LAMP -> LIMP -> LIME -> LIKE

pg 91

## SOLUTION

Though this problem seems tough, it's actually a straightforward modification of breadth-first-search. Each word in our "graph" branches to all words in the dictionary that are one edit away. The interesting part is how to implement this—should we build a graph as we go? We could, but there's an easier way. We can instead use a "backtrack map." In this backtrack map, if B[v] = w, then you know that you edited v to get w. When we reach our end word, we can use this backtrack map repeatedly to reverse our path. See the code below:

```
1    LinkedList<String> transform(String startWord, String stopWord,
2                                   Set<String> dictionary) {
3        startWord = startWord.toUpperCase();
4        stopWord = stopWord.toUpperCase();
5        Queue<String> actionQueue = new LinkedList<String>();
6        Set<String> visitedSet = new HashSet<String>();
7        Map<String, String> backtrackMap = new TreeMap<String, String>();
8
9        actionQueue.add(startWord);
10       visitedSet.add(startWord);
11
12       while (!actionQueue.isEmpty()) {
13           String w = actionQueue.poll();
14           // For each possible word v from w with one edit operation
15           for (String v : getOneEditWords(w)) {
16               if (v.equals(stopWord)) {
17                   // Found our word!  Now, back track.
18                   LinkedList<String> list = new LinkedList<String>();
19                   // Append v to list
20                   list.add(v);
21                   while (w != null) {
22                       list.add(0, w);
23                       w = backtrackMap.get(w);
24                   }
25                   return list;
26               }
27               // If v is a dictionary word
```

```
28              if (dictionary.contains(v)) {
29                  if (!visitedSet.contains(v)) {
30                      actionQueue.add(v);
31                      visitedSet.add(v); // mark visited
32                      backtrackMap.put(v, w);
33                  }
34              }
35          }
36      }
37      return null;
38  }
39
40  Set<String> getOneEditWords(String word) {
41      Set<String> words = new TreeSet<String>();
42      for (int i = 0; i < word.length(); i++) {
43          char[] wordArray = word.toCharArray();
44          // change that letter to something else
45          for (char c = 'A'; c <= 'Z'; c++) {
46              if (c != word.charAt(i)) {
47                  wordArray[i] = c;
48                  words.add(new String(wordArray));
49              }
50          }
51      }
52      return words;
53  }
```

Let n be the length of the start word and m be the number of like sized words in the dictionary. The runtime of this algorithm is O(n*m) since the while loop will dequeue at most m unique words. The for loop is O(n) as it walks down the string applying a fixed number of replacements for each character.

**20.11** Imagine you have a square matrix, where each cell is filled with either black or white. Design an algorithm to find the maximum subsquare such that all four borders are filled with black pixels.

pg 92

## SOLUTION

*Assumption:* Square is of size NxN.

This algorithm does the following:

1. Iterate through every (full) column from left to right.

2. At each (full) column (call this currentColumn), look at the subcolumns (from biggest to smallest).

3. At each subcolumn, see if you can form a square with the subcolumn as the left side. If so, update currentMaxSize and go to the next (full) column.

4. If N - currentColumn <= currentMaxSize, then break completely. We've found the largest square possible. *Why? At each column, we're trying to create a square with that column as the left side. The largest such square we could possibly create is N - currentColumn. Thus, if N-currentColumn <= currentMaxSize, then we have no need to proceed.*

Time complexity: O(N^2).

```
1   public static Subsquare findSquare(int[][] matrix){
2       assert(matrix.length > 0);
3       for (int row = 0; row < matrix.length; row++){
4           assert(matrix[row].length == matrix.length);
5       }
6
7       int N = matrix.length;
8
9       int currentMaxSize = 0;
10      Subsquare sq = null;
11      int col = 0;
12
13      // Iterate through each column from left to right
14      while (N - col > currentMaxSize) { // See step 4 above
15          for (int row = 0; row < matrix.length; row++){
16              // starting from the biggest
17              int size = N - Math.max(row, col);
18              while (size > currentMaxSize){
19                  if (isSquare(matrix, row, col, size)){
20                      currentMaxSize = size;
21                      sq = new Subsquare(row, col, size);
22                      break; // go to next (full) column
```

```
23                    }
24                    size--;
25                }
26            }
27            col++;
28        }
29        return sq;
30  }
31
32  private static boolean isSquare(int[][] matrix, int row, int col,
33                                  int size) {
34      // Check top and bottom border.
35      for (int j = 0; j < size; j++){
36          if (matrix[row][col+j] == 1) {
37              return false;
38          }
39          if (matrix[row+size-1][col+j] == 1){
40              return false;
41          }
42      }
43
44      // Check left and right border.
45      for (int i = 1; i < size - 1; i++){
46          if (matrix[row+i][col] == 1){
47              return false;
48          }
49          if (matrix[row+i][col+size-1] == 1){
50              return false;
51          }
52      }
53      return true;
54  }
55
56  public class Subsquare {
57      public int row, column, size;
58      public Subsquare(int r, int c, int sz) {
59          row = r;
60          column = c;
61          size = sz;
62      }
63  }
```

**20.12** Given an NxN matrix of positive and negative integers, write code to find the sub-matrix with the largest possible sum.

pg 92

## SOLUTION

### Brute Force: Complexity O(N^6)

Like many "maximizing" problems, this problem has a straight forward brute force solution. The brute force solution simply iterates through all possible sub-matrixes, computes the sum, and finds the biggest.

To iterate through all possible sub-matrixes (with no duplicates), we simply need to iterate through all order pairings of rows, and then all ordered pairings of columns.

This solution is O(N^6), since we iterate through O(N^4) sub-matrixes, and it takes O(N^2) time to compute the area of each.

### Optimized Solution: O(N^4)

Notice that the earlier solution is made slower by a factor of O(N^2) simply because computing the sum of a matrix is so slow. Can we reduce the time to compute the area? Yes! In fact, we can reduce the time of computeSum to O(1).

Consider the following:

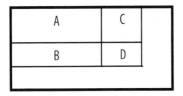

If we had the sum of the smaller rectangle (the one including A, B, C, D), and we could compute the sum of D as follows: area(D) = area(A through D) - area(A) - area(B) - area(C).

What if, instead, we had the following:

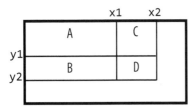

with the following values (notice that each Val_* starts at the origin):

```
Val_D = area(point(0, 0) -> point(x2, y2))
Val_C = area(point(0, 0) -> point(x2, y1))
Val_B = area(point(0, 0) -> point(x1, y2))
Val_A = area(point(0, 0) -> point(x1, y1))
```

With these values, we know the following:

```
area(D) = Val_D - area(A union C) - area(A union B) + area(A).
```

Or, written another way:

```
area(D) = Val_D - Val_B - Val_C + Val_A
```

Can we efficiently compute these Val_* values for all points in the matrix? Yes, by using similar logic:

```
Val_(x, y) = Val(x - 1, y) + Val(y - 1, x) - Val(x - 1, y - 1)
```

We can precompute all such values, and then efficiently find the maximum submatrix. See the following code for this implementation

```
1   public static int getMaxMatrix(int[][] original) {
2       int maxArea = Integer.MIN_VALUE; // Important! Max could be < 0
3       int rowCount = original.length;
4       int columnCount = original[0].length;
5       int[][] matrix = precomputeMatrix(original);
6       for (int row1 = 0; row1 < rowCount; row1++) {
7           for (int row2 = row1; row2 < rowCount; row2++) {
8               for (int col1 = 0; col1 < columnCount; col1++) {
9                   for (int col2 = col1; col2 < columnCount; col2++) {
10                      maxArea = Math.max(maxArea, computeSum(matrix,
11                          row1, row2, col1, col2));
12                  }
13              }
14          }
15      }
16      return maxArea;
17  }
18
19  private static int[][] precomputeMatrix(int[][] matrix) {
20      int[][] sumMatrix = new int[matrix.length][matrix[0].length];
21      for (int i = 0; i < matrix.length; i++) {
22          for (int j = 0; j < matrix.length; j++) {
23              if (i == 0 && j == 0) { // first cell
24                  sumMatrix[i][j] = matrix[i][j];
25              } else if (j == 0) { // cell in first column
26                  sumMatrix[i][j] = sumMatrix[i - 1][j] + matrix[i][j];
27              } else if (i == 0) { // cell in first row
28                  sumMatrix[i][j] = sumMatrix[i][j - 1] + matrix[i][j];
29              } else {
30                  sumMatrix[i][j] = sumMatrix[i - 1][j] +
31                      sumMatrix[i][j - 1] - sumMatrix[i - 1][j - 1] +
```

```
32                          matrix[i][j];
33                     }
34                  }
35              }
36          return sumMatrix;
37  }
38
39  private static int computeSum(int[][] sumMatrix, int i1, int i2,
40                                int j1, int j2) {
41      if (i1 == 0 && j1 == 0) { // starts at row 0, column 0
42          return sumMatrix[i2][j2];
43      } else if (i1 == 0) { // start at row 0
44          return sumMatrix[i2][j2] - sumMatrix[i2][j1 - 1];
45      } else if (j1 == 0) { // start at column 0
46          return sumMatrix[i2][j2] - sumMatrix[i1 - 1][j2];
47      } else {
48          return sumMatrix[i2][j2] - sumMatrix[i2][j1 - 1]
49                  - sumMatrix[i1 - 1][j2] + sumMatrix[i1 - 1][j1 - 1];
50      }
51  }
```

**20.13** Given a dictionary of millions of words, give an algorithm to find the largest possible rectangle of letters such that every row forms a word (reading left to right) and every column forms a word (reading top to bottom).

pg 92

## SOLUTION

Many problems involving a dictionary can be solved by doing some preprocessing. Where can we do preprocessing?

Well, if we're going to create a rectangle of words, we know that each row must be the same length and each column must have the same length. So, let's group the words of the dictionary based on their sizes. Let's call this grouping D, where D[i] provides a list of words of length i.

Next, observe that we're looking for the largest rectangle. What is the absolute largest rectangle that could be formed? It's (length of largest word) * (length of largest word).

```
1   int max_rectangle = longest_word * longest_word;
2   for z = max_rectangle to 1 {
3       for each pair of numbers (i, j) where i*j = z {
4           /* attempt to make rectangle. return if successful. */
5       }
6   }
```

By iterating in this order, we ensure that the first rectangle we find will be the largest.

Now, for the hard part: make_rectangle. Our approach is to rearrange words in list1 into rows and check if the columns are valid words in list2. However, instead of creating, say, a particular 10x20 rectangle, we check if the columns created after inserting the first two words are even valid pre-fixes. A trie becomes handy here.

```
1   WordGroup[] groupList = WordGroup.createWordGroups(list);
2   private int maxWordLength = groupList.length;
3   private Trie trieList[] = new Trie[maxWordLength];
4
5   public Rectangle maxRectangle() {
6       int maxSize = maxWordLength * maxWordLength;
7       for (int z = maxSize; z > 0; z--) {
8           for (int i = 1; i <= maxWordLength; i ++ ) {
9               if (z % i == 0) {
10                  int j = z / i;
11                  if (j <= maxWordLength) {
12                      Rectangle rectangle = makeRectangle(i,j);
13                      if (rectangle != null) {
14                          return rectangle;
15                      }
16                  }
```

```
17                }
18           }
19      }
20      return null;
21 }
22
23 private Rectangle makeRectangle(int length, int height) {
24      if (groupList[length - 1] == null ||
25          groupList[height - 1] == null) {
26          return null;
27      }
28      if (trieList[height - 1] == null) {
29          LinkedList<String> words = groupList[height - 1].getWords();
30          trieList[height - 1] = new Trie(words);
31      }
32      return makePartialRectangle(length, height,
33                                  new Rectangle(length));
34 }
35
36 private Rectangle makePartialRectangle(int l, int h,
37                                        Rectangle rectangle) {
38      if (rectangle.height == h) { // Check if complete rectangle
39          if (rectangle.isComplete(l, h, groupList[h - 1])) {
40              return rectangle;
41          } else {
42              return null;
43          }
44      }
45
46      // Compare columns to trie to see if potentially valid rect */
47      if (!rectangle.isPartialOK(l, trieList[h - 1])) return null;
48
49      for (int i = 0; i < groupList[l-1].length(); i++) {
50          Rectangle org_plus =
51              rectangle.append(groupList[l-1].getWord(i));
52          Rectangle rect = makePartialRectangle(l, h, org_plus);
53          if (rect != null) {
54              return rect;
55          }
56      }
57      return null;
58 }
```

NOTE: See code attachment for full code.

# Index

## Mock Interviews

Studying helps, but nothing can prepare you like the real thing. Each CareerCup interviewer has given over a hundred interviews at Google, Microsoft, or Amazon. To nail your interview, sit down with a trained interviewer and get their experienced feedback.

*See www.careercup.com/interview for more details.*

## One Hour Interview with Real Interviewers

Our interviewers will give you a real interview, just like you'd get at Google, Microsoft or Amazon. We'll test you on the same types of questions that they do. We'll grade you the same way they do. How can we do this? We've done over 100 interviews each for these companies. We've screened resumes. We've been part of their hiring committees. We know what they want.

## We'll Also Give You...

» An .mp3 recording of your interview.

» Feedback on where you shined and where you struggled.

» Specific suggestions on how to improve.

» Instructions on how to approach tough problems

» Lessons on what interviewers look for in your code.

## Schedule Your Interview Today!

See www.careercup.com/interview for pricing and details. Check out our special student rates!

Gayle Laakmann's interviewing expertise comes from vast experience on both sides of the desk. She has completed Software Engineering interviews with - and received offers from - Microsoft, Google, Amazon, Apple, IBM, Goldman Sachs, Capital IQ, and a number of other firms.

Of these top companies, she has worked for Microsoft, Apple and Google, where she gained deep insight into each company's hiring practices.

Most recently, Gayle spent three years at Google as a Software Engineer and was one of the company's lead interviewers. She interviewed over 120 candidates in the U.S. and abroad, and led much of the recruiting for her alma mater, the University of Pennsylvania.

Additionally, she served on Google's Hiring Committee, where she reviewed each candidate's feedback and made hire / no-hire decisions. She assessed over 700 candidates in that role, and evaluated hundreds more resumes.

In 2005, Gayle founded CareerCup.com to bring her wealth of experience to candidates around the world. Launched first as a free forum for interview questions, CareerCup now offers a book, a video and mock interviews.

Gayle holds a bachelor's and master's degree in Computer Science from the University of Pennsylvania.

10352936R0